The Future of Retail Banking in Europe

The Future of Retail Banking in Europe

A View from the Top

Oonagh McDonald and Kevin Keasey

UNISYS

JOHN WILEY & SONS, LTD

Other Wiley Editorial Offices

John Wiley & Sons Inc., 111 River Street, Hoboken, NJ 07030, USA

Jossey-Bass, 989 Market Street, San Francisco, CA 94103-1741, USA

Wiley-VCH Verlag GmbH, Boschstr. 12, D-69469 Weinheim, Germany

John Wiley & Sons Australia Ltd, 33 Park Road, Milton, Queensland 4064, Australia

John Wiley & Sons (Asia) Pte Ltd, 2 Clementi Loop #02-01, Jin Xing Distripark, Singapore 129809

John Wiley & Sons Canada Ltd, 22 Worcester Road, Etobicoke, Ontario, Canada M9W 1L1

Library of Congress Cataloging-in-Publication Data

McDonald, Oonagh.
   The future of retail banking in Europe : a view from the top / Oonagh McDonald and Kevin Keasey.
      p.   cm.
   Includes index.
   ISBN 0-471-89277-7 (alk. paper)
   1. Banks and banking—Europe.   I. Keasey, Kevin.   II. Title.
   HG2974 .M39   2002
   332.1′2′094—dc21
                                                                        2002071302

British Library Cataloguing in Publication Data

A catalogue record for this book is available from the British Library

ISBN 0-471-89277-7

Typeset in 10/12pt Times by TechBooks, New Delhi, India
Printed and bound in Great Britain by Biddles Ltd, Guildford and King's Lynn
This book is printed on acid-free paper responsibly manufactured from sustainable forestry in which at least two trees are planted for each one used for paper production.

Contents

Foreword

There is no reason to presume that banks are more immune to change than any other business or institution, or more reason to presume that banking itself will go ahead as it is now.

Over the last fifty years we have seen dramatic changes in many industries. New industries have emerged—information technology, air travel and tourism—and older industries have declined—railways, coalmining and canal transport—or at the very least changed substantially. If this is the case then we can be confident that the future holds changes we will find hard to imagine today.

In this book the authors have laid bare the changes and challenges within the banking industry in Europe. The very question once posed and received with such shock that the world needs banking but does not need traditional banks is debated and discussed here. The 'new entrants', non-traditional banks, have entered the market and are having some success. There has been and there remains a strong sense that financial institutions want to broaden their product lines to include investment and insurance offerings.

There remains the ever present need for growth, by increasing the customer base, through attracting new customers and retaining the present ones, through new initiatives and propositions and through the ever continuing record levels of mergers and acquisitions.

So what's changing? We are. We're living longer and we're remaining healthier longer. We're wealthier younger. Our lifestyle patterns have changed. There are more single-adult households than ever before, as the extended family continues to decline as the preferred way we share our lives with others. Most importantly, banks need to look at the entire life cycle of their customers to better address the changing demands for financial products and advice.

We are becoming more demanding as consumers. We want good service from our financial providers. We want flexibility in our products to match our individual lifestyles. With the divorce rate now at 50% in some European countries, we need flexible and independent financial solutions for pensions, savings and assets. We 'know' we can always get our financial needs met elsewhere and expect our banks to know that, and behave as if they know that. We want access to our banks any time, from anywhere by many different means. And we are very happy now to have multiple banking relationships.

Our technology changes dramatically, all the time. Moore's law stated that the power of technology would double every eighteen months. This has held true for decades. Maybe change here is even accelerating. Banking has relied heavily on technology since the first commercial mainframe computers in the 1950s. The automatic teller machine (ATM) sparked a great debate about how customers preferred to do their banking. It turns out most people are happy to get money out of a 'hole in the wall'. Today we see people managing their financial affairs on home computers over internet connections and even from their mobile phones. But we also see a growing need for advisers to help people with the complex choices presented to them when making financial decisions.

The role of the regulator is also changing. The need to protect the industry, the participants, the customers and the state is changing. The need to protect individuals' privacy is being challenged by the need for justice and the need for the security of the state. The eurozone single currency is now in place and the European Union continues with its plans to expand.

Much is changing; little remains the same for long now. I commend this book to you if you wish to become more familiar with these issues and the other issues the banks across Europe are grappling with.

Guy Warren
Head of Banking, Europe
Unisys Corporation

Preface

Banks will never be popular. They might do more to explain themselves.

The Banker, April 2000

That bald and uncompromising comment was made in response to the publication of the Cruickshank Review, a critical review of banking in the United Kingdom. Banks may not always be unpopular, but it might still be desirable for banks to 'explain themselves' to their customers. This book is designed to allow the banks to explain their aims and objectives and the strategies designed to fulfil them through the mouths of their senior executives. At a time of rapid change, banks need to explain the purpose and also the value of the changes they are introducing or which are being forced upon them by fierce competition at national and international level.

Their aims and objectives have to be understood in the context of developments in the European Union. These include a decade of change in banking regulation as central banks and banking supervisors have sought to remove restrictive, old-fashioned regulations with the aim of making their banking systems more competitive. The introduction of the euro has required more efficient and reliable banks, able to provide the necessary liquidity for a single market. At the same time, banks have faced increased competitive pressures from a global financial market and declining profits from their traditional sources of income—credit and deposits. New technology has opened up the possibility of new methods of dealing with retail customers, but has also allowed for new, apparently low-cost entrants to banking, challenging the role of the traditional banks and enticing their customers away. The book provides an analysis and a description of the retail banking strategy adopted by leading European banks, informed by discussions with leading bankers and illustrated by their comments on the challenges they face.

Acknowledgements

The authors are grateful to Unisys for their support, without which it would not have been possible to create this work. Unisys have a long heritage of meeting the needs of banks and financial institutions across the world, particularly in Europe. They continue those relationships today and are heavily engaged in helping their banking clients to be more successful, using their own capabilities to work alongside the skills of their clients. This partnership approach generates the creativity needed to address today's issues, and Unisys provides the technical capability and capacity to see the projects through.

The authors would like to express their grateful thanks to Dr Laura Costanzo, Research Fellow, International Institute of Banking and Financial Services, for her invaluable assistance in providing research support for this book. We would also like to thank the many senior managers and directors of banks, central banks and academics who kindly gave freely of their time to discuss the issues involved in European retail banking. The following banks and individuals were represented:

Abbey National plc
ABN-AMRO
Allianz-Dresdner
Banca di Roma
Banca Intesa BCI
Banca Sabadell
Banco Español de Credito
Bank of Italy
Bank of France
Bank of Spain
Banque National de Paris
Barclays Bank plc
BBVA
BSCH
Bundesverband deutscher Banken

Caisse d'Epargne
Central Bank of the Netherlands
Commerzbank
Commission Bancaire
Crédit Agricole
Crédit Mutuel
Deutsche Bank AG
Deutsche Bundesbank
Deutsche Sparkassen und Giroverband
Dutch Bankers Association
ForeningsSparbanken
French Banking Association
Groupe Banques Populaires
Handelsbanken
HSBC

HVB Group
ING
Skandiabanken
Skandinaviska Enskilda Banken
   (SEB)
Swedish Bankers Association
Swedish Financial Services Authority
Société Générale
Spanish Banking Association

Unicredito Italiano
Professor Aglietta, Centre d'Etudes
   Economique et Bancaires, Paris
Professor Mottura, Professor of
   Financial Markets and Institutions,
   Universita
Commerciale Luigi Bocconi
Professor Bruni, Universita
   Commerciale Luigi Bocconi

1
Setting the Scene

The purpose of this book is to explain the changing role of banks, sometimes through the mouths of senior executives in the industry. Their views will be set in the context of the developments of the last decade, which has revolutionised banking in some member states of the European Union (EU), and the challenges to come. Banking in the EU has undergone a transformation in the last decade. That transformation has been partly due to the introduction of the European Directives on Banking Supervision and the impact of first the Basel Accord of 1988 and then its subsequent recommendations on banking supervision. The net effect has been to ensure a gradual move towards a uniform approach to banking regulation: the regulatory impact will only form part of the analysis of banking strategy, where deregulation has contributed to the present structure of banking.

The structure of the banking system has changed rapidly and the pace of change will continue to accelerate not only as consolidation gathers momentum, but also as the development of new technology continues to alter markets and facilitate cross-border expansion. It will reshape the environment and allow for the existence of niche players and pan-European banks. But much will depend on how banks use new technology to enhance services for customers and thus retain them. The arrival of the euro and the development of online technology have already brought about significant changes in the conduct of banking business, which may yet constitute a financial revolution. Just what the extent of those changes will be is as yet unclear, but some take the view that banks themselves will not survive. That may seem to be an extreme view but the possibility that banks will disappear depends on what a bank is understood to be and how far its traditional functions are or could be taken over by non-banks or non-bank financial institutions. The first step is to outline the reasons for such a claim and then to look at the entities which may take over banking functions and assess the true extent of the threat to traditional banks.

BANKS, MONEY AND THE PAYMENTS SYSTEM

The claim that banks will cease to exist in anything like their present form rests on the argument that some or all of a bank's functions may be taken over by other processes or entities. The traditional business of banking is usually considered to be taking deposits and granting credit and playing a unique role in the payments system. Indeed many central bankers regard this as the most important function which banks perform. It provides the rationale for banking supervision, which arises from the need to safeguard the payments system on which the economy depends from 'systemic shocks'; namely, the inability of the banks to guarantee payments to individuals or companies.

It is an extension of the use of electronic money—a vision of a future in which payments are made directly between individuals and businesses without the intervention of a third party, one in which the individual is his own banker using his computer, mobile telephone or interactive television. Transactions would be handled directly and each individual would carry out his own investments, buying and selling shares or selecting investment products.

The apparently straightforward transfer of money from one individual to another as payment for goods or services is not as simple as it seems. The process depends on the acceptability of the payment (whether that is made by a cheque, cash, debit or credit card, a smart card, an electronic purse or any other form of electronic money) and the enforceability of the payment. In addition there must be an audit trail; if the recipient does not receive the payment, he must be able to demonstrate that he has not received it. The person making the payment must have a way of telling that the payment has been received.

Then it must be possible to show that the money transferred from one to another belonged to the person making the payment and that it was properly and legally in the possession of the person making the payment. There must be a guarantor of the safety and security of the transfers of money from one to another, otherwise the essential trust is broken that enables payments to take place and thus the whole economy to function. Whatever form the payments system takes, it must conform to these criteria. Otherwise the payments system simply will not work, and that will be the case even if the system never involves the transfer of paper or money in a physical form.

Electronic money is a payment instrument which allows a monetary value to be stored electronically and allows for transactions to take place without involving a bank account; payments are not settled by transfers between bank accounts. Technically, it is defined as a prepaid bearer instrument, and is accepted as a means of payment by individuals and companies besides the organisation which issued it. To be electronic money, it has to be used in paying for more than one type of purchase, so a prepaid telephone card does not count as electronic money. Other payment instruments might be limited-purpose payment instruments, such as those used in paying for bus transport in a particular city.

Electronic money is simply another retail payment instrument, analogous to notes and coins, cheques, bank transfers or credit and debit cards. Each of these has certain features which make them more or less attractive to certain customers or for certain types of transactions. All of these methods of payment compete with each other, from the viewpoint of the customer and the viewpoint of the bank and the banking system generally. Some EU countries, such as Sweden and the Netherlands, have virtually eliminated cheques, for example, because of the costs and difficulties involved in transporting vast quantities of paper and the need to retain them for a number of years. They have imposed costs on the use of cheques which make them unattractive to customers, while providing cheaper alternative methods of payment. Each method has costs attached to it. For credit and debit cards, the main costs arise from the bookkeeping in relation to bank accounts, including the verification of accounts, transfers between accounts and sometimes the fraudulent use of cards.

Electronic money has the advantage of low marginal costs, but the fixed costs (the purchase and maintenance of the cards, software and/or dedicated merchant terminals). It is possible that this new payment instrument will develop and eliminate others. That will depend on the possibility of reducing the fixed costs and widespread acceptance of a particular instrument. The total amount of electronic money has increased since 1994 and reached a level of €140 million by the end of June 2000, but was only 0.04% of banknotes and coins. It is possible that electronic money will become a very close substitute for banknotes and coins, and if it offers attractive interest, it might almost become an attractive alternative to holding short-term bank deposits.

What is interesting about the emergence of electronic money is the reaction of the European Central Bank and the reasons for it. 'Society reaps substantial benefits from using a single, well-defined and stable unit of account for conducting transactions, irrespective of the issuer or the form in which money is issued,' both domestically and internationally.[1] The latter aspect is ever more important, given the global economy. There are risks: electronic money could lead to the emergence of multiple units of account in the economy, so that the prices of goods and services would be entirely unclear. Electronic money issuers might start to issue excessive amounts of electronic money so that they can make profits. They could get involved in risky investment activities, which could lead to electronic money instruments being traded at variable exchange rates, which would undermine the role of money as a single unit of account.

The organisation which is responsible for the transfer of money is part of a payments system, namely a bank, and the external guarantor of its smooth functioning is generally the central bank. Indeed in some countries the central bank not only regulates the payments system but also sponsors it. This is the fundamental function of a bank, from which flows its role as a deposit-taker and provider of credit. Electronic money issuers, if they came to play a substantial role in the economy, could 'jeopardise either the smooth functioning of payment systems or the stability of the financial

---

[1] Issues arising from the emergence of electronic money. *ECB Monthly Bulletin*, November 2000, p. 55.

system,' unless an appropriate framework of regulation is put in place. The concerns expressed by the European Central Bank led to the adoption of EU legislation on electronic money.

What this does is to limit the issuance of electronic money to traditional credit institutions and to a new type of credit institution known as an electronic money institution (ELMI), specialising in the electronic money business. Interestingly enough, the application of existing banking directives to the ELMIs allows them to benefit from a European passport which enables them to carry out their activities throughout the EU. Electronic money need not be confined to a small group who agree and accept its terms; it can become a convertible currency as well, another vital element of money. But these advantages come at a price: they must be subject to prudential supervision; electronic money schemes must have solid legal and transparent legal arrangements and must maintain adequate technical, organisational and procedural safeguards to prevent, contain and implement electronic money schemes. They must agree to supply the central bank with whatever information may be required for the purpose of monetary policy. Those who issue electronic money must accept the legal obligation to redeem it at par value. The fact such regulation is necessary indicates that electronic money is simply money in a new form, not a replacement for money. If they were a practical means of exchange for modern living, conch shells would be subject to similar regulation and would fulfil the same functions.

The function of the ELMI shares one of the fundamental functions of a bank. This function is reflected both in the definitions of a bank in the banking laws of the EU and elsewhere and in the concerns of regulators. The payments system has to be protected from possible systemic shocks, since domestic and foreign exchange payments lie at the heart of all economic systems. If the ability to make and receive payments collapsed, then all other markets with their own separate activities would be put at risk. Such risks are intensified by the network of interbank linkages both directly via banks and indirectly through the markets, whereby a failing bank may well be a large debtor to other banks, partly and necessarily because of their central role in the payments systems. Moves towards real-time gross settlement systems, such as Target (the trans-European automated real-time gross settlement express transfer system) enhance the risk.

BANKS AS INTERMEDIARIES

Arising from their function in facilitating payments, banks acquire deposits, but must return the money their customers have deposited with them on demand, even though that money has been invested in long-term credit, extended to other individuals or institutions. As a consequence of that, the debt/asset ratio for banks is higher than for other financial institutions (e.g. insurance companies) as well as non-financial institutions, and compared with non-financial firms, a far larger proportion of bank debt is short-term and directly demandable from the issuer.

A bank provides liquidity services, because it accepts deposits and extends loans. By doing this, it enables depositors to have better access to their funds than if they had invested directly in the firms to which the banks have lent the money. It would be neither easy nor possible for other financial institutions or the capital markets to take over this role entirely. Banks are still seen as the most important intermediary between the investor and the firm requiring investment, between buyers and sellers. In the words of Ricardo, the distinctive feature of a banker is 'that he uses the money of others'; hence the need for regulation.[2]

Modern banking theory stresses the important function of banks in screening and monitoring loans, loans to companies and consumer credit. In the case of consumer credit, banks gain valuable information through management of personal customers' bank accounts as all the transactions through the account which reflect customers' income, wealth and expenditure patterns. In the case of companies, banks act as financial intermediaries between savers and borrowers. They are able to do so primarily because they have access to information about companies who do not want to make the information publicly available or borrowers who do not want their strategies subject to public scrutiny and market pressures. In addition, borrowers' behaviour should be monitored so that the probability of their repaying the loans is maximised. It is much easier and far less costly for banks to undertake that task than the investors, who are depositors with banks. Banks have the advantage of economies of scale in monitoring, perhaps through long-established relationships with the borrowers and direct knowledge of the state of the company through interlocking directorships.

This brief outline of the traditional function of banks explains their key role in the economy and the reason for banks being subject to special regulation and insurance in the form of deposit insurance, designed to protect depositors and to prevent runs on banks. Similarly, to prevent such runs and to enable banks to manage the range of risks involved in their business (market and credit risk, interest rate risk and liquidity risk), banks are required to retain an appropriate level of capital. At the moment, just what that should be is the subject of intense debate and policy-making by the Bank for International Settlements. At the same time, it is recognised that if banks were to set aside sufficient capital to cover all eventualities, then they would be unable to contribute to economic growth. So public funds may be injected through the central bank, acting as lender of last resort.

The overall aim of banking regulation is to ensure the safety and soundness of the financial system and to ensure that credit is distributed in a neutral way from an economic viewpoint, but above all it is to safeguard *confidence* in the financial system. The relevance of that even now and the role of the government and the central bank in establishing and maintaining stable monetary policies was seen on our television screens in December 2001. Anxious and angry crowds in Argentina thronged the streets outside the banks with their doors firmly closed against a run on the banks.

---

[2] W. Bagehot, 1978, *Lombard Street: A Description of the Money Market*. New York: Arno Press, p. 100. Original edition 1873.

Withdrawals when allowed would be limited to $1,000 per person. Very often, though, banking regulation is strengthened and increased following banking crises, such as the 1987 Banking Act in the UK after the collapse of Johnson Matthey Bank and again after the BCCI debacle. That could follow when the banking system is finally restored in Argentina as well.

THE ROLE OF A BANK

It is worth getting a clear view of what it means for a financial institution to be regarded as a bank. In the traditional paradigm, banks are the main providers of all financial services, a dominance based on five aspects of banking business. They were the only ones to act as market intermediaries, providers of capital, providers of transaction services, providers of market information and providers of know-how.

- As market intermediaries, banks collect money from depositors and lend money to customers seeking financing, thus matching lenders and borrowers. Furthermore, they play a role in matching both sides of the transactions; for example, sellers and buyers of securities or of firms. In this role, banks give customers access to capital markets.
- Besides securities markets, as providers of capital, banks are the sole or main source of financing, and provide services for managing financial risks.
- As participants in the capital and money markets, banks can advise their customers on the basis of the information received in real time. They play a role in monitoring the markets on the basis of company information as well as fundamental economic information.
- In addition to holding market information, banks also have the ability to analyse information and develop an understanding of markets and trends; they also have experience in dealing with complex financial issues and analyses of business opportunities for their clients.

These are matched by the values to the clients who rely on the banks to be market intermediaries, providers of capital, providers of transaction services, providers of market information and providers of know-how. Those who see non-banks as undermining the traditional role of banks see the banks' dominance as being underpinned by their proprietary branch network; their exclusive role in the economic system, protected by regulation; their proprietary infrastructure for transaction processing; their position as the sole source for market information and proprietary knowledge owing to their knowledge of transaction flows. Regulation, of course, applies to all financial services companies or to all companies offering financial services, even if the holding company is a non-financial company.

It is only then that the nature of the pressures on banks during the 1990s and the potential and continuing pressures on banks in this decade can be understood. Then the extent to which other financial institutions and even non-banks have begun to nibble away at the banks' traditional role can be seen in the appropriate context. Some would say this process is inexorable and that banks themselves will disappear. But banks fought back during the last decade and many emerged as stronger, more efficient and more profitable institutions as a result. Their chances of survival in Europe in the twenty-first century look good.

THE THREAT FROM NON-BANKS AND NEAR-BANKS

The terms 'non-bank' and 'near-bank' refer to a wide category of entities and institutions which include consumer credit companies, credit cards, insurance companies, and on the internet, established general portals and start-ups, as well as internet brokerages and stand-alone internet banks. The current threat from non-banks may be more apparent than real. The term 'non-bank' is somewhat misleading, since in most member states apart from the UK, at least some of these entities, such as consumer credit companies, are classed as banks and are regulated as such.

Consumer Credit Companies

Consumer credit companies are not new, but what is changing is the increased use of consumer credit. They can be seen in opposition to banks in the UK, because the banking legislation defines a bank rather narrowly as an authorised 'deposit-taking' institution in the Banking Act 1987. Banks were supervised by the Bank of England under that Act until the responsibility for their supervision was transferred to the Financial Services Authority (FSA) under the Financial Services and Markets Act 2000. Companies offering consumer credit alone are not regulated by the FSA but fall under the aegis of the Consumer Credit Act 1974. If such companies take deposits then they have to have special authorisation and become a bank. If they simply lend money to consumers in the form of loans, credit agreements and mortgages, they have to be licensed by the director general of the Office of Fair Trading, who keeps a public record of licensed traders and anyone who has ever applied for a licence. The Act also applies to those who hire out goods, run credit agencies, collect credit debts or provide debt counselling or debt adjusting. These companies are not authorised or supervised by the FSA but by local authority trading standards officials. This is the background for the description of new entrants to banking being described as non-banks.

France

Consumer credit companies do not form a different category in other EU member states. For example, France's 1984 Banking Act defines a bank as an institution carrying out any one of the three activities set out in Article 1 of the act: the 'receipt of funds from the public; credit operations and making available to customers or administering means of payment'. According to the Commission Bancaire, all of these activities are regulated by the banking authorities in the same way, so setting up a company which specialises in any one of these activities does not carry any advantages.

Consumer credit companies are by no means insignificant, highly specialised companies, as indicated by the following brief survey of some major companies and their role in the banking system. France, for example, has a wide range of specialised *société financière*, including 64 consumer credit companies and 69 consumer leasing companies, but it is hard to see these as providing real competition to the traditional banks. Almost all the consumer finance companies are owned by banks, despite some misgivings in certain parts of the industry. The leading finance companies, such as Cetelem, Sofinco and Cofinoga, are all owned by large banking groups. Cetelem is owned by BNP Paribas; Cofinoga is jointly owned by Galeries Lafayette/Cetelem; S2P is owned Carrefour and Cetelem; Sofinco is owned by Crédit Agricole/Indosuez; and Sovac is owned by GE Capital. It is true that they may have considerable independence within the group; for example, over 70% of Sofinco's business is outside the orbit of Crédit Agricole. Some of the leading store cards and related banking operations are owned by banks; for example, S2P at Carrefour and Edel at Leclerc. In addition, Carrefour, with over 600,000 customers, offers loans and deposit services either in-store or through electronic channels through an exclusive arrangement with Cetelem.

Cetelem has extensive operations in Spain, Italy and Portugal with a network of partnerships and subsidiaries such as Findomestic (Italy), the launch of an Aurore–Mastercard partnership in Spain and partnerships with banks such as Caixa Galicia, Bankinter and Banco Zaragozano. Early in 2001 Cetelem and Dresdner Bank signed a partnership agreement, and Cetelem acquired a 70% share of WKV Bank, a Munich-based company specialising in consumer credit, with the remaining 30% being held by Dresdner. In the same year, Cetelem and the Halifax signed an agreement and set up a joint subsidiary handling personal loans. In France, Banque Populaire renewed its agreement with Cetelem and the Scalbert-Dupont Bank began marketing the Allure card with the group. The company works throughout Europe and sees a potential market of some €700 billion. It does not, however, operate separately from the banking system but is part of it. It is a wholly-owned subsidiary of a bank and has established a complex network of profit-sharing agreements with other banks. It does, however, point out the differences in attitudes to consumer credit in the leading EU member states.

Spain and Italy

The definition of banking in Spain includes both deposit-taking institutions and, under the new legal framework for credit institutions introduced in 1996, financial credit institutions are prohibited from taking deposits but are allowed to engage in a restricted range of operations, such as lending, factoring, leasing, issuing and administering credit cards. Given the restricted nature of their activities, credit companies are exempted from membership of the deposit guarantee scheme and the capital requirements are lower, but they are regulated in the same way as banks, and the differences are regarded as being minimal and justified by their specialised business. They are authorised and supervised by the Bank of Spain.

Non-banks such as large retailers can own a maximum of 20% of a credit institution, but this does discourage new entrants to banking. Many large retailers, such as El Corte Inglés, have their own consumer finance companies and these could become significant competitors to banks if the opportunity arose. They not only provide store cards but also loans and investment services. These specialised credit institutions are not exclusively owned by banks. Some of these finance companies are owned by industrial groups and retailers but the majority are owned by banks.

Consumer credit legislation (Law 7/1995) may also limit the profits to be made by finance companies. The law does not allow overdraft interest rates to exceed a certain limit (the effective interest rate derived from such interest cannot be more than two and a half times the legal interest rate, which is a little less than the market rate). This is not the only restriction placed on consumer credit. The law imposes a limit on the level of commissions which credit companies can demand in the case of cancellation or advance refund of consumer credit. All in all, consumer credit companies do not pose a threat to Spanish banks.

Italy's 1993 Banking Act restricts the granting of consumer credit to banks and financial intermediaries, and these institutions are also supervised by the Bank of Italy. The act also specifies the level of the annual percentage rate of charge (APR). However, there are complications in Italy arising in part from the application of the 1996 anti-usury law, which prevents lenders from charging borrowers more than 1.5 times the current rates. The law applies, among other things, to mortgages and personal credit.

The governor of the Bank of Italy indicated that the effect of the usury laws is a matter of concern in a speech to the Association of Italian Bankers in July 2001:

Usury is found where there is social and economic degradation. It flourishes outside the legal credit system. The Bank contributes to the scrupulous application of the statutory rules in this field. But I have already had occasion to recall that, although administrative limits on bank high interest rates reduce their dispersion, they worsen the allocation of financial flows. Ceilings on lending rates that are the same throughout the country may have the paradoxical effect of reducing the volume of legal credit, where credit risk is highest and leads to the expansion of illegal lending. Banks must improve their procedures for granting loans, ensure that valid initiatives do not end up outside the legal credit system. It is necessary to increase the awareness of households and enterprises of the consequences of making inappropriate use of money and borrowed funds.

The main sources of consumer credit and personal loans are some 41 companies, 8 of which are car makers' finance houses, 24 are non-captive finance houses and 9 are banks, responsible for 65% of the total consumer credit granted to Italian households. That amounted to L48.3 billion in 2000, of which about L25 billion was for car finance. It is a rapidly growing sector, and although the consumer credit companies and credit card companies are supervised by the Bank of Italy, they do have an advantage in the reluctance of the banks to provide unsecured loans. The financial institutions, consumer associations and the Bank of Italy are all concerned about the growth of the *strozzini* (literally 'stranglers') or 'loan sharks', who have taken advantage of the restrictions on interest rates and accessibility of credit, and who have thrived because of weak competition from legitimate lenders. Their activities are now the subject of an inquiry by a special commission.

Banks in Italy also face competition from Poste Italiane, which was established as a bank in 1999 and has now expanded into financial services, a move which it expects will enable the group as a whole to break even in 2002. Its banking division, BancoPosta, accounts for 37% of its total revenues. By March 2001 it had over 1 million retail banking clients (out of Italy's 29 million current accounts) and 230,000 corporate accounts. It is in a good position to take advantage of the growth in the financial services sector, since it still has about 14,000 branches, many of which are in rural areas from which the banks have withdrawn through branch closures. It has also set up a payments card business, established a life insurance company and has started selling equity-linked bonds. But again, BancoPosta has become a fully-fledged universal bank and is another new entrant.

Germany

The banking market in Germany is large and fragmented and also one in which the large banks are unable to dominate the retail sector. In theory it should be wide open to competition, but in practice it is not quite as simple as that. Once again, banking legislation does not allow for the possibility of separate consumer credit companies. According to the Banking Act (as amended in 1998), the definition of a credit institution covers deposit-taking; granting of money loans and acceptance credits (lending business); the execution of cashless payment and clearing operations (giro business); the issuance of prepaid cards for payment purposes, unless the card issuer is also the service provider and hence the recipient of the payment using the card (prepaid card business); and the creation and administration of units and payment in computer networks. The definition is both up to date and comprehensive. Both credit institutions and financial services institutions (brokers) are authorised and regulated by the Federal Banking Supervisory Office working in cooperation with the Deutsche Bundesbank.

However, non-traditional banks do exist in Germany. They are often subsidiaries of insurance companies, household retailers or car manufacturers. Among the largest car manufacturers, Volkswagen and BMW have already established consumer banks and DaimlerChrysler launched a combined banking operation, Debis, at the end of 1999. The 'auto banks' account for 42% of new car financing. The BMW bank has an established credit card and deposit banking operation alongside its traditional leasing and finance business with 500,000 customers in Germany. It has extended its services to asset management and through its partnership with the Frank Russell Company offers a range of funds to its customers. The Volkswagen finance company, which has been in existence since 1949, was transformed into a bank in 1995 to take deposits, issue credit cards and develop a range of saving and loan products through Volkswagen Bank Direct. By 2000 the bank had €2.6 billion in deposits and over half a million customers. It is now an independent unit, but it is still closely related to the purchasing and financing of cars. Preparations were made in good time for the loss of the exemption from EU competition rules in 2002, which the car distribution business had long enjoyed. Leading retailers have also emerged as 'non-bank' competitors; for example, Quelle, a mail-order company, set up Entrium Direct Bankers in 1990, which was then revamped as the first internet bank in Germany in 1995. The bank grew rapidly in balance sheet and payroll terms and now has over 700,000 customer. Entrium acquired Austria's largest direct bank and established a branch in Luxembourg. Metro Group, owner of Kaufhof, the largest retailer, did not send up its own bank, but was one of a group of international investors in First-e, a stand-alone internet bank established in Dublin in 1999. All the back-office operations were outsourced: bank clearing to the Royal Bank of Scotland, broking execution to Dresdner Kleinwort Benson, and settlement to Pershing. For regulatory purposes it operates as a branch of its Paris-based partner, Banque d'Escompte. It set out to target a specific and narrow markets, 25–35 year olds. However, although it acquired about 250,000 UK clients, the bank was closed in October 2001.

Given the distribution of retail banking accounts in Germany—about 50% with savings banks and another large slice, about 16%, taken by the top four banks—it is hard to see any of these developments as being more than peripheral competition. Certainly, German bankers dismiss the 'non-banks' as being irrelevant.

Sweden

The banking market in Sweden has undergone radical changes in the past decade. It is dominated by four large banks (possibly about to be reduced to three), which control 90% of the market. The remaining 10% of the market is split between four banks and small savings banks, including SkandiaBanken, Wasabanken, GE Capital Bank and Ikano Banken. Ikano is based in Amsterdam and offers a range of banking and investment services via the internet, telephone and Ikea stores. Ikano Finans has several lines of business, including advancing credit for Ikea's store customers and running store cards for other groups. Its banking interests are mainly in Sweden, where apart from Ikano Banken it owns 20% of JP Bank, Sweden's sixth largest bank.

United Kingdom

The UK market is quite different from the major continental European markets in that it defines a bank as a deposit-taker, thus leaving the consumer credit market more open than in other EU member states. However, many of the so-called non-banks engage in traditional banking activities, such as deposit-taking as well as the provision of credit. The new entrants are subsidiaries of companies with an established brand name in a wide range of other areas. The newcomers include the supermarket banks (Sainsbury's, Tesco, Safeway, Asda, Marks and Spencer), the subsidiaries of insurance companies, (Standard Life, Scottish Widows, Prudential, Legal & General) and the utilities (Centrica, Thames Water), transport companies (British Airways and Easyjet) and even football clubs, such as Leeds United and Chelsea. Some build on their established brand names and existing client relationships to diversify into financial services. Virgin Direct is one such company, which since the launch of its services in 1995 has established a customer base of 270,000, and a 15% share of the personal equity plans (PEPs) market. It is a joint venture with the Royal Bank of Scotland (RBS), whereby Virgin provides its marketing skills, and the RBS provides the 'execution' of banking services and customer care from its call centre.

Many of the supermarket banks are joint ventures with long-established existing banks: Safeway's partnership with Abbey National was set up in 1996; Sainsbury's bank is a joint venture with Bank of Scotland (55% + BOS 45%); and Tesco has a 50:50 partnership with the Royal Bank of Scotland. They jointly have 2.5 million customers, or 7% of the retail market in the UK. They offer a fairly complete range of banking products from mortgages to cheque and savings accounts. Marks and Spencer is the only retail company which established its own financial services company, and all the insurance companies established their own banks, often savings accounts only, in order to attract funds. Given the fact that the latter offered higher interest rates, they were very successful at first. They competed very heavily on price with cheaper loans and more attractive savings rates than the high-street banks, enabling them to attract a huge inflow of funds in the early months of their existence. Interest rates soon declined so that savers moved their funds again, and low-cost consumer credit is offered in an extremely competitive market. Not all of these banks have succeeded in becoming profitable or in retaining their customers.

The New Banks

The so-called non-banks are better described as new non-traditional entrants to the banking industry. Even that description disguises the relationship between traditional banks and the new entrants. In the UK many of the new entrants are partnerships with existing banks where the retailers look for further profits and strengthening of the relationships with their customers, and the banks are taking advantage of strong brand names and thus gaining access to the distribution network of the supermarkets.

They offer only a limited range of products—loans or deposits—and they avoid current accounts. Unlike some of their continental European counterparts, they have not ventured into investment products, such as broking services and mutual funds.

But the non-banks have had more of an impact on established banks in the UK than they have had or are likely to have in continental Europe. By the middle of 1999, the new banks had acquired deposits of about £15 billion, which amounts to about 5% of the UK's £320 billion interest-bearing bank deposit total and about 1% of the total mortgages outstanding, but more importantly, they gained a 10% share of new lending in the first half of 1999. They achieved such rapid expansion because they focused on a limited range of activities in very narrow market segments where their low costs and their special delivery channels would ensure that they made significant advances very quickly. They also drew attention to the existence of a market segment composed of those who had the time and energy to switch deposits from one account to another in pursuit of higher interest rates. But moving their savings from one account to another does not preclude the retention of the current account with their own bank, and customers of the new entrants still look to their main bank to manage their income.

Non-banks did have an immediate impact on established banks, who viewed them as a serious threat. The established banks have responded in a variety of ways, by offering a wider range of deposit accounts with varying interest rates, highly competitive mortgage packages and competing with each other over interest paid on current accounts. However, since then the new entrants have been unable to sustain the attractive interest rates offered initially or to sustain their share of the mortgage market. They are no longer leaders in the league table of mortgage or deposit rates.

The new entrants have had less impact on established banks in the leading EU member states. This is partly because companies offering consumer credit count as banks and have no regulatory advantages and also because of the ownership patterns of such companies in France, Spain and Italy. The UK new entrants have in general concentrated on a strategy: attract clients by offering initially attractive products and a very limited range of banking services. For a number of new entrants, the strategy has not brought the expected success. The high interest rates could not be sustained. The cost of acquiring clients has not been sufficient to retain them. Other new entrants offer a wider range of banking and investment services, but have failed to provide more than peripheral competition for the established banks. The sources of pressure on banks are much more fundamental than on new entrants, which often provide a limited range of services. The new entrants are not perceived as a serious threat; indeed some of them have been in existence for at least a decade and have only succeeded in gaining a small market share.

However, banks do need to be aware of the factors which could lead to the non-banks becoming a more serious threat to the traditional banks. Customer behaviour has begun to change as customers have developed more sophisticated product needs; customers are placing higher demands on the quality and performance of financial services products, and they are becoming more price sensitive. They are determined to maximise value for money. Convenience has become much more important and may not be defined in terms of geographical convenience but also on availability in terms of opening hours and the choice of channels. They are less likely to accept standardised products and look for round-the-clock convenience. A survey of 2,000 small businesses conducted in August 2001 indicated that they wanted not just 24-hour banking services, they wanted 24-hour telephone-based advisers as well. This seems to be driven by the difficulties in obtaining appointments and inflexible hours.

It is an example of what customers are currently seeking, namely solutions designed for them plus an individual bundle of products, services and delivery. The solutions have to offer high product quality in terms of functionality, performance, speed and flexibility; they must leverage technical possibilities and be specifically adapted to the client's needs. They must be suitably priced and easily accessible.

Of these, the near-banks (auto banks, supermarket banks, finance subsidiaries of retailers, credit card specialists and insurance companies) present the most competition. They are providers of financial services with a banking licence but their range of services is often limited and they can draw on their skills and, perhaps more important, they can build on critical mass and economies of scale. The competition from near-banks and non-banks lies in the provision of intelligent agents (internet) and networking through third-party networks, as an element in the market intermediary services provided by banks. They also provide transaction services, including electronic transaction services. They may also act as third-party processors or become specialised players.

Information, a strength of traditional banks, is available over the internet and indeed there are now multiple sources of information. Banks have recognised the competition by establishing alternative methods of distribution (multichannel approach) or they have formed strategic alliances with the competitors or acquired them (e.g. the BNP Paribas acquisition of Cetelem in 2000). The principles which banks will need to apply, where they have not done so already, include developing innovative products, alternative channels of distribution and a strong brand. They should also unbundle activities which require different business systems and thus ensure that they remain competitive in every market segment and streamline the internal organisation in line with their new business developments and partnerships with the near- or non-banks. They may need to be willing to leverage another strong brand name instead of their own.

The leading banks in the EU have emerged from a decade of much more fundamental challenges than a few companies offering limited banking services. They have developed strategies which enabled them to survive a turbulent decade and some are ready to take on pan-European or even global competition.

ARE CREDIT CARDS A THREAT TO BANKS?

Credit cards are sometimes seen as another kind of new entrant in that they divert consumer lending from banks. Once again the UK is quite different in that 'revolving' credit cards are the norm and continue to proliferate; for most other EU member states, debit or payment cards, perhaps with a limited period of credit are the norm. The credit card business (in the form of debit or payment cards) in the EU has continued to grow over the past decade with ever-intensifying competition. Even before the advent of the euro, credit cards emerged as being entirely suited to the cross-border delivery of financial services, as long as they bore a universally recognised logo, such as Visa, Mastercard or American Express.

But although the credit card market continues to grow throughout the EU, it has not fulfilled the hope so many credit cards providers have entertained for the past decade—that the rest of the EU would follow the UK's lead, where 60% of the population hold one or more credit cards. Instead of credit cards, banks in mainland Europe issue debit cards, either direct or deferred, which are linked to the cardholders' current accounts, rather than stand-alone credit cards with separate and revolving lines of credit attached.

At first, few banks issued credit cards, so retailers throughout Europe developed their own extremely successful card-based credit programmes; for example, Aurore developed by Cetelem, which dominates the French credit card market. It emerged as a general-purpose credit card in France and is increasingly important in markets such as Italy, Belgium and Spain. As a result, Cetelem companies are in a strong position to develop credit cards throughout the EU.

The French banks established Cartes Bancaires in 1984 as an interbank organisation to manage the national cards network. Cartes Bancaires can claim considerable success: the card, bearing the CB logo, is essentially an interbank card, which means it will be accepted even if the issuing bank is different from the merchant's bank or the bank managing the automatic teller machine (ATM), provided the financial insitution is a member of the CB network. The card is multifunctional: ATM cash withdrawal, cash advance, electronic payment, mail/telephone order and payment at vending machines. The date at which the account is debited depends on the contract agreed between the bank and the customer, which can take the form of immediate debit, deferred debit or credit card. These cards have attained high levels of ownership and usage with three out of four adults owning the card and high levels of usage for cash withdrawals and payments.

In Germany consumers are still very conservative in their choice of payment methods. Consumers and retailers have a strong preference for cash, partly because of the high merchant discount charges imposed on card payments, and also because current account holders can borrow up to three times monthly earnings without being overdrawn and penalised for an unauthorised overdraft. The banks are keen to ensure that the overdraft remains as the consumers' main source of short-term finance, since credit cards with stand-alone revolving lines of credit attached would open up further disintermediation. The current account has become the cornerstone of the customer—bank relationship, and provides a further reason for the limited effect of non-banks and near-banks on the banks' traditional retail market.

Ownership and therefore the profits of card usage are complex; they are shared between banks or owned by banks, directly or indirectly. For example, Maestro (formerly Mastercard) is jointly owned by European banks and the newly listed company, which acts as a cross-border or a cross-regional network brand. In Europe, cross-border ATM access on debit cards was introduced in the late 1980s, and by 1998 the number had grown to 80 million a day. The growth rates for cross-border transactions of all kinds will grow rapidly with the introduction of notes and coins. The banks' involvement in the use of debit cards and other forms of money transmission may have to be extended, given the ever-increasing demand for cross-border retail money transmission services at a reasonable price to the user. The banks already have a share in the profits of these companies, but they should ensure they have at least a share of the potential growth of such mechanisms currently managed by Maestro, Visacard, American Express and others.

Efficient payment systems, especially cross-border systems in Euroland, will be an increasingly important part of the service banks can offer their customers and an important source of revenue, provided they make sure they have at least a stake in their development. Ease of provision of consumer credit will also grow in importance.

Some domestic banks in continental Europe see that there may be a potential for revolving credit in continental Europe, but they know better than their US and even UK competitors that there is a deeply felt aversion to debt. It is markedly less in some countries than others, so that card products are divided into two categories: 'pay now' and 'pay later', but the 'pay later' cards only cover a limited period of credit, such as 90 days or 6 months. It is an attempt to change consumer behaviour on the part of US banks and card issuers in the same way as it was achieved in the UK. The American banks which entered the UK market in the 1970s and 1980s made a long-term commitment to change consumer behaviour and gain an acceptance of the 'buy now and pay later' culture, and they were extremely successful in that market.

But revolving credit card issuers may face a tougher market in continental Europe. First of all, they may not be able to charge high interest rates on outstanding credit so easily, since some member states have regulations in place governing the level of interest charged. In addition, card issuers and payments associations may well be re-quired by the regulatory authorities to enhance transparency in the payments system, especially with regard to interchange fees. If the banks can ensure that such develop-ment takes place through partnerships such as Cetelem's complex web of partnerships, including a newly established partnership with HBOS (the bank resulting from the merger between the Halifax and the Bank of Scotland) and Postbank, a subsidiary of the ING group, then the threat to the banks' profits will be much reduced. Postbank launched Eurocard, a Mastercard-branded revolving credit card, in the Netherlands in 1999 and followed this by launching a Visa-branded online credit card, called E-Go. Other initiatives may be expected to follow.

E-BANKING: COMPETITION FROM NON-BANKS AND NEAR-BANKS

Competition in the banking market has been intensified by the appearance of non- and near-banks on the internet. These include general portals, such as money central.msn.com, which offer information enabling users to compare products and prices at different banks. Such portals do not offer financial products but there are links to online providers. The information is based on income from advertising and fees paid by providers for placing their products or links to the site. Other general portals include AOL, Yahoo! and T-Online. Some of these are set up by non-banks to act as intermediaries for a limited number of financial services companies and a limited range of products. From the viewpoint of banks, they represent a new distribution channel, and some banks are considering using some of the general portals for that purpose. Online business by banks may be achieved through cooperative ventures or by the creation of financial portals by banks.

For banks, 'attractors' such as general portals could well become established distribution partners of banks. The selection will depend on which portal has the most frequently visited home page and as such offers the best platform for selling financial products to the bank's target group. Banks have had to face the fact that the internet gives customers much easier access to the products of other financial services providers and allows rapid comparisons. Traditional customer ties are also losing value, so the problem for banks, as bank products become more homogeneous and interchangeable, is to retain and attract customers.

E-banking has contributed to the greater transparency in the provision and costs of banking and insurance products, customers' increasing price sensitivity, and aggressive pricing strategies. The ensuing battle for market share could also squeeze bank margins. This is the case even though the internet reduces the prices and costs per transaction.

On the other hand, the prospects of margin erosion might be mitigated by mergers and acquisitions (M&A) among the companies providing portals. The e-banking market might well be limited to a few large providers of financial portals, since these depend on large traffic volumes. It is also clear that advice will continue to be vital for the majority of customers. Banks with direct customer links through a branch network and which use the internet as an extension of their distribution channels will continue to have advantages over stand-alone internet banks. The threat of competition from e-banking cannot, however, be lightly dismissed and banks have been re-examining their strategies in the face of competition from non-banks, near-banks and new entrants. These new challenges have arisen after a decade in which the banks have experienced a decline in net interest margins and developments in the capital markets, which could undermine their traditional role as intermediaries. These issues will be explored in the next chapter.

CONCLUSIONS

The first issue to be considered in looking at the future of retail banking in the EU is the continued existence of the banks themselves. But when the alleged new threats are examined more closely, they do not seem to offer the replacement for traditional banks which many academics and futurologists expect. The universal or integrated model, the typical continental approach for banking, may well be better placed to absorb new technology and the existence of alternative sources of credit.

E-money is still very much in the early stages of development, but it has the potential for growth, even a rapid growth. Although the volume of e-money in circulation currently remains very low in the euro area, the number of devices already in circulation suggests that its usage could expand very quickly. That does present a challenge for the banking system. Domestic payment systems in some countries have eliminated paper transfers in the form of cheques (paper giros are still much in use in these countries) but the minimum period of time for retail payments is still two days. In other countries, such as the UK, the Clearing House Automated Payment System (Chaps) is subject to frequent and sustained criticism. The European Commission has successfully established Target for large transfers between member states, but has subjected retail transfers to sustained criticism over the costs and time taken. At present, banks do not see e-money systems as posing a threat to them, but as the volume of e-money in circulation begins to rise, they may well do so.

Customers will begin to demand a comparable level of service for both domestic and cross-border transfers in Euroland in terms of speed and cost of transfers. Individual banks could match that for certain payments by setting up e-money devices, but a wholesale increase in efficiency would require a consolidation of interbank infrastructure and improved internal procedures for processing all payments, domestic and cross-border. Competitive pressures will increase along with external pressures for improved efficiency on the domestic front and from the European Commission. Banks will have to respond immediately to lower cross-border costs and in the longer term to compete with e-money. They will still have an advantage over the e-money devices; customers do not just want to be able to make rapid payments or to receive credits to their accounts, they also want to be able to manage their income. The bank plays a key role in that, and if it wishes to retain the customer and that relationship of trust, it will have to prepare to meet that new challenge.

E-money and the development of internet banking certainly intensify the franchise value of banks as they contribute to the intensification of competition in the banking sector. Some commentators have taken the view that the internet could lead to the separation of typical banking activities, such as deposit-taking, payment services and lending being split up, because internet banking would reduce the traditional synergies between them. So far that has not happened and banks have absorbed new technology. Advances in technology, such as data processing and business models, allow banks to make more efficient use of information about their customers and to offer them a more efficient and profitable service. This book aims to explore the way in which the leading banks have responded to the challenges of technology, the innovations which have taken place, and where they believe their strengths lie.

This chapter has also explored a different challenge to the very existence of banks—the development of the so-called non-banks and the new entrants. First of all, the non-banks would be described as banks in the banking legislation in most EU member states (the UK is unusual in this regard), since they offer credit, although they do not take deposits, and are subject to banking regulation. Secondly, almost all of these are either owned by or operate in partnership with existing traditional banks and can be regarded as a means of retaining customers and providing the bank with additional profits. This is true of most credit cards, where the credit card often has the bank's logo and is issued by the bank in a profit-sharing arrangement. The use of credit cards as a means of borrowing is extremely limited in most continental European countries, where people either do not borrow or they use the overdraft facilities offered by their banks. Finally, new entrants are not seen as a serious competitive threat to the leading retail banks, since they are only too well aware of the costs of acquiring new clients themselves. Offering a specific service, as most new entrants do, whether in the form of car loans, credit for retail purchases or high interest rate accounts means that they do not compete with the main banks. This is partly because their relationship with the new entrant is limited and sometimes temporary. The leading retail banks have other challenges to face.

2
The Challenges

Banks have traditionally played a key role in the financial system by acting as financial intermediaries between ultimate savers and borrowers. Most banks in the European Union (EU) have been the main, if not the only source of credit for households and the corporate sector. That role has come under increasing pressure over the last decade and the same pressures show no sign of diminishing in this decade. The squeeze on the banks' traditional sources of income has several causes, and has led to the banks seeking other sources of profit. The main challenges facing banks during the last few years have included:

- The squeeze on bank interest income
- The developments in the capital markets
- The decline in corporate bank borrowing
- The euro and the customer

THE SQUEEZE ON BANK INTEREST INCOME

Banks' lending margins declined throughout the 1990s and there is every sign that the trend will not be reversed. Germany, Denmark, Spain, Italy, Sweden and the UK in particular emphasised that the downward trend had been evident for a long time. The decline is partly due to the convergence of interest rates towards the common levels for European Monetary Union (EMU), followed by the adoption of a single interest rate for Euroland, and first to the stability of exchange rates in EMU and then the elimination of exchange rate risk. Interest rate volatility has a significant effect on bank net interest margins, as a 1% increase in volatility increases net interest margins by 0.2%.[1] Bank margins are also affected by low inflation and the consequent fall in

---

[1] Anthony Saunders and Liliana Schumacher, 2000, The determinants of bank interest rate margins: an international study. *Journal of International Money and Finance*, vol. 19, pp. 813–32. This study is based on a comparison of 614 banks in six selected European countries and the US.

nominal interest rates. Higher market interest rates make it easier for banks to pass on changes in the market rates to the customer. On the other hand, it is much more difficult for banks to pass on very low interest rates on deposits to their customers, so their margins are narrower than the nominal interest rates would otherwise suggest.

The decline in bank margins has not only been brought about by macroeconomic factors of these kinds. Most leading banks have reported that stiff competition from new entrants, such as foreign banks, insurance companies, supermarket chains and car manufacturers or car dealers, and internet banks, have forced them to compete harder on price terms. Some countries, such as the UK, have seen the most significant reductions taking place in the personal sector, that is, the mortgage and consumer credit markets, including credit cards. Others, such as France, Italy and Sweden, saw the greatest squeeze in the corporate sector; but for the rest, the effects on margins have been much the same across all sectors.

A leading UK banker described Egg as an example of such competition, but one which reversed the usual banking procedure of lower rates for deposits than for loans, a business plan which cannot last. Part of his bank's strategy was not to respond with the same ill-advised approach, but to develop its own ways of attracting and retaining customers. Most traditional bankers talked about stand-alone internet banks and their customers in somewhat derogatory terms. One leading banker called them 'interest rate tarts' with time on their hands to pursue an additional half-percent of interest: 'They are not worth pursuing, because they will continually move'. Very often these customers remain with their banks but move part of their assets from one high-interest account to another, thus depriving the bank of fees or income-earning opportunities.

There are interesting differences between the margins for banks in various member states. Belgium, Ireland, Austria, Portugal and the UK all reported that the most significant reductions in margins took place in the personal sector, that is, for mortgages and consumer credit, with the UK reporting that the major squeeze on margins was in the area of credit cards. On the other hand, France, Italy and Sweden experienced the most significant changes in the corporate sector, but for most member states the reduction in margins was more or less the same across all sectors of the credit market. Italy faces competition from new entrants; it has come from foreign banks in the mortgage and corporate markets. In Sweden, mortgage banks, insurance companies and retail firms have all entered retail banking. For France and Germany, telephone or, more important, internet banks have had an impact, although the market shares for all these new entrants are small. The fear is that, although they have a long way to go before they match the size of the well-established banks, they will cherry-pick the best-quality customers.

Competition has significantly tightened over the longer term, partly as a result of deregulation and other basic tendencies generating more competition in the banking industry. Interest rate levels and changes obviously have the most important impact on margins, especially the margins on deposits. There can be marked temporary effects on bank income; for example, banks often delay changing their own rates in response to changes in the market rates, so they may continue to benefit from high lending margins for a short time even though market rates have fallen. Changes in the market rates may have the greatest impact on deposit margins as banks typically react to market rates more slowly than lending rates. Banks take a judgement on how quickly their competitors will respond to changes in market rates. Typically, once one bank alters its deposit rates, the others follow rapidly. In general, banks charge more for household lending than for lending to companies, though this is not necessarily justified by the credit risks involved. In some countries, however, like Denmark and Spain, where a high proportion of personal lending is mortgage lending with low risks of default on the loan, the lending margins can be very narrow.

Banks have also started to charge fees for servicing bank accounts and payment services, as a way of lessening the effect of tightening bank margins. The margins then cover a smaller part of the banks' operating expenses with the same level of charges for the risks involved. In Sweden this has happened at the same time as competition from niche players, who only offer loans or deposits, not payment services. The Spanish banks have also increased the income they receive from the fees they charge their customers. Then they price loans much more competitively as a way of locking in customers with profitable accounts. Their focus is on the profitability or otherwise of all the business a customer brings to the bank.

Most banks claim that increased competition, partly as a result of deregulation, is the main reason for much more careful pricing of bank lending. Of course, bank margins are primarily affected by changes in market interest rates, because banks do not wish to change all their lending and deposit rates as soon as the market rates have changed. The reasons for that are familiar enough: the costs of changing the rates for customers; to keep or obtain market share; or the banks may regard the interest rate change as only a temporary one, so there is no point in changing the rates. Obviously this affects lending margins on a temporary basis, but in the longer term the margins are not affected by sudden changes once the banks' new lending rates have fully reacted to any reduction or increase in interest rates.

There are interesting differences between the margins for banks in the various member states. Belgium, Ireland, Austria, Portugal and the UK all reported that the most significant reductions in margins took place in the personal sector, that is, for mortgages and consumer credit, with the UK reporting that the major squeeze on margins was in the area of credit cards. On the other hand, France, Italy and Sweden experienced the most significant changes in the corporate sector, but for most member states the reduction in margins was more or less the same across all sectors of the credit market.

Household lending margins are usually higher than the margins in corporate lending in most countries. Assuming that corporate lending is at least as risky as household lending, the lower margins suggest that competition for corporate lending is tougher than for personal clients. This is not the case in all member states, such as Belgium, Germany, Spain and Ireland. Here household lending margins are lower than those for corporate lending in the case of mortgages, which shows that the margins on mortgage lending can be quite low, where the risks of default on the mortgage are very low.

Banks have responded in various ways to the changing environment—characterised by low interest rates, low inflation and increased competition—but predominately they have looked for other sources of income and at ways of retaining customers by improvements in the quality of service. That will be set out more fully in the next chapter, which explores the ways in which banks have tackled the changes in their own domestic retail environments. The main issue for the banks is how to deal with the reduction in margins which, according to the analysis by the European Central Bank, is largely due to the 'tightening of pricing conditions due to competition'.[2]

Deregulation of the Spanish and Italian banking systems has also had the effect of reducing margins. Banks had to seek the permission of the central bank to open branches, and banks were often restricted to a particular geographical location or a particular range of banking services. That, however, simply led to banks being able to exercise a monopoly in the area and charge higher rates of interest. A study of bank competition and regulatory reform in Italy spells out the effects of reform on the Italian banking systems. Italy adopted the Second Banking Directive in 1993, which led to a spate of mergers and acquisitions (M&A). The banks that emerged from this process gained market share, introduced major reforms and were able to reduce costs. Indeed they have consistently lower marginal costs than other banks, but have still been able to offer their clients better service.

They slowly pulled out of the profitability crisis which hit the Italian banking system in 1993. The crisis arose from three factors: the reduction in price-cost margins, very rigid cost structures preventing a reduction in costs, and a rapid increase in bad and doubtful loans. The average mark-up in the supply of banking products throughout every region of Italy had remained unchanged until 1992. From 1993 onwards, banking slowly became more efficient, when the removal of administrative barriers clearly contributed to the improvements in competitive conditions. The drive for that came from privatisation and the regulatory reforms introduced by the central bank. The impact of the deregulation process is still going on and is still producing increased competition; for example, banks have been allowed to distribute products through other channels more freely. The reforms have continued to drive down interest rate margins.[3]

In a much more competitive world, banks may well be tempted to lend at lower margins as a response to the aggressive pricing of some new entrants, and as a response to increased competition arising from the introduction of the euro, as it has become easier to borrow and invest abroad. That is especially the case during an economic boom, when demand for credit increases, by competing heavily for new customers coming into the market for the first time or customers of other banks. Banks may

---

[2] *EU Bank Margins and Credit Standards*, December 2000, p. 5. This is an analysis of contractual lending rates offered on new loans by banks in the EU between 1997 and 2000. It shows there was a significant reduction in banks' margins on lending in the personal sector and in the corporate sector. Corporate sector lending margins began to decline more obviously towards the end of the decade.

[3] P. Angelini and N. Cetorelli, *Bank Competition and Regulatory Reform: The Case of the Italian Banking Industry*, Document 380, Bank of Italy Research Department, October 2000.

even give up short-term profits if they believe they will be able to sell other products to their new customers in the future. Banks may also offer higher interest rates on deposits so that they can finance the growth in lending.

Borrowers may well borrow more on the strength of rising asset prices, but banks have to assess the risks of a fall in value during a cyclical downturn. As the intense competition continues, banks may be tempted to relax lending standards or to base their customer rating systems on current conditions rather than pricing on the basis of changes in asset quality over the business cycle. Against that, the development of internal risk management and pricing systems has brought about a closer alignment of credit to the risks inherent in the loan proposal. Leading banks have put much time and effort into developing these systems over the past decade.

In mortgage lending and consumer credit, credit scoring techniques are being used in conjunction with a more streamlined and centralised processing of information. Some banks have an unsophisticated approach to credit scoring, and this could lead to increased risks. Banks apply a wide range of rating systems to corporate customers, allotting firms to risk categories depending on the probability of a default on the loan. With increasing competition, banking supervisors have to encourage banks to take a long-term approach to their credit rating systems. That would involve assessing the borrower's current position and his future situation over the course of the loan. The internal credit rating could well change over time as the borrower's situation changes. Most of the leading banks adopt these approaches or have been encouraged to do so under the watchful eyes of the banking supervisors.

The reported decline in bank net interest margins is therefore one of the key factors in explaining the strategy banks have adopted throughout the 1990s and will expect to follow during the coming decade. New sources of profit must be found as banks face not only the decline in interest rate margins but also the attractions of developing capital markets and investors seeking higher returns on their savings.

DEVELOPMENTS IN CAPITAL MARKETS

Structural changes in the capital markets in continental Europe were already under way before the introduction of the euro in 1999. The somewhat sleepy continental European equity markets had already begun to change and develop long before that. Annual growth rates of volumes reached over 30% per year between 1995 and 1999. Turnover in the European stock exchanges reached record levels in 2000, further evidence of an emerging equity culture. However, the capitalisation of the European stock exchanges remains behind the US, at about half the size.

Obviously the introduction of the euro eliminated currency risk. It has also contributed to the relaxation or the gradual unification of technical, regulatory and other constraints, which have led to the segmentation of the markets along national lines. There is still a long way to go to build an integrated European market. The Report of the Committee of Wise Men (the Lamfalussy Report, published in February 2001) identified a wide range of factors, which slow down market integration.[4] They prevent the EU from realising the full benefits of the single currency and they could risk the diversion of European savings into foreign markets. European companies need to be able to tap deep, liquid and innovative European capital pools centred around the euro for the financing they require to develop their business activities. The proposals on regulation form part of the European Commission's Financial Services Action Plan, which the European Council meeting in Lisbon agreed should be implemented by 2005 at the latest. If achieved, the impact of the plan on existing financial services businesses will be substantial.

Borrowers and investors now have the opportunity to diversify their financial strategies; financial markets in the euro area have deepened; and cross-border activity has increased rapidly. Borrowers have a much wider choice of investors, and savers are now in a position to place their funds in a wide range of instruments and across borders. It has transformed the fixed-income markets because banks and investors no longer consider the currency and local interest rate risk but attention is focused on the characteristics and qualities of the individual borrowers rather than the nationality of the issuer. As far as borrowers are concerned, the euro has increased the potential for market-based financing methods by allowing debt issuers to tap institutional portfolios across the euro area. Large corporations have begun to seek to lower their borrowing costs by improving their credit ratings and tapping the capital markets. They want to take advantage of what is expected to become a large pool of investment capital, as pension funds and other institutional investors seek out more attractive yields (at least relative to sovereign debt) on corporate offerings. The market is already large and has huge potential for growth. The capitalisation of European insurance, investment and pension funds alone was equivalent to €10 trillion in 2001—the size of European gross domestic product (GDP).

When it comes to banks' sources of income, the two most important developments are the fixed-income and equity aspects of the capital markets. The impact of the euro has been felt more quickly and in a more pronounced way on the bond market. The bond market already had an international flavour even before the euro, since government debt securities from the euro area were the main source of international diversification for institutional investment portfolios. Continental institutional investors (such as pension funds) were, and often still are, constrained by legal and prudential restrictions in terms of the size and composition of their foreign exchange and credit risk exposures, so government securities were often their only means of diversification.

With the removal of currency risk and a unified monetary policy, it was expected that the government bond market would explode and it did, reaching $2.8 trillion by the end of 2000, almost level with the US market of $3 trillion. It poses a real

---

[4] The report lists a wide range of factors, including the absence of clear Europe-wide regulation, such as market abuse and prospectuses, an inefficient regulatory system, a large number of transaction and clearing and settlement systems, differences in legal and taxation systems, and cultural barriers.

challenge to the US market for global leadership. But it still cannot compete with the US market in terms of being a reference point for international asset managers. It has also become a more competitive market from the viewpoint of individual governments; each monitors the other governments' issues as they are all competing for a share of the same investor base, indicating the absence of a single established reference yield curve for the new currency. The range of issuers and the differences in their credit standing distinguish the market from the US, though it is possible that such convergence would emerge over time.

Convergence will require a determination on the part of member governments in Euroland to ensure a single market in government bonds, but there are obstacles in the way. Each government wishes to manage its own government debt and wishes to retain, or is at least unwilling to change, its legal frameworks for the issuance of debt. Everyone would gain from the increased liquidity of the market, which would in turn enhance the market's appeal to investors outside the euro area. It has transformed the fixed-interest markets, because banks and investors no longer face currency risk and can concentrate on the individual borrowers.

There was rapid development in the issuance of corporate bonds denominated in euros from borrowers within and outside the euro area. Its timing coincided with the advent of the euro in January 1999. By August 1999 private sector borrowers within the euro area issued 75% of their international debt in euros, compared with 10% between 1990 and 1998; and private borrowers outside the euro area issued 21% of their international debt in euros, compared with 2% in the legacy currencies in the same period. Not all of this was due to the impact of the euro, but to the positive outlook for growth then and the wave of mergers and acquisitions in which European companies were involved. The advantage of the single currency to these developments has been in the form of widening the range of investor portfolios that could be tapped with a single issue, thus reducing the costs of capital market financing.

The euro immediately became the second most important widely used currency for international financing and investment. By the end of 1999 there was a clear and sustained increase in the volume of the issuance of international debt securities in the euro by non-residents in the euro area. Indeed an ECB working paper showed that new euro-denominated issuance of bonds and notes exceeded the issuance of bonds and notes denominated in US dollars for the first time in the last six months of that year.[5] The paper's authors, Carsten Detken and Philipp Hartmann, point out that the data about investment currency use are much more limited and also the quality of the available data is lower, partly because it is based on an *Economist* survey involving a small number of global fund managers.

But the survey indicated that early increases in euro investments turned out to be short-lived. The difference between the development of the euro's external financing role in comparison to its external investment role implies that the demand for euro debt securities supplied by non-residents is still domestic, that is, by Euroland residents.

---

[5] *The Euro and the International Capital Markets*, ECB Working Paper 19, April 2000, p. 23.

But despite these differences, what emerges from this analysis of the data is that the euro is established in all important segments of the international markets; in fact, its emergence is what could be regarded as 'normal' and its role in the international capital markets resembles what was then known about the euro's role for other functions of a currency in the international monetary and financial system.

This surge in euro-denominated corporate bonds has been taken to suggest the beginning of a new stage in the structure of the financial markets in Euroland. It would signify a shift from bank-based finance to market-based finance, but it is too early to say whether or not such a major shift has yet taken place. Yet it does follow a period in which banks have found it increasingly difficult to lend profitably to large companies. Since the early 1990s corporate borrowers had found it more cost-effective to pay agent banks to arrange, syndicate and administer loans. Loan fees began to pick up again towards the end of the decade, but large loans are still not a major source of profitability for most banks, and the euro and euro-denominated bonds will put pressure on this aspect of bank activity.

Banks still dominate the issuance of bonds in euros; for example, during 1998–2000 banks issued 60% of all euro-denominated bonds, accounting for 53% of the total volume. This is a feature of the continental market, as banks are still the main channel for corporate finance and thus use the capital markets to finance their own lending. The banks also issue bonds representing securitised mortgages and government loans, mainly by German banks in the form of Pfandbriefe.

In 1999 and 2000 the 'new economy' sectors of telecommunications and the media were the most active borrowers in the eurobond market. The introduction of the euro coincided with a strong demand for funds, especially with the telecommunications companies following privatisation and the deregulation of national markets. During that period, bond issuance was driven by the growth of mobile telephones and the cost of licences and infrastructure investments that were thought to enable operators to provide the next generation of wireless-operated services. Olivetti's issue of €5 billion in bonds during summer 1999 was regarded as a trailblazer. The proceeds of the bond issue financed the takeover of Telecom Italia and allowed the company to cancel the syndicated loan it had arranged to finance the transaction. The size of the issue set the scene and was followed by other major issues, despite the difficulties faced by the telecommunications industry.

The financial institutions still play an important role, but companies themselves are becoming more active in the bond market. There were 144 issues in 2000, which raised more than €50.7 billion. The first half of 2001 saw 101 bond issues totalling €40.7 billion. This included an issue of €8 billion by Deutsche Telekom to pay for third-generation mobile telephone licences, and the industrial group Siemens issued a €4 billion multi-tranche bond to refinance maturing debt. What is interesting is the number of smaller companies tapping the markets for funds, sometimes using complex products such as puttable reset securities, which allow financing rates to be reset after each year. The companies concerned include BMW, Bayer, Lufthansa, Deutsche Flugsicherung (the air traffic control authority), Volkswagen and Sudzucker.

These are all significant straws in the wind as far as German companies and banks are concerned, and indicate the response on the part of German companies to competitive pressures to optimise capital structures.

Investment strategy has been transformed by the introduction of the euro and is no longer based on cross-currency yield arbitrage and directional bets on national interest rates. European institutional portfolio managers are now in a position to evaluate and manage credit risk, and investors now focus more closely on the assessment and pricing of credit risk. The consequence is that the market has widened to include borrowers other than those rated AA or higher.

The increasing use of the bond market might indicate a shift from relationship banking to a market-oriented financial structure. It is perhaps too early to say whether the bond issues mark a clear trend that will rapidly intensify in the future. Banks may be facing a reduction in income from lending to the commercial sector, but that does not necessarily deprive them of income. Commercial banks, under pressure to increase returns to shareholders, are repricing loans, limiting unprofitable lending and striving to sell higher-margin investment banking products to their customers.

The rapid growth of Europe's bond markets since 1999 has not been driven by economic growth or low interest rates but by regulatory reform. The removal of currency risk opened the way for regulations to allow for wider options and enabled issuers the chance to escape from local and often small markets. The consequent burgeoning of M&A activity introduced issuers to the possibilities of tapping into a wider range of opportunities for raising capital. 'The main drivers of growth are likely to remain intact as the bond market offers competitive financing and European credit becomes securitised-in the broadest sense of the term.'[6] Even in the first half of 2001, private corporate issuance in euros continued to rise and was nearly a fifth higher than the corresponding dollar volumes. However, the euro corporate bond market is still about one-third the size of the corresponding US dollar market. And in what is described in the same quarterly report as 'another milestone along the road to the disintermediation of the banking sector,' private corporations raised virtually the same amount of cash as private banks. The exceptional volumes from the telecommunications industry were €9 billion, closely followed by cars and electrical/electronic at €7 billion; industrial and retail companies also accounted for significant volumes.

Mergers and acquisitions have provided the major impetus on non-government bond issuance from 1995 to 2000. An analysis recently published by Robert Fumagalli found that changes in M&A volumes anticipate changes in issuance by about two quarters, which suggests that M&A transactions are first founded in the loan market and only at a later stage in the bond market.[7]

The development of the equity markets could also have a detrimental effect on bank income. Some of these changes occurred before the introduction of the euro,

[6] Graham Bishop, *2001 Second Quarter: Euro Corporate Bond Issuance Passes another Milestone*, Schroder Salomon Smith Barney, July 2001.
[7] Robert Fumagalli, *European Corporate Credit Outlook Second Half 2001*, Schroder Salomon Smith Barney, July 2001.

but its advent did help to create the perception of a single European equity market, which in turn led to an increase in the issuance of international equity. Companies in Euroland issued shares worth $199 billion between 1999 and 2000, double the value issued in the previous two years. It was, however, still lower than the increase of 119% achieved by all industrialised countries during the same period. Both retail and institutional investors showed a vastly increased readiness to invest in equity, and equity-based mutual funds grew rapidly.

The new markets consist of a network of exchanges, established in most member states during the latter part of the 1990s to provide equity finance for small dynamic companies with growth potential. Investors and entrepreneurs alike seized the opportunity to invest in the new economy, mainly internet, biotechnology and media companies. These include Nouveau Marche (1996), Nuovo Mercato (1999) and Neuer Markt (1997), the leading growth markets in the EU. The Neuer Markt continues to hold the dominant position among Europe's growth markets in terms of market capitalisation, exchange turnover, the number of initial public offerings (IPOs) and transparency standards, despite the massive correction in share prices in the global stock markets since spring 2000. That has been exacerbated by the continuing decline in company profits during 2001 and the impact of September 11. The global economic slowdown continued to be felt throughout 2001 most strongly in technology stocks, as profit and sales forecasts factored into the prices could no longer be achieved in the market conditions prevailing then.

The European growth markets played a vital role in increasing the number of listed companies in the EU. The number of IPOs continued to increase year on year until 2001, rising from 19 in 1996 to 436 in 2000 with a drop to 79 in 2001 in response to the economic circumstances and market reactions. Annual turnover increased from €451 million in 1996 to €22,067 million in 2000, but fell to €5,765 million in 2001.[8] The total market capitalisation of the five growth markets reached €167 billion in December 2000, although developments in 2001 were dismal.

The growth markets in general have attracted retail investors, although some have been more successful in this drive than others. They either invest directly through brokers, including internet brokers, or indirectly through investment funds. Having retreated to cash during 2001, retail investors have retained the resources to invest again; for example, during 2001, customers of the online brokers, such as Comdirect, Consors and DAB, alone held cash of over €5.2 billion. Europe as a whole still has substantial development potential as indicated by the relatively low market capitalisation to GDP ratios in Europe; the figure for Germany was 49% compared with 163% in the US at the end of 2000.

What has not yet happened is the development of a pan-European equity market. Companies have sought to increase opportunities for international access to their securities; for example, the issue of depository receipts, international equity offerings and by listing shares in international exchanges. Continental European equity markets

---

[8] Figures from Deutsche Börse.

are smaller than their counterparts in other industrial countries, and they account for a comparatively smaller share of trading activity as measured by the ratio of average monthly turnover to overall size. This is partly due to the segmentation of national markets and the absence of an integrated trading infrastructure covering the entire EMU area. Some of these problems have been addressed in the Lamfalussy Report and are a matter for the European Commission and national governments and regulators.

Several attempts were made to create an alliance involving the leading stock exchanges, but some collapsed under the pressure of the complexities of integrating historically independent markets and the strength of local interests. That has now been replaced by a gradualist programme, beginning with the harmonisation of opening hours and would lead to a common trading infrastructure as well as uniform settlement and clearing arrangements. But progress has been slow and often hindered by the reluctance to change on the part of individual exchanges. Disappointment with the lack of progress and the competition from the new electronic trading systems led some of the exchanges to bring about closer cooperation. However, the London Stock Exchange and Deutsche Börse merger plans fell apart, but Paris, Amsterdam and the Brussels exchanges succeeded. The Euronext merger took place in September 2000 and work commenced then on the migration of the three Euronext systems. The merger has created an important competitor within Europe. It is the second largest exchange but it needs more blue-chip stocks trading there to enhance its prestige. Clearly such a fragmented system of exchanges cannot continue to exist. Not only competitive pressures but also investor and issuer demand will help to bring about a single exchange. Cross-border transactions are very expensive, up to 60% of the overall transaction costs, so a unified platform would obviously slash these costs.

The immediate impact of the euro even before 1999 was to change investors' and fund-raisers' attitudes towards capital financing. The euro was also introduced in a particularly favourable economic climate in Europe and the US, and that assisted the growth of portfolio investment in Europe and directed attention away from bank-intermediated credit. It suggests that banks can no longer rely on credit as their major source of income and need to refocus their banking strategies in response to these trends.

DECLINE IN CORPORATE BANK LENDING

Loans are still the main source of debt financing in the euro area, but it is possible that a shift is taking place in the euro area, both with the issue of corporate bonds and high-yield bonds issued by borrowers with poorer credit worthiness. It is difficult to identify a clear trend over such a short time period; most detailed analyses precede the real developments in the equity markets, which have taken place since 1996 and have continued to grow since then. The enhanced opportunities for access to capital markets by new sectors of the economy which have previously been absent from it may well draw small and medium-sized enterprises away from reliance on bank borrowing. More efficient price formation and improved secondary market liquidity are likely to speed up this process.

Corporate issuance is generally facilitated by banks. The increased focus of shareholder value by corporate managers, the new Basel regulations on bank capital, and the stronger competition in the European financial sector prompted banks to use their balance sheets more efficiently so that they could increase their return on equity. The result is that banks are increasingly facilitating direct access by companies to the capital markets. They take the lead in managing bond issues. However, there are limitations on the use of the eurobond market, since companies may have low credit ratings or unrated debt. Furthermore, many European companies do not have a credit rating at all, and this will obviously limit their access to the bond market and price information is still lacking. However, other measures are afoot: the impact of the euro itself in terms of price transparency and the adoption of international accounting standards, as well as the general demands for increasing transparency concerning a company's financial strength and profitability.

THE EURO AND THE CUSTOMER

Euro notes and coins were immediately accepted following their introduction on 1 January 2002, and will undoubtedly have an important psychological and practical impact on consumer attitudes. In the retail sector, banks expect significant changes to the industry in structure, consolidation, average bank size and methods of competing.

It is worth looking in some detail at what banks expect to happen and then later at the way in which the leading banks expect to tackle competition. Customers still do not change their basic banking relationship very easily, if at all, but most banks regard service, personal relationships, branding and geographical accessibility as the means of customer retention, closely followed by price. These are still seen as strengths by European banks. Other factors such as transparency of pricing and business hours are currently far less important.

However, euro notes and coins have arrived at a time when the internet and other forms of direct banking will have the effect of increasing price transparency and change the relative value of banking brands. Many bankers believe that margins and fees are likely to be hit differentially across the range of products and services and others believe that at the very least prices will generally drift downwards with current accounts/deposits, credit cards, mutual funds and stockbroking being particularly at risk of lower prices. Lower interest rates and intense competition over commoditised products will drive prices down. The cost of 'execution-only' securities business and brokerage services could fall, whereas analytical and advisory services will continue to be high value-added services.

Banks face an uncertain future in other respects. Expanding the customer base is increasingly difficult, and for many leading banks it is made more difficult by the constraints they face in their domestic markets. They are not sure how retail customers will react to a much more visible 'single market' for financial services in the form of 'notes and coins'. Many bankers believe that, unlike corporate or investment banking, retail banking within Euroland will remain segmented along national or even regional lines for some time, but they cannot be entirely sure. Transparency and remote accessibility may change that, provided accessibility can engender trust and reliability.

SOME CONCLUSIONS

The banking sector has faced a much tougher and more competitive environment for the past decade and there are no signs of a reduction in such pressures in the foreseeable future. Its traditional sources of income—current accounts, deposits, retail and corporate lending—have declined as the capital markets have developed in the context of the single market. Companies, especially large companies, have turned to the capital markets as a cheaper source of capital. Bank lending, even where relationship banking is part of a strong and long-established tradition, is beginning to decline. Retail customers have gradually turned to the equity markets as low interest rates on their savings deposits provided inadequate returns. Banks have seen a decline in their interest margins over the past decade and have looked to fees and commissions on alternative means of retail savings, and to their fees as bond issuers and organisers of IPOs. Further challenges arise from the process of consolidation in the retail banking sector, and the creation of a visible single market for retail banking services, supported by advances in technology. Taken together, these factors ensure that the banks have to continually review their strategies, especially in the retail sector, where the traditional approach to retail banking may no longer be sufficient.

The problems facing banks were summed up by Manfred Caesar, a director of the German investment bank Sal Oppenheim. Quoted in *The Banker*, April 2001, his analysis was with reference to German banks in particular, but it has a wider application to the continental banking system in general:

> The old business model of taking in cheap funds and using them in the traditional loan business is not working any longer. In view of the ongoing deregulation, the arrival of new competition such as e-banks, online brokers and insurance companies, new technologies with fast rising IT costs, and the need for multichannel distribution, banks have to redefine their strategies and adopt a clear focused approach. (P. 72)

The subsequent chapters will examine the banks' current strategies in the light of these changes.

3
Transparency and Accountability

The broader context in which banks operate has been undergoing further changes as well. Governments, regulators, international bodies, such as the Organisation for Economic Cooperation and Development (OECD) and the Basel Committee on Banking Supervision, and the financial services industry itself have begun to establish new standards for transparency and accountability. Many of the leading banks have already anticipated changes and have adopted international accounting standards, since they are listed on international exchanges (or US GAAP if listed on the New York Stock Exchange).

NEW ACCOUNTING STANDARDS

As a key part of the European Union's Financial Services Action Plan, it is expected that all listed EU companies should use international accounting standards by 2005 at the latest. The proposal for a regulation on the application of international accounting standards in the EU was published on 13 February 2001 by the European Commission. It aims to harmonise financial reporting in the EU on the basis of globally agreed accounting standards by 2005 and to enhance EU companies' access to international capital markets.

The proposed regulation requires all companies to prepare their consolidated accounts on the basis of standards adopted and promulgated by the International Accounting Standards Board (IASB) from 2005. The regulation also provides for a mechanism whereby international accounting standards can be 'endorsed' for use in the EU within the European legal framework. A regulation would apply directly to companies and would not need to be implemented by national legislation.

At the time of writing, only the German, Austrian and Swiss banks have adopted the international accounting standards, and not all of them. Other leading banks already apply international accounting standards and so the regulation would not have any impact on them. The impact on banks in other member states depends on the current state of their accounting standards and the extent to which they conform to international accounting standards (IAS); for example, 'hidden reserves' were abolished in the Netherlands some four years ago. IAS 39, which sets out the requirement that all financial instruments should be disclosed, a move which is intended to provide users of financial statements with information that will enable them to understand the significance of on- and off-balance-sheet instruments to an enterprise's financial position and performance, so that they can assess the amounts, timing and certainty of cash flows was introduced. There should also be information about the extent to which financial instruments are used, the risks involved and the business purposes served. The risks involved cover price, currency, interest rate risk and market risk, credit and liquidity risk. The financial instruments involved include all derivatives, including hedging instruments and securitisation. All of these have to be recognised on the balance sheet when the company or the bank becomes party to the contract.

Examining and understanding the range of risks to which the bank is exposed is an essential element of banking supervision. The governor of the Bank of Spain outlined the advantages of the adoption of such standards in a recent speech:

> As regards the introduction of the International Accounting Standards (IAS) in the EU, the aim is to promote the convergence of accounting practices across European countries. This is certainly a desirable goal, which should pave the way for progress towards the creation of a single financial market. The practical experience of banking supervision over the last twenty years in Spain has demonstrated that accounting regulation has been a fundamental element in achieving a solid and stable financial system and effective supervision. Moreover, accounting standards based on prudential criteria and conservative principles are not only essential for prudential supervision, but also for individual investors, who thereby have a guarantee that the information they receive is well-founded. That is why it is extremely important that accounting principles be reconciled with good banking practices, with modern risk management techniques and with the nature and time horizon of all types of banking operation.

It is a good summary of the effects. It will help to create the single market. But the greater transparency resulting from the application of the regulation would reveal the true financial strength of many small and medium-sized banks and may lead to further domestic consolidation or even cross-border acquisitions, as large banks seek a foothold in other member states.

DEVELOPMENTS IN CORPORATE GOVERNANCE

A corporate governance system may well be defined as a framework of legal, institutional and cultural factors shaping the patterns of influence that stakeholders (variously identified) exert on managerial decision-making. What is significant is the nature and extent of the changes in corporate governance which are taking place and the extent to which these will affect the future development of banking in the EU.

From the viewpoint of the banking industry, such developments have been encouraged by the Basel Committee on Banking Supervision. *Enhancing Corporate Governance for Banking Organisation* was published in September 1999. The key issue from the viewpoint of banking supervision involves the way in which the business and affairs of individual institutions are governed by their boards of directors and senior management. Basel points out that the approach to corporate governance affects how banks:[1]

- Set corporate objectives
- Run the day-to-day operations of the business
- Consider the interests of recognised stakeholders
- Align corporate activities and behaviours with the expectation that banks will operate in a safe and sound manner, and in compliance with applicable laws and regulations
- Protect the interests of depositors

Clearly Basel focuses on the relevance of corporate governance to bank supervision. This cannot function properly if sound corporate governance is not in place, so banking supervisors have a strong interest in ensuring that there is effective corporate governance at every banking organisation. The experience of banking supervisors suggests that it is necessary to have the appropriate levels of accountability and checks and balances within each bank. It makes the work of banking supervisors easier. Besides the Basel Committee and the OECD, which also published *Principles of Corporate Governance* in June of the same year, various government- or industry-inspired bodies in the EU published their own versions of corporate governance.[2] Each of these applies the more general principles set out by the international bodies to their own legislative and regulatory frameworks. The developments in the form of the introduction of new principles only took place in the late 1990s, so their full impact has yet to be felt. They will have an impact not only on the work of banking supervisors, but on the banks themselves and the reaction of the markets to more open information about the management of the bank they will acquire as a result.

It is possible to identify three main strands of corporate governance in Europe: (1) the German model, in which the company is seen as being accountable to a range of stakeholders; (2) the Anglo-Saxon model, characterised by the institutionalisation of shareholder value; (3) the concept of the firm in France, Italy and Spain, which falls between (1) and (2) but seems to share more of the characteristics of the German model.

---

[1] *Enhancing Corporate Governance for Banking Organisations*, Basel Committee on Banking Supervision, September 1999.

[2] The OECD principles cover five main areas: the rights of shareholders and their protection; the equitable treatment of all categories of shareholder; the role of employees and other stakeholders; timely disclosure; and transparency of corporate structures and operations.

Germany and the German Model

For the German model, the company is perceived as an autonomous economic entity responsible to various stakeholders such as shareholders, corporate management, employees, suppliers of goods and services, suppliers of debt and customers. Germany has a two-tier board system: the management board (Vorstand) and a supervisory board (Aufsichstrat), which separates management and the supervision of management; indeed it is the legal duty of the supervisory board to monitor the competence of the management board and to advise on major policy decisions. Technically, the management board is appointed and dismissed by the supervisory board.

The structure reflects the fact that employees and shareholders are significant stakeholders, able to exert considerable influence on decision-making. This is particularly the case with the commercial banks, whose ability to influence decision-making arises from their role as providers of capital as well as equity ownership, typically holding large blocks of shares in industrial and commercial firms and seats on supervisory boards. As far as the banks are concerned, the members of their own supervisory boards are not independent of the bank but represent the interests of the companies in which the banks have large shareholdings.

The OECD estimated that the largest five shareholders held on average about 40% of the outstanding shares. The potential influence of banks in their role as shareholders is magnified by the Depostimmrecht, that is, the right banks have to bring together voting rights conferred on them by their custody of the bearer shares of individual investors who have surrendered their proxies. Bank representatives hold 10% of the total number of seats on the supervisory boards of large German companies. In addition the chairman of the supervisory board may also be a representative of a bank.

Mutual cross-shareholdings between firms are the norm and interlocking directorships frequently accompany the cross-shareholdings; there is an implicit agreement that cross-shareholdings are not used as a launching pad for hostile takeover bids. However, the role of banks in Germany is gradually becoming less important. The ownership of blocks of shares in non-financial companies and the numbers of interlocking board seats have been subject to criticism by both policy-makers and practitioners. Some banks have begun to dispose of their shares in advance of legislative changes.

Similar corporate governance structures prevailed in the Netherlands, Sweden, Denmark and Norway among others. The Netherlands has a two-tier structure with the supervisory board providing some form of codetermination for all stakeholders, because the supervisory board has to serve the interests of all the stakeholders. The management board, as the company's management team, reports to the supervisory board and is responsible for attaining the company's objectives, its strategy and policy, and the company's performance. An important aspect of the Dutch board system is the structured regime, which can take full or mitigated form. The full form is a legal requirement for all Dutch companies with more than a hundred employees, a legally established works council and a book value of shareholders' equity of Fl 25 million or more.

The supervisory board in this context is responsible for the publication of the annual accounts and the election of the managerial board; it monitors the major decisions made by the management board. This still provides scope for technical takeover defences since some shares, priority shares, have superior voting rights. Furthermore, preferred shares may serve as a takeover defence device, whereby firms with preferred shares may have an arrangement which allows further preferred shares to be issued without the approval of shareholders and for which only 25% of the nominal value of the shares has to be paid up. If there is a hostile takeover attempt, the firm can place these with another party and pay for them through debt. The use of these defence mechanisms persisted for much of the 1990s, but a takeover panel was established in 1995 with the powers to suspend attempted defences of this nature.

The French Model

In France the concept of the company shares some of the characteristics of the Anglo-Saxon view and the institutional view outlined above. In France companies may select either a one-tier or a two-tier system but the majority of listed companies (some 98%) have selected the one-tier system. Indeed the second Vienot Report on Corporate Governance in France (1999) noted that the two-tier system was perceived to be costly and not necessarily very efficient. Because the definition of independent administrators is not very clear, the composition of the supervisory board does not ensure that it is fully independent from the management board. The Vienot Report proposes a change in French law to allow listed firms with a single board to separate the functions of the chairman and the chief executive officer (CEO).

That would be a radical change, given the authority of the company president (*président directeur-générale*) with his wide powers in relation to the management of the company. In theory, however, that power may be limited given that shareholder sovereignty is an important element in company law in France as well as in Italy and Spain. One of the fundamental principles, known as *revocabilité ad nutum*, is that directors can be removed by the shareholders at will, but the influence of shareholders on management decision-making is in practice relatively small for a variety of reasons. This includes the fact that bank shareholdings are important, especially in France and Spain, and also because cross-shareholdings, government and family control are extremely significant. In France financial holdings can take a variety of forms, which are in effect similar to cross-shareholdings, including mutual cross-shareholdings.

The structure of ownership in France, Spain and Italy is in the process of change, partly due to the privatisation process which began in the mid to late 1990s in each of these three countries. However, the concentration of ownership is still relatively high in both listed and unlisted companies; on average, the largest shareholder of a non-listed company owns 66% of the capital and this increases with the size of the firm. A survey of 680 listed companies indicated the largest shareholder holds on average more than 50% of the equity. For the 40 firms belonging to the CAC 40, the share of the largest identified stake is about 29%. Estimates based on the Global Equity ownership database show that although foreign firms hold on average only 3–4% of listed firms' capital as a whole, when they are effective owners their holding rises to almost 30%. Concentration of foreign ownership is high in France and increasing, which can and does give foreign shareholders an important role in influencing the structure of the French banking system.[3]

The Company in Italy

Public companies are still rare in Italy and banks and financial companies have only a limited role in ownership structures. Ownership is still extremely concentrated; for example, in 1999 the largest shareholder in listed companies owned on average 44% of the voting rights (weighted by market capitalisation) and shareholders owned 50% in the three largest companies. The role of the state has declined rapidly as a result of the process of privatisation, which began in 1993. In 1996 the voting rights share of the state represented about 30% of the Italian stock market, but fell to 19% by the end of 1999. Family control is even more important in Italy; more than 90% of Italian employees work in firms with less than 10 employees. Banks were not allowed to own shares in non-financial companies until 1992 but they have not taken up this opportunity to any great extent. They have, however, played a more informal role, through interlocking directorates for example.

The Company in Spain

In Spain there were 600 listed companies in 1997, half of which operated in the financial services sector. Effective market turnover is highly concentrated, with about 70% attributed to 10 companies on the electronic market. A recent survey by CNMV, the Spanish Securities Commission, shows that share ownership is still highly concentrated in Spanish listed companies. In terms of listed companies, about 49% of them were found to have one single shareholder with over 50% of share capital, which may be a financial institution (bank or savings bank), a founding family or the government. A further 26% of the remaining companies had 25–50% of their share capital in the hands of a single shareholder. But change is taking place rapidly, as 'core shareholders' have not kept pace with the capital increases required and even divest

[3] L. Bloch and E. Kremp, 2001, Ownership and control in France In F. Barca and M. Becht (eds), *The Control of Corporate Europe*. Oxford: Oxford Univ. Press.

part of their holdings. Share ownership is becoming more widely spread, as Spanish 'blue chips' emerging from privatisation have relied on domestic retail holders and non-Spanish institutional investors to raise funds.

By the end of 2000, Spanish institutional shareholders accounted for only 6% of the shares in Spanish companies, as a result of the relative underdevelopment of the asset management industry in Spain. Foreign institutional investors doubled their investments in Spain in 2000, following a 76% increase in 1999, and accounted for 36% of the market. Privatisation, coupled with declining interest rates, encouraged households to invest in shares up to 34%, with a further 24% owned by the various groups: founding families, banks, savings banks and the government. The government still retains control over most listed companies.

Changes in Corporate Governance

France, Germany, Italy, the Netherlands, the Nordic countries and Spain have all adopted corporate governance rules. In general, the concentrated shareholdings in continental Europe are associated with two groups of investors: families and other companies. Large family holdings are still much more prevalent on the Continent than they are in the UK and the US. Holdings by companies are complex, sometimes taking the form of pyramids in which companies have controlling shareholdings of other companies lower down the pyramid, and in other cases there are cross-shareholdings or complex webs of holdings. These intercorporate holdings create a system of 'insider ownership' by which companies and financial institutions have controlling shareholdings in each other.

Various methods are used to concentrate control among insiders, such as dual-class shares, with different classes of shareholder having different voting rights. Insiders hold shares with a high ratio of voting to cash flow rights. In some countries, such as Germany and Italy, pyramid structures are commonplace and allow the owners at the top of the pyramid to exert control over companies lower down in the pyramid at comparatively low cost to themselves.

Dual-class shares and pyramid company structures are comparatively rare in the UK. There are very few cross-shareholdings and control is dispersed among a large number of external investors. Shares are typically held through financial institutions—pension funds, life assurance companies and mutual funds—but no one institution holds a substantial proportion of the shares of one company.

Obviously the question arises concerning the significance of these differences in corporate ownership and their association with corporate governance issues. The continental 'insider' systems are easily able to monitor and control management, at least lower down the pyramid, though whether other stakeholders are able to monitor management effectively through the supervisory boards is less obvious. Large shareholders can certainly exercise control and are well informed but their control may well lack transparency. Minority investors may be at risk of their interests being ignored by the large shareholders, so a key issue for corporate governance rules in these countries is the protection of minority investors. On the other hand, the typical continental system promotes close relations between companies and between investors and companies. Since there are large identifiable blocks of shares attributable to particular investors, responsibility of formulation and implementation of policy can be left to the controlling shareholders. However, since the markets are in the process of change in the leading continental European countries, the system of corporate governance is in the process of change as well.

In France there have been three reports on corporate governance. *Le Conseil d'Adminstration des Sociétés Cotées*, chaired by Marc Vienot, was followed by the *Recommendations of the Committee on Corporate Governance*, published by the Association des Entreprises Privées (AFEP) and the Mouvement des Entreprises de France (MEDEF) in July 1999. In the same year AFG-ASFFI, representing the mutual funds industry in France, also published the recommendations of their own commission on corporate governance. French company legislation, dating from 1966, allows companies to have a one-board or two-board system with a supervisory board and a management board. In fact, almost all companies have adopted a one-board system. The Vienot Committee considered the proposals of the justice ministry (July 1999) to separate the roles of chairman and chief executive officer and disclosure of the compensation and options granted to corporate officers of listed companies. The committee considered and accepted the proposal but argued that the separation of roles and the reasons for it should be stated in the annual report.

The committee also proposed limitations on directors' terms of office (four years) and made recommendations concerning the working of committees of the board, the role of the audit committee and the publication of annual accounts. AFG-ASFFI, on the other hand, focused their attention on the role of and preparations for the annual general meeting (AGM) and queried the offering of 'gifts' to shareholders attending the AGM and the 'loyalty premiums' to shareholders who have held their shares for a specified period of time. The recommendation is for a maximum of 16 directors, of which at least 2 should be entirely independent of the company. Some of the Vienot proposals became law in 2000; in particular, companies will be allowed to split the role of chairman and chief executive. In addition a director may only sit on five boards, another of Marc Vienot's recommendations.

In other respects, French companies have moved forward: most cross-shareholdings between large listed companies have been unwound; most companies have appointed independent directors; and managers' renumerations are usually vetted by committees dominated by three non-executive directors. Annual reports for the financial year 2000 contained details of managers' pay, including the value of stock options and fringe benefits.

On other important issues, France has not yet moved forward. France remains one of the few countries which does not recognise the one share, one vote principle. The 1966 company law allows companies to distribute voting rights unevenly or even deprive shareholders of their voting rights. Thus, Crédit Lyonnais removed voting rights from

Dresdner Bank recently. Under pressure from other large investors, including Crédit Agricole, Crédit Lyonnais invoked an obscure clause in its statutes forcing investors to notify the bank when they increase their stake above 0.5% of Lyonnais's capital. Last year Société Générale recently decided to cap the votes of any investor or group of investors at 15%, regardless the size of their stake. Although the bank's shareholders had voted in 1999 to scrap double-votes, Société Générale decided to keep them, realising that employees' double-votes had protected the company in its defence against BNP's attempted hostile takeover in 1999. Double-votes become important when they allow a minority of shareholders to control a majority of shares. It was a disappointment that the government did not tackle this issue when it introduced other corporate government reforms. Shareholders are, however, attacking the managers' power to issue shares during takeover battles, and thus dilute existing shareholders without consulting them. One success was the withdrawal of a resolution of this kind by Suez Lyonnaise des Eaux.

In Germany the first law on corporate governance, the Law on Control and Transparency in the Corporate Sector (KonTrag), was passed by the Bundestag in 1998. The government introduced corporate governance in that year partly in response to various crises in the corporate sector, but mainly because of the recognition that national capital markets are no longer isolated. Banks are gradually withdrawing from their long-term holdings in industrial companies, and face increasing pressure to maximise profits and invest in growth in their core businesses.

KonTrag was linked with changes in securities legislation and the acceptance of internationally recognised accounting standards for German companies and the Third Law for the promotion of the German financial market. Sweeping changes to company boards were introduced, including a reduction in the maximum number of supervisory board seats an individual may have (currently 10) and an annual report to shareholders stating frequency of meetings and describing the work of its committees.

Radical changes were made to voting rights: plural voting rights are no longer permissible and existing plural voting rights are to cease after five years, although they may be cancelled at the AGM before that. Maximum voting rights are no longer allowed in quoted companies and existing rights have now ceased. Listed companies must also declare all shareholdings of 5% or more in large listed companies in the annual report. There are full voting rights for each ordinary share, and shares are transferable at any time. All of this is embodied in legislation (the German Stock Corporation Act and the Securities Trading Act as well as a voluntary Takeover Code, which will also become law).

The OECD principles of disclosure and transparency are met by the full range of legislation, including the German Commercial Code, the Antitrust Act and the Banking Act. This is the assessment of the current state of corporate governance in Germany, provided by the German Panel of Corporate Governance in January 2000. Further changes in the structure of German listed companies will come about as a result of the tax reform measures announced by Chancellor Schroder in July 2000. They will eliminate by 2002 the current 50% tax on capital gains imposed on corporate sales of shares in other companies. This will do much to encourage the unwinding of cross-shareholdings among German companies and open them to a wider shareholder base. It may in the future lead to an increase in mergers and acquisitions (M&A).

Italy has undertaken significant reforms to securities laws and market regulation over the past decade. In 1998 the parliament approved a decree based on the work of the Draghi Commission with provisions designed to discourage cross-ownership between companies listed on the stock exchange. Shareholder agreements were permitted and rules for tender offers were simplified. Shareholder rights were strengthened by enabling minority shareholders to call a shareholders' meeting and enabling them to appoint a member of the board of statutory auditors. The rights and duties of the board of statutory auditors were extended to include the duty to engage in a dialogue with various elements of the company, and they must require information from directors and independent auditing firms, and reports from the internal controllers. They also have the right to call a general meeting of the company. Minority shareholders (less than 10% of the voting rights) may call a general meeting. All shareholders have the right of access to all documents at the company's offices. Shareholders with over 2% of the share capital of a listed company must notify the company and CONSOB, the securities regulatory authority. A shareholding of over 30% requires the holder to launch a bid for the company. CONSOB issued a further set of rules implementing the decree in 1999 and in the same year, the Borsa Italiana issued a further set of non-mandatory governance guidelines for listed companies.

In the Netherlands, the Peters Committee on Corporate Governance, established by the Association of Securities Issuing Companies and the Amsterdam Stock Exchange Association, issued 40 recommendations on corporate governance in 1997. It is a code of best practice for effective corporate governance, but compliance with the code is entirely voluntary. A survey of companies in the following year indicated that few companies were following the Peters recommendations, and the Dutch government announced various initiatives to improve corporate governance with reforms due to be introduced in 2001. The board structures of listed firms operate under a two-tier management structure consisting of a supervisory board and a managerial board. The supervisory board is independent of the company, and its members are responsible for the supervision of management policy and the company's general management of its affairs. It is meant to provide some form of codetermination for all stakeholders, though in a somewhat limited way. By law, most of the Netherlands' top companies have all non-executive supervisory boards, but just 5% of the members of such boards are thought to be independent of management.

Corporate structures in the Netherlands are also characterised by technical takeover defences, which effectively means that shareholder power is limited and managers are protected from full monitoring or disciplining by the market via shareholder decisions. Shareholders may have no votes at all or limited voting power, or specific shareholders may be given exclusive rights to vote on specific decisions. Changes are under way which will give shareholders the right to elect supervisory board members.

But in terms of accounting standards, the leading Dutch companies are moving ahead in that the large listed companies have accepted international accounting standards and disclosure of pay of members of the management board will soon be a legal requirement.

In Spain a special committee set up by the Securities Commission (CNMV) published a report on corporate governance in 1998. Known as the Olivencia Report, after the chairman of the committee, it includes a series of recommendations which mainly draw from the UK's Cadbury Report and other European guidelines. The Olivencia Report seeks to provide corporate governance recommendations within the framework of an ambiguous Companies Act, clarifying the concepts of board independence and shareholders' voting rights. The consequence has been that many companies have appointed former executive directors as being 'independent', when they may still have connections with the founding family or relevant banks, or may have been government officials in the industry concerned in the case of privatised companies. It is difficult for shareholders to find representation on the board of many Spanish companies through properly independent directors. Similarly, about 70% of Spanish listed companies restrict shareholder voting rights in a variety of ways, of which the most usual is the voting cap, typically at 5% or 10% of share capital, irrespective of the real level of investment in the company.

However, the current legal framework of the Companies Act does permit these practices. The work of the second Corporate Governance Committee has been suspended due to internal disputes. However, the following elements of corporate governance are contained in companies legislation and the committee's report. Listed companies have to meet strict disclosure requirements regarding earnings, significant holdings, market transactions and other price-sensitive information. Companies must be independently audited and reported on in accordance with Spain's general accounting rules, with only a few companies providing additional statements following US generally accepted accounting principles (GAAP).

All holdings exceeding 5% of share capital must be disclosed to the CNVM, but access to such information may be difficult, as this information is kept by the local clearing house and can be made available only to the issuers, that is, to the same listed companies on request. There are no specific provisions on related party transactions, but work is under way on a draft bill which will govern such transactions and also a more severe regulation on insider trading practices.

These are the listing requirements. The listing requirements and the Olivencia Code do not form part of the Listing Rules, but all listed companies are required to submit a report to the CNVM on compliance with these principles. Not all companies are compliant.

The same bill will also introduce the obligation to disseminate relevant information to all market agents and shareholders, thereby banning privileged access for analysts and money managers. The Spanish Takeover Code is contained in the Financial Law of 1987 and allows for partial takeover bids. If the bidder owns less than 25% of the outstanding equity, it may launch a takeover aimed at gaining control over 51% of share capital; only if the bidder already owns over 25% of share capital is it legally bound to tender for 100% of share capital. Almost all takeover bids are by agreement and there have been very few hostile takeovers.

AGMs take place as routine meetings, but the short notice period (usually two weeks), unclear legal provisions and long-established corporate practices make it difficult for shareholders to exercise accountability and control. Full financial information may be presented actually at the AGM. A large number of votes at the AGM may be issued through proxies held by board members or the chairman of the board, so it is possible to determine the outcome of the AGM.

Quoted Spanish companies have a unitary board with both executive and non-executive directors and tend to be rather large by international standards, with 15–20 members and sometimes more than that. This is partly as a result of the adoption of the Olivencia Code of 'best practice' in 1998, which led to the addition of independent directors, and mergers and acquisitions have led to the amalgamation of boards rather than the establishment of a new board of an appropriate size. This results in much of the work being delegated to committees of some 5–10 directors, which report directly to the chairman. The 'best practice' rules require the committees to reflect the same balance between executive and non-executive directors. They should be appointed by formal and transparent procedures for nomination, and the Companies Act includes the right of shareholders with more than 5% of share capital to nominate a director, although in practice the procedure is complex.

One feature has not yet commanded the attention it deserves, given the development of strong chief executives in France and now in Germany. The UK interpretation of corporate governance places great stress on the separation of the roles of chairman and chief executive. These titles are often adopted in descriptions of the roles of leading bankers, but they do not necessarily have the same connotation as they have in the UK context. In Germany the title 'chairman' or 'chief executive' is used, but strictly speaking, it refers to the person elected by the supervisory board as the spokesman for the board. That may be set to change, as Deutsche Bank plans to break with tradition when Josef Ackermann takes over from Rolf Breuer in May 2002. There will be a new executive committee, running all the bank's operations; the Vorstand will be slimmed down and will be chaired by Dr Ackermann. He will effectively become a new-style chief executive with full control over the bank's strategy. Such moves may turn out to be less acceptable to the markets and to banking supervisors in the future.

These changes in corporate governance are first of all a testimony to the 'growing dominance of equity holdings by institutional investors, both domestic and international,' which 'cast a sharp focus on owners and monitors of firms'. Banks rely on private information acquired from ongoing credit relations, knowledge of the borrowers' deposit history and their use of transaction services, whereas 'securities markets must rely on public information'.[4] At the same time, the requirements of the markets are a

---

[4] E. Philip Davis, 2001, Institutional investors and corporate governance. In E. Philip Davis and Benn Steil (eds), *Institutional Investors*. Cambridge MA: MIT Press.

catalyst in bringing about changes in corporate governance in continental European countries. Those changes have a further effect in that they increase the likelihood of further concentration in the banking sector (as well as other sectors of industry) by opening up the possibility of hostile takeovers as well as mergers and acquisitions, given the greatly increased transparency and the shareholders' acquisition of power.

The sheer size and financial strength of British and American institutional investors and their increasing interest in foreign equity are illustrated by the results of a recent study by Conference Board.[5] Institutional investors hold $24 trillion in financial assets in the world's top five markets, and over two-thirds of these assets are held by UK and US investors. The 25 largest pension funds account for two-thirds of all foreign equity investment by US investors. Finally, the percentage of foreign equity held in individual portfolios of these top 25 US pension funds continues to rise, reaching 18% of the individual portfolio in 2000. It is not just the size and strength of these funds that will force the pace of change, but also the investors' demands for the disclosures and transparency to which they are accustomed.

These general trends will have their effects on the banking system in each of the countries concerned. Interlocking directorships and the consequent lack of independent scrutiny of management decisions, and the strategy of the bank concerned, are features which the market will increasingly take into account. The independent assessment of the bank's risk management strategy and internal controls provided by the independent members of a board will provide comfort not only to banking supervisors but also to the markets. They form part of the criteria by which the market assesses shareholder value. Some banks have realised the necessity of changing the structure of their boards as a result of bitter experience—shareholdings in industrial companies and the consequent interlocking directorships have become both an embarrassment and a cost. Foreign institutional shareholders and their expectations will also affect the shareholder value of the bank. The combination of legislative changes, the imposition of codes of conduct and market expectations will force the pace of change and consequently help to bring about changes in the structure of banking.

---

[5] *Institutional Investment Report: International Patterns of Institutional Investment, 2000*, Conference Board, New York, p. 27

4
France: Seven Slices of the Cake

France has seven national banking groups, each with a sizeable market share of at least 5%, and sometimes a larger share of the retail market, but only Crédit Agricole can claim to have a leading position. Table 4.1 shows the top six banking groups in terms of tier 1 capital in December 2000 (measured in dollars).

The French Banking Association's January 2001 comparison of the market share of each of these banks shows Crédit Agricole clearly in the lead with 27.4% of the market, followed by BNP Paribas at 10.3%, closely followed by Société Générale at 9.9% and Groupe Caisse d'Epargne at 9.3%; Crédit Lyonnais trails at 5.9%. That is taking the ranking in terms of tier 1 capital, but if the ranking is in terms of assets then Groupe Banques Populaires and Crédit Lyonnais become the sixth and seventh, respectively.

French banks have to compete more effectively on the European stage and to meet the challenges facing all European banks. Pressure from the non-banks and from internet banks presents less of a threat in France, but most of the banks consider that they face severe competition from long-established, government-sponsored savings products. They face the same problems as most banks—bank lending and bank deposits have declined with the consequent squeeze on interest rate margins, although the banks claim that their interest rate margin environment is particularly tough.

French banks are in a stronger position than ever before, but may now only have achieved sufficient size and strength to 'deal with European competition', according to Laurent Fabius, the French finance minister, commenting on the merger of Caisse des Depots et Consignations (CDC), the state-owned financial institution with the Caisse Nationale des Caisses d'Epargne (CNCE). in June 2001. He added, 'With €17 billion of capital, the new group approaches the size of Crédit Agricole and BNP Paribas, the French leaders . . . and will have the size to deal with European competition. Its aim is to grow beyond our borders in order to reinforce firmly the international dimension to which it can lay claim'.

Table 4.1   The top six banking groups in terms of tier 1 capital

Name	Tier 1 capital ($)	Size ($)	Soundness (%)	Pre-tax profits ($)	Cost/income ratio (%)
Crédit Agricole	26,383	498.4	5.29	3,541	59.76
BNP Paribas	18,889	645.7	2.92	5,754	64.20
Société Générale	13,679	424.1	3.22	3,940	68.99
Crédit Mutuel	10,880	270.2	4.03	1,974	66.50
Caisse d'Epargne	10,000	245.5	4.07	930	74.56
Crédit Lyonnais	7,902	174.9	4.52	1,522	70.65

Source: *The Banker*, July 2001

The merged bank will exploit its existing partnership with San Paolo IMI in Italy and Germany's Bayerische Landesbank. But the new alliance has a complex and unwieldy structure, which may only be resolved if and when La Poste is added to the group.[1] La Poste is precluded from offering credit but it can offer investments and has 15% of the retail market.

THE BANKING SYSTEM

It has taken some time to reach this position. The banking system was transformed by the introduction of the Banking Act 1984, which brought in the notion of a 'credit institution' and replaced the principle of specialisation with that of universal banking. The Act defines a 'credit institution' as an institution which engages in at least one of three banking operations: (a) collecting deposits from the public, (b) granting credit and (c) issuing the system's means of payment, such as credit cards, traveller's cheques or banker's drafts. Finance companies also fall within the remit of the Banking Act, which means that they are regulated in the same way as banks but are not allowed to accept demand or term deposits with a maturity of under two years. In other words, consumer credit companies or non-banks specialising in consumer credit do not have the advantage of escaping banking regulation.

The French banking system has had an unusual history in the post-war period; it has remained relatively stable with familiar names dominating the scene. The three largest depositary institutions, Crédit Lyonnais, Société Générale and Banque Nationale de Paris (BNP), were nationalised in 1945, and by the end of the 1980s these three banks accounted for 49% of total bank credit and 55% of demand and time deposits together with the commercial banks. With Crédit Agricole, Crédit Industriel et Commercial,

---

[1] Caisse des Depots et Consignations (CDC) was founded in 1816 and it has a unique and vital role in the French banking system. It is an autonomous public institution which carries out a variety of tasks in the public interest, such as investing a substantial proportion of deposits collected by Caisse d'Epargne and investing them in social housing, local development and the management of social security funds. Both CDC and La Poste, which offers a wide variety of instruments to collect investment but cannot offer credit, are excluded from the Banking Act.

Banque Indosuez, Banque Paribas and Banque Populaire, they accounted for 90% of the banking activity in France.

The chequered history of the banking sector consists of two waves of nationalisation, the first in 1945 and the second in 1982, followed by two waves of privatisation. The 1982 wave of nationalisation was justified by the then socialist government as a means of influencing the banks to favour investment in small and medium-sized enterprises and by the need to have a more coherent industrial and monetary policy. The first wave of privatisation was implemented by Prime Minister Jacques Chirac and his finance minister, Edouard Balludar. This was justified by the pressures of competition and the need for French banks to increase their capital, but it was halted by the crash of 1987 and a change of government in 1988. Société Générale, Paribas and Indosuez were privatised.

It was resumed in the 1990s with the privatisation of Banque Nationale de Paris and is nearing completion with the government's decision to sell its remaining 10% share in Crédit Lyonnais.[2] However, the privatisation programme does not necessarily mean the end of government influence on the formerly publicly owned banks, owing to the retention of a kind of golden share and the strategy of selling large stakes in a bank to a stable core group of reliable shareholders as a form of protection against hostile takeovers. The 1998 deal itself was the result of complex and difficult negotiations with the European Commission regarding the vastly expensive rescue plan for the troubled bank, considered to be a form of state aid, in which the bank was forced to sell off many of its assets and allowed only to retain those which the bank believed were essential to maintain its role as a universal bank in France and a corporate bank around the world.

Other privatisations included the sale of CIC, the state-owned regional banking network to Crédit Mutuel, a mutual bank with a strong presence in eastern and northern France in 1998. Crédit Mutuel won in a competitive bid in which Société Générale and ABN-AMRO also took part. Société Générale was widely expected to win, but its highly centralised management structure would have clashed with the decentralised structure of Crédit Mutuel, and risked opposition from the trade unions and employees. It is thought that the sale of the bank to ABN-AMRO shortly after Allianz had acquired Assurances Generali de France would have been difficult from a political viewpoint. However, the funds raised by the sale had to compensate for losses incurred by GAN, the state-owned insurance group, which owned CIC and which was the subject of a massive rescue plan. GAN retains its 20% stake in CIC and Crédit Mutuel was prepared to sell GAN products through its increased network, which as one banker pointed out, Société Générale was not prepared to do.

In 1999 BNP launched a takeover bid for both Société Générale and Paribas, an unprecedented move in an attempt to create a trillion-dollar bank, the world's largest bank in terms of assets. It was also designed to frustrate the proposed merger of Société Générale and Paribas, which had gained official approval. The bid to take over Société Générale ultimately failed, and BNP took over Paribas. Although the bid

---

[2] At the time of writing, the date of the sale of the 10% share has yet to be announced.

failed, it did fulfil various useful functions, first in exposing the conflicts of interest in many boardrooms owing to interlocking directorships, and then in its impact on government and the regulators. The initial reaction on the part of the minister of finance and the governor of the central bank was to issue a joint statement saying that they would act 'in the national interest' and 'scrutinise the impact of the bid on the proper functioning of the French banking and financial system'. There was no legal reason to oppose BNP's bid for Paribas, which was then given formal approval.

The effect of the battle, which dominated the French banking system for most of 1999, was to destroy the belief that hostile takeover bids would not succeed in the banking sector. It also marked the end of a period of the process of consolidation in French banking, which the Jospin government considered essential in order to create 'national champions'. In addition the government also made it clear that it would no longer oppose cross-border mergers involving French banks. The government, however, considered that at least a balanced banking system had been produced in which both BNP Paribas and Crédit Agricole, the largest mutual bank, have equity of over €20 billion. According to Christian de Boisse the Société Générale–BNP battle 'shows that France is entering what for her is a new form of capitalism. The market economy is finally taking root in France'.[3]

Another significant step was taken in 1999, a crucial year for French banking. The *caisses d'épargne*, the savings banks, were privatised and the state-controlled CDC was reformed. These banks were often criticised by the private sector banks because they did not face any constraints in terms of profitability. The privatisation of Caisse d'Epargne took the form of a three-year process of selling its own shares, 'social stakes' to its clients and employees. The process was completed in January 2001, and Caisse d'Epargne finally became a mutual bank operating under similar statutes as Crédit Agricole and Crédit Mutuel. At that time the CDC did not change hands, since the state was still the controlling shareholder. The bank was, however, reorganised and was given two different functions. The Livret A funds will be channelled to organisations which build and operate social housing. CDC Finance was established with responsibility for four core businesses—custody, asset management, financial intermediation, and securities origination and syndication—with allocated capital of €5 billion and a mission to achieve after-tax returns of over 10%.

For some time French banks have been regarded as vulnerable to competition; indeed one leading banker predicted that there would only be 'three of France's five largest banks left within two years'. That has not happened. Crédit Commerciale de France (CCF), although it is only a second-tier bank in terms of size and a niche player in investment banking and securities acquisition, was seen as a real asset and ripe for acquisition. As one analyst commented, 'It is the only acquisition in France that would not dilute the earnings of a foreign bidder'. It was duly acquired by HSBC in 2000 for €11 billion. Both banks took care to retain the support of the Bank of France. The chairman of CCF, Charles de Croisset, kept the governor of the central bank informed throughout the whole process, and the terms of the deal were planned to avoid job cuts,

---

[3] *Time*, 30 August 1999, p. 14.

which would have aroused union opposition. The two banks gave a firm commitment to retain CCF's headquarters and management team in Paris. At the same time, the Bank of France made it clear during the whole process that regulatory clearance would only be granted if the deal provided a 'clear and concerted solution'; in other words, a hostile takeover would be blocked if it disturbed the financial stability of the system. Meanwhile in 2001 Deutsche Bank acquired Banque Worms, a bank specialising in investment services, corporate banking and asset management to national and multinational companies, institutional investors and high-net-worth private clients worldwide. It has 17 branches in France and a worldwide network of international offices.

In June 2001 the merger was announced between Caisse des Depots et Consignations (CDC) and Caisse Nationale des Caisses d'Epargne (CNCE).

The mutual banks, CDC and CNCE, had already agreed to pool their assets to form France's third largest bank with shareholder funds of €17 billion. It will operate in six European countries and will have the critical mass to become a major force in Europe through partnerships. Laurent Fabius, the minister of finance, made it quite clear this was designed to accelerate consolidation among French banks in the face of European competition. With €17 billion of capital, the new group approaches the size of Crédit Agricole and BNP Paribas. The CDC-CNCE alliance came into operation at the end of 2001 and was expected to build on its existing partnership with San Paolo IMI of Italy and Bayerische Landesbank in order to extend its activities in other EU member states.

Much of the restructuring so far has strengthened the cooperative banks, and the change in the legal status of the savings bank will intensify that trend and enable the cooperative banks to play a key role in the changing banking system. That role is not always welcomed; as one leading banker put it, the French banking market is 'blocked by nationalised and mutualist banks'. Although outside France, BNP Paribas and Société Générale are seen as the leaders in retail banking, the mutual banks in fact have three-fifths of the market. The CDC-CNCE alliance will operate in six European countries and will have the critical mass to become a major force in Europe through partnerships. The private banking sector has reacted sharply against the 'emergence of the semi-public body' formed by the alliance and especially with the possibility of a further alliance with La Poste. Indeed the French Banking Association (AFB) called for a review of the legal status of La Poste, so that it is put on the same footing as other banks and is subject to the same regulation.

That leaves the issue of Crédit Lyonnais unresolved. July 2001 marked the end of the pact which required the core shareholders to guarantee the stability and independence of the bank since its privatisation in 1999. The pact requires these shareholders to sell their shares first of all to other shareholders in the pact. The government still retains its 10% share and any decision about the disposal of this share is now unlikely to be taken before the election in June 2002, but the sale of this share could trigger a takeover battle.

Crédit Lyonnais almost collapsed in the early 1990s and had to be rescued by the government to the tune of some €20 billion; it has spent the last five years undergoing restructuring and has restored profitability above the cost of equity, but trails behind the other leading banks. It is aiming at a cost/income ratio of 70% in 2002 in its domestic retail market, down from 76% in 2000, but may not reach its targets in a weaker economic situation. The bank itself recognises that it is too small to remain independent, and the government regards it as a key asset because it cost so much to rescue, so once more the government looks as though it will have a role in the decision. One banker described the difficulties involved: 'Any interested candidate has to consider how the others [core shareholders] will react and whether this could spiral into a takeover battle'.

The continuing process of consolidation since 1996 has been successful in that weaker banks have been gradually integrated into financially stronger banking groups. It has resulted in increased operational efficiency, which has improved as a result of network rationalisation, early retirement plans and staff reallocation to commercial duties. Cost savings have resulted, but the savings have been absorbed by technology spending and the introduction of the 35-hour week. Their strong position in the domestic retail market, both in banking and non-banking, is the main asset of all the leading French banks. The banking system in France, however, is unusual in that the mutual banks continue to occupy a dominant position in the market, due to their close community ties, arising from local ownership and their broad branch distribution networks. They control about 60% of savings and about 50% of loans, and their share of the mortgage and consumer finance markets has increased. They have also diversified their activities into areas such as insurance, asset management and wholesale banking, often by making large acquisitions. The 'alliance' of CDC-CNCE is a powerful challenge to the commercial banking sector, since combination of the two groups' interests in retail and investment banking, asset management, insurance and real estate could be mutually beneficial. The integration of CIC with Crédit Mutuel Centre Est Europe will also lead to a strong competitor in the long-term.

GOVERNMENT-SPONSORED SAVINGS

Crédit Mutuel, Caisse d'Epargne and La Poste have the advantage of being the only banks able to offer two of the array of savings products designed by the government to encourage savings. Given the continuing popularity of these products, selling them gives these banks the opportunity to gain or retain customers. These are Livret A, first introduced in 1904, and Livret Bleu, introduced in 1947 (with improvements in 1979), two of the most popular savings products in France. The maximum which may be invested in these products is €15,300. Other products were introduced in the 1960s and the 1980s and these can be sold by other banks, provided they have an agreement with the state and La Poste.

Codevi is the industrial development account introduced in 1983 and currently offering 3% interest. The *compte d'épargne logement* (CEL) and the *plan d'épargne logement* (PEL) were introduced in the 1960s. CEL has a minimum contribution

Table 4.2   Government-sponsored savings

Name	December 1996	December 1998	December 2000
Livrets A and B	117.5	123.3	114.5
Livret Jeune	3.9	4.9	5.0
LEP	26.0	41.3	44.4
Codevi	30.7	35.1	35.8
CEL and PEL	23.3	25.8	27.8

Source: French Banking Association

level of FF 2000 and a maximum of €15,300. PEL has a minimum of FF 1,500 at the beginning and annual contributions of FF 3,600 to a maximum of €61,200. Another important savings product is the *plan d'épargne populaire* (PEP); introduced in 1989 it has a maximum of €92,000. The *compte sur livret d'épargne populaire* (LEP) is restricted to those who pay less than FF 4,260 income tax and has a maximum of €7,700. Livret Jeune was introduced in 1996 and has a maximum of €1,600. These are all designed to encourage people to save for a variety of purposes; for example, PEL for house purchase and PEP for retirement. Livret Jeune was introduced to help young people between the ages of 12 and 25 to save money and get used to handling a bank account. The advantage to the government is to have substantial funds at its disposal with the right to change the rate of interest at will, provided the rate is not lower than Livret A.[4]

These products show no sign of any decline in popularity; indeed Livret A is held by about 50 million individuals, or 80% of the population, because it guarantees tax-free returns well in excess of money-market interest rates (Table 4.2).

Not surprisingly, the commercial banks have long resented the unfair advantage enjoyed by Crédit Mutuel, La Poste and Caisse d'Epargne. Bankers consider that these instruments, which pay artificially high interest rates set by the government, take savings away from other riskier investment products. Crédit Mutuel, with its extensive branch network in both rural and urban areas, was selected for this scheme. The bank was required to distribute the savings products to the public without cost to the consumers, who benefit directly from the tax exemption. A complaint was laid before the European Commission (EC) by the French Banking Association, Crédit Agricole and Banque Populaire in 1991 to the effect that Crédit Mutuel received state resources in the form of commission paid by the state-owned CDC. The net costs borne by Crédit Mutuel take into account all the benefits and costs linked to the service and allow for a normal commercial margin. The EC found that, for the years 1991–1998, the commission paid to Crédit Mutuel for the public service exceeded its

---

[4] This does not apply to PEL and Livret Jeune. The announcement of the interest rate change is placed in the Official Journal in the form of a *décret* or *arrêt*, essentially unchanged since their introduction. The only change is the introduction of a committee in 1998 to advise the government on the rate change. The current rates of interest range between 3% for Livret A and Livret Bleu to 4.5% for PEL and 4.25% for LEP, with CEL at a low rate of 2%.

net costs, resulting in an overcompensating of Crédit Mutuel by €164 million. Crédit Mutuel would also have to pay interest up to the recovery on the funds it was unduly awarded by the government. At the time of writing, both the government and Crédit Mutuel are contesting the judgement.

The existence of these products and the restrictions on the outlets illustrate the particular competitive pressures in the retail banking market in France. Foreign banks have tried to penetrate the market, but with limited success, because of the entrenched position of the existing major players. The growing preoccupation with shareholder value for the commercial banks and with financial discipline for the mutual banks has helped to eliminate some of the more aggressive pricing practices, but it has also made the market a tough one in which to operate. But these are not the only challenges. French banks are also tackling the challenges faced by banks throughout Europe, such as the squeeze on margins brought about by greater competition and low interest rates; the shift in traditional patterns of banking away from deposit-based savings and corporate lending. All of these factors have an impact on bank profitability. Profitability is much more open to view than before, exposed in the harsh light of domestic and global capital markets. From the customer's viewpoint, the euro reveals comparative costs and encourages the customer to look for better and more efficiently delivered banking services.

BANKING STRATEGIES

Significant domestic consolidation has already taken place, resulting in the establishment of financially stronger banking groups. There is obviously more to come, given that the position of Crédit Lyonnais is still uncertain, and the bank itself recognises that it will not stand alone. According to Jean Peyrelevade, the chairman, the bank is currently focused on strengthening itself through cost-cutting and productivity improvements before the time comes for a merger with a French or European partner. The other remaining independent players are likely to join larger groups.

The Search for Profitability

'The interest rate margin environment is harsh,' perhaps largely because the banks face competition from government-sponsored, and some say, subsidised savings. Furthermore, 'interest rates are more controlled than in the UK. We cannot charge more than the legal rate'. That is not, of course, the only problem. According to one leading banker, 'Banks recognise that the margins between credits and deposits have declined sharply over the past ten years.... The trend is clearly supporting fees rather than interest rate margins, but that was a trend for which we were rather well-prepared'. For some years, French banks have developed alternative strategies to ensure profitability. Such strategies involve cutting costs; indeed, one banker suggested that this dominated their thinking too much: '[The] focus for French banks is on cutting costs rather than battling for market share, at least, for the time being'.

Service Delivery

Profitability is not the only element in banking strategy. Cutting costs clearly does not include a branch closure programme. All the banks interviewed were firmly convinced that branches still have an important role to play in retaining and providing services for clients. One senior manager stated firmly that 'we do not plan to close many of our 4,700 branches, but we plan to integrate the branches with our information technology systems so that we can establish a customer relationship management system within the branches ... [but] not in a way which kills the personal relationship with the customer.... We're actively exploring ways in which we can link the customer with the bank and so improve our competitiveness and productivity'.

Another banker endorsed the value of the branch: 'We are not engaging on a programme of branch closures; in fact, we have opened 50 new branches and plan to open a further 150 branches. We shall close unprofitable branches. We retain branches because they are good for our business. It means that we have a visible presence throughout the country. We use branches for cross-selling life and general insurance, the products of our partner, a mutual life insurance company'. Here it is the client who dictates, said another: 'The client requires the branch network, so it's maintained and planned. These are slow-moving changes. We shall not embark on any massive or brutal movement [in terms of branch closures]'.

This is not to suggest that the French banks have ignored the importance of new technology or have failed to recognise the impact of internet banking on their business. Their response depends partly on the way in which the bank concerned has developed, so one bank refers to the 'big challenge' it faces with 'two business models, one is bricks and the other is the internet, call centres and ATMs'. The challenge for his bank is 'to build a real integrated multichannel model'. The problem for his bank is that 'when you put together two banks, you find that the tools for customer relations management are used separately'. The bank also has a 'pure internet player', but has since wondered 'whether it is in our interests to set up such a model. We have hesitated for a few months ... because the advice we have received from our consultants is that we should not launch such a pure player'.

Alternative strategies are under consideration. One leading banker indicated that 'we have been asking ourselves whether it might not be better to ally ourselves with a large non-bank player to launch an internet bank ... [but] there is a risk in pooling data,' and until that issue has been resolved, the bank will not proceed. Another confirms that his bank is 'now able to propose free access to the internet to all its retail clients'. The bank 'expects that 80% of the day-to-day transactions of 1 to 1.5 million customers will be conducted on the internet'. Another recognises that 'we could make real gains if we combined the platforms into a single one. The UK or

Spanish examples suggest that large cost synergies can be derived from merging two retail platforms'.

These statements might suggest that French banks have not adopted new technology, but in fact they have all moved in the same direction. One banker summed it up: 'The main revolution is multi-access.... We are developing the multichannel approach—branches, the internet/WAP/call centres and mobiles'. Another reports, 'We have adopted multichannel, real-time access: branch ATM/telephone and internet with interactive TV as a remote possibility'. The adoption of the internet may be slower in France because of the existence of Minitel, which was introduced by the French government in 1982. It has been an important element for mainstream French banks since then, because the users pay a fee for each Minitel service they access: 'There is less drive to use the internet in France because of Minitel, but internet use is growing'.

'All the banks are investing in multichannel access. That is why the new players are relying on the internet. But multichannel is requested by the French consumer.' The banks are clearly unwilling to countenance becoming pure internet players, since they do not see any sign that their customers wish to use the internet alone, and indeed they do not consider this is the way to offer services other than transactional services: 'For simple transactions, e-banking is fine, but as soon as you need financial advice, you need to talk to someone'. French banks 'no longer see the internet as a tool to conquer clients'. Instead internet banking is regarded as a useful tool for retail banks, rather than a substitute for a traditional bank network. The strategy is not without its difficulties. As one leading banker said, 'We operate in a saturated market. We are overbranched and branches are the strategy of most French banks'.

Cross-selling

One large cooperative bank commented, 'All the large banking groups have the same policy. We are all universal banks, serving all categories of customers with retail banking as a major part of the business'. It is a 'highly competitive' market: 'All the banks sell the same products. It is a very difficult market as we have too many banks and now foreign banks are trying to enter the market.... The retail market is increasingly characterised by the standardisation of products and specialisation in product distribution.... Retail banking is more stable [than investment banking], but we have some of the lowest margins in Europe. The UK and Italy have better margins'.

Not all the bankers took quite such a gloomy view. Another leading banker said, 'We are revitalising its universal banking model and are reallocating capital, growing our higher-value-added activities, such as asset management and private banking, and improving cross-selling.... [The] strength of our diversified banking model [is demonstrated by the fact that] we sold 6.7 products per current account in 2001 as compared with 6.4 in 2000'.

Another states, 'We have one of the few banking alliances that works well. It's not just a cross-shareholding.... We still aim to be one bank for all, offering a wide range of financial services, mutual funds, life assurance and risk assurance. . . . We are looking for the critical mass for some activities to find those where we can generate economies of scale. Asset management is where we can find economies of scale, can establish production centres and so distribute our products more widely'. None of the banks interviewed were prepared to consider selling third-party products—'open architecture' has not reached France. The banks either sell their own products or products of companies within the group or an alliance with an insurance company.

Despite misgivings and anxieties about intense competition on the part of some bankers, bancassurance in France is extremely successful. French banks control 60% of the life insurance market, partly because the tax incentives make it an attractive form of saving. Furthermore, the banks' extensive branch networks provide them with a more efficient method of reaching customers and potential customers than the network of agents which insurance companies have at their disposal. Insurance sales contribute between 2% and 16% of the banks' domestic revenues, but up to 30% of pre-provision income. In terms of asset management, the French domestic position is strong and profitable, but few asset managers are important players in European asset management. Fee and commission income continues to grow as a proportion of the banks' operating income—up to 32% in 2000 from 25% in 1996, and for some banks the proportion is much higher at up to 50%.

France is the most developed bancassurance market in Europe, selling 60% of life and pensions business, but also makes a significant contribution to general risk insurance and health insurance, the second highest after the Netherlands. These sales are seen as making an important contribution not only to banks' income but also to the retention of customers: 'The sale of insurance products uses the distribution capacity of the banks' networks to full effect, but also enhances the loyalty and profitability of the relationship between the customer and the bank'. They 'tie the customer to the bank'.

The Centrality of the Customer

The mutual banks and the banks which have recently acquired mutual status have a somewhat different approach to customer retention from that of the commercial banks. They 'aim to build up a feeling of ownership among customers where it did not exist before, and to explain the financial consequences of ownership,' but without a clear idea as to how that might be achieved. They will not, of course, rely solely on developing that sense of ownership, but as one such banker said, 'Our bank serves largely middle-class customers, so we have teams of specialised advisers, offering solutions to their customers, as well as specialised fund managers'.

All recognise that 'the key in terms of competition is the current account and the mortgage loan'. Both are a 'source of loyalty for the client', but the current account is fundamental, since 'it is the capacity to have a relationship with the customer'. Mortgages have disadvantages: 'Mortgage loans are seen as a means of attracting clients, but they are not profitable in themselves, and the most aggressive are losing out at the level of margin of interest'. The current account is seen as a more valuable tool. It may be a more expensive tool in the future. French banks have historically neither paid interest on customer deposits nor charged for basic banking services, the 'ni, ni' approach. Although it is an important consumer issue, the government has refused to countenance any change. If changes do take place, and it is expected this will happen in 2002, the cost of paying interest on sight deposits is likely to be covered by account maintenance fee packages, including the cost of cheque processing.

An analysis of the current account provides vital information about the customer, and French banks are as aware of the possibility of using this information as anyone else. One banker after another emphasised the importance of customer relations management. One said, 'We shall strive to improve our cost base through applying customer relations management'. Another large bank seemed to adopt a more cautious approach, 'We are focused on customer relationship management, and we are developing a model, but it is a long process. . . . [We shall achieve our aims] through a process of domestic restructuring'.

The French banks seem much less certain about customer segmentation. According to one banker, 'We are not inclined to talk about the "mass affluent" as we believe in more diversified products and a much wider range of more sophisticated products in a highly competitive market'. Another banker intends 'to devote resources to independent advice and maximise the opportunities of the Banque de Proximité'. And yet another claims to 'target the mass affluent, even though this group is not yet well-defined', but perhaps it covers 'our typical customers in small towns or rural areas with €50,000 or more to invest'. They do seem to be certain about the need to provide private banking facilities for high-net-worth individuals and see that as an important market in a country characterised by increasing wealth.

CONCLUSION

French banks regard themselves as being strong. As one leading banker put it, 'A recession would have to be very deep and last a number of years before it will have consequences for the French banking sector'. They have tackled domestic competition by acquiring alternative suppliers of their product range, such as consumer credit companies and stockbroking firms, including electronic banking. The acquisition of electronic banking is not only to avoid competition but also the consequences for profitability. According to one banker, 'Electronic banking has a destructive effect on commissions. The drop in distribution costs is passed on to the customers and everybody is involved in cost-cutting. The big problem for the networks is how to avoid losing customers. Already stockbroking commissions have been cut in half in the space of a year'.

The banks have avoided competition in the domestic market in other ways. 'The focus for French banks is on cutting costs rather than battling for market share,' according to one leading banker, who then added meaningfully 'for the time being'. The French banks operate in a market in which it is difficult for the commercial banks to expand, given the presence of the mutual banks. There is no legal process of demutualisation and no means of encouraging such a process by the offer of 'compensation' for loss of 'membership'. Customers are not members of a mutual organisation in the same way as UK clients are members of a mutual bank. The possibilities of growth by acquisition are limited but available, and may be the only way of acquiring new clients. Another banker explained that the 'cost of acquiring a new client is far too high'. So high, in fact, that 'it is impossible to close the gap between the cost of acquiring a new client and the return of equity'. That serves to push the leading French banks in the direction of domestic and cross-border mergers, since the 'French financial industry has one weakness: the small size of its participants,' according to a former finance minister.

5
Germany: A Level Playing Field

The structure of banking in Germany is complex and unusual, dominated by universal banks, both publicly and privately owned. They usually offer a wide range of banking services besides the traditional activities of taking deposits and lending. The full range of activities is set out in the Banking Act, whose provisions apply to credit institutions and also to fund management companies, credit card companies, investment advisers, portfolio managers and investment banking among others.[1] All are subject to banking supervision, so no one escapes banking supervision by specialising in consumer credit, for example. That is a partial explanation for the fact that neither the large commercial banks nor the publicly owned banks need fear competition from non-banks or non-banking new entrants.

The real competition is between the commercial banks and the Sparkassen (savings banks), owned by local or regional authorities, and the Landesbanken, the state-owned wholesale banks. The commercial and savings sector is divided into the 'big banks', regional banks, branches of foreign banks and private banks. Naturally, the big banks dominate the scene: Deutsche Bank, Dresdner, Commerzbank and Hypovereinsbank, (now owned by Allianz) now known as HVB, following its merger with Bank Austria.[2] Deutsche Bank is one of the top ten banks in the world. The HVB group deserves a particular mention as the first cross-border merger involving retail banking; it now has the largest banking network in Central Europe, spanning Germany, Austria, Poland, Hungary, the Czech Republic, Slovakia and Croatia, a fulfilment of Dr Albrecht

---

[1] The Banking Act, which is continually updated and amended in line with EU directives, sets out the definition of a bank. It includes institutions taking deposits, granting credits, issuing payment or credit cards; discount; safe custody; investment funds; underwriting and network credit business. Financial enterprises such as credit card companies, broking, portfolio management, money transmission and foreign currency dealing are all included in the act.

[2] The 187 regional banks and other commercial banks used to restrict their services to a particular region, but this is no longer the case. National-Bank, Essen, and Westfalen Bank still do but others such as BfG operate nationally. They account for a significant volume of business and provide a comprehensive range of financial services. This category also includes various group banks, such as Opel Bank, Fiat Bank and foreign banks such as American Express Bank and Chase Manhattan Bank. The number of foreign banks has increased rapidly over the past few years and now stands at 82. There are about 50 private banks, few of which operate independently, and most operate without a branch network.

Table 5.1   The retail market share
of German banks

Cooperative banks	22%
Major private banks	16%
Regional and other	11%
Mortgage banks	8%
Sparkassen	35%
Landesbanken	8%

Source: JP Morgan

Schmidt's cherished vision of a European bank of the regions. HVB's frustration in the retail market can easily be seen when comparing the market shares of the various groups (Table 5.1).

To understand the nature of the competition between the public and the private sector banks, it is necessary to describe the respective roles of the cooperative sector and the Sparkassen. Some banks bitterly resent the role of the public sector banks, the Sparkassen, seeing this system as a way of legitimising loss-making; others resent the government guarantee which provides the Landesbanken with a AAA rating, and their close relationship with the Sparkassen, which makes it difficult for competitors to gain access to the retail market.

THE COOPERATIVE BANKS

The cooperative banking sector is worth mentioning first of all. Germany has a vast array of cooperative banks (operating under a variety of titles; Volkesbanken, Raiffeisen-banken, Spar-und-Darlehenskassen, Spardabanken and Apother-und-Artzebanken). They have a close-knit network of branches, offering universal banking services to many small businesses, such as tradesmen, small-scale manufacturing firms and farmers, who still rely on their local Volksbank or Raiffeisenbank. They continue to depend on deposit-taking and lending, and manage to retain customers with large deposits on which the banks offer interest rates of 1.5%. Centralised services, including the payments system, fund management and investment facilities, are provided by a clearing and settlement bank, such as the Deutsche Genossenschaftsbank (DG), as well as issuing bonds, which are sold to customers though the branch network. DG had to increase its risk provisions at the end of 2000, owing to the agricultural impact of the cattle brain disease BSE, and then merged with another clearing bank, GZ, to create the sixth largest bank in terms of assets. The third clearer, WGZ, pulled out of the deal on the grounds that it did not wish to increase its risk provisions.

The small cooperatives often cause banking supervisors concern, owing to their limited management capabilities, especially in the area of credit risk management. German cooperatives are no exception and such skills are often provided centrally; they are still fragile. Many German families do not realise that their liabilities for losses are much higher than their equity holdings as shareholders of the cooperative banks. Changes are afoot, however, as the most fragmented and most conservative sector of German banking is consolidating with some speed. There were 240 mergers in 2000, when the number of cooperative banks was still over 2000 in 1999 with average assets of DM 450 million.

THE SPARKASSEN

Far more important than the cooperative banks are the savings banks, or Sparkassen. They are owned by local or regional authorities, usually limited to a well-defined area, normally a city or a rural district, thus avoiding competing with each other. Savings banks are not in fact allowed to operate outside the jurisdiction by which they were incorporated. This rule has its roots in history; the funds deposited with the savings banks should be used to fund loans in the same area. The local authorities act as the bank's guarantor and assume full liability towards its creditors. The functions of the Sparkassen are defined in the savings bank laws of each state.

They cooperate closely with their respective regional Landesbanken. These are owned by the savings banks and regional governmments and act as clearing houses to the Sparkassen, holding excess liquidity, putting together large loans for them, financing foreign trade, dealing in foreign exchange, and more recently, structured finance and investment banking. These functions are provided centrally by Deutsche Girozentrale–Deutsche Kommunalbank which (with the Landesbanken) actss as a clearing house for the banks and provides them with fund-raising and investment fund facilities. It has a balance sheet of DM 131 billion and fund assets of DM 250 billion.

Altogether there are about 562 savings banks with a close-knit network of branches, numbering 18,781. Together with the cooperative banks, they ensure that even small villages have a savings bank or a cooperative bank, and they make up for the absence of the commercial banks, which have very few branches in such tiny villages and small towns. By having such a wide network of branches, the savings banks can fulfil their explicit public mission: to ensure access to financial services for all social groups, to promote savings and to provide small and medium-sized businesses with funding and access to financial services. Cooperation with the Landesbanken enables them to provide a full range of services, enabling German enterprises to conduct all their foreign and domestic business. In fact, the Sparkassen state that they can assist firms at all stages of their development, from the start-up phase to the sale of the company, purchasing another company or raising equity capital by means of an initial public offering (IPO).

Bank loans continue to be an important source of finance for small to medium-sized businesses, especially when they are sufficiently flexible to allow for adjustments to be made to the loans to be made over time. These more flexible arrangements are the hallmark of the 'hausbank' relationship, that is, a long-standing relationship between the bank and the company, which ensures that the bank will be able and willing to cover the costs arising from such an arrangement. Just how important and popular that is can be seen from the fact that about 75% of small and medium-sized businesses have a hausbank relationship with the savings bank and that the savings banks are responsible for about half of the loans to this segment of the economy and over two-thirds of the loans to craft businesses. On top of that, the savings banks cofinance about 1 in 2 business start-ups.

Three out of four Germans still have a checking account at a Sparkassen or at DG, the lead institution of the cooperative banking sector. Together the cooperative banks and the Sparkassen present a formidable challenge, since the former have 22% of the retail market and the latter have a sizeable chunk of 35%.

THE MORTGAGE BANKS

The battle for market share is intensified by the existence of a wide range of specialist banks, 33 private mortgage banks and 5 public sector mortgage banks. The private mortgage banks have grown up under the Mortgage Bank Act, which only allows certain institutions to issue Pfandbriefe, the collateralised bonds widely used in Germany for funding public sector loans and mortgages, and thus to engage in public sector and mortgage lending. The commercial banks established specially designated mortgage banks, but the pressure on margins has increased, leading to consolidation in the sector. As a result, Hypovereinsbank combined four of its five mortgage banking subsidiaries into one unit in March 2001, and in November 2001 the chief executives of Deutsche Bank's Eurohyp, Allianz-Dresdner's Deutsche Hyp and Commerzbank's Rheinhyp announced that the three mortgage lending companies were being merged to form a giant with an estimated €243 billion in assets. The reason given at the time was the 'tough competition and narrow margins which have made things more difficult for each of the banks to achieve the necessary profitability in the German market'. Strategic decisions of this kind have to be seen in the context of the public/private sector divide in banking provision in Germany.

THE EC JUDGEMENTS

The four big banks have a market share of almost 16% measured in terms of business volume. This shows that in spite of the falling number of banks (just over 2,800 in April 2001, a fall of about 40% during the 1990s), there is still very little concentration in the German banking sector, making it one of the most fragmented in Europe. Mergers and acquisitions (M&A) among the four largest banks have been difficult, if not impossible, to achieve, because the crowded retail banking sector (with one bank branch per 1,777 of the population) remains largely in the hands of the cooperatives, savings banks and other public sector banks. The role of the savings banks and the Landesbanken has undergone marked changes over recent years, greatly helped by the existence of the guarantees. The German Banking Association, representing the commercial banks, finally decided that the time had come to take their complaints to the European Commission. As one leading banker put it: 'I'm not too sceptical about the profitability of retail banking, but we're competing with the public sector. We do not have a level playing field'.

While private banks had to raise additional capital by issuing new shares after the EU directives on banking supervision were implemented in 1993, in six German states, state-owned housing development group assets were transferred to Landesbanken at below market rates. In June 1999 the European Commission (EC) established that in the case of WestLB this amounted to an illegal state subsidy because interest at market rates had not been paid. This was a test case but the judgement went in favour of the commercial banks. The EC agreed and WestLB was ordered to pay DM 1.6 billion for the years from 1992 to 1998 to the state of North Rhine–Westphalia (NRW).

The substantial complaint on behalf of the commercial banks was brought before the EC in 1999 by the Banking Federation of the EU. Their main argument is that the entire German savings bank system represents an anti-competitive monopoly with state subsidies. This charge strikes at the heart of the link between the savings bank and the public sector, legally established in 1897, and the local community capital guarantee, dating from 1931.[3] The private banks were further angered by the activities of larger savings banks, such as WestLB, which have moved into investment banking and foreign activities and are competing actively for market share. On the capital markets, the public sector guarantees allow savings banks to attract AAA credit ratings from the rating agencies such as Moody's and Standard & Poor's for all the Landesbanken with the exception of Berlin and Saxony, while the four major German banks had only second- or third-category ratings (at the time of submission in July 2000). The unlimited state guarantees effectively safeguard public sector banks against bankruptcy indefinitely. Apart from the 22 public sector credit institutions in Germany and the 4 in Austria, only 5 banks in the EU, 2 in the Netherlands and 3 in France command AAA ratings.

The Landesbanken and the leading savings banks owe their rating to the first-class standing of the federal government, as shown by the fact that the rating agencies would consider downgrading these banks in the long term if the guarantees were abolished. The main effect of such a high rating is to enable the bank to reduce the cost of borrowing funds in terms of issue price and interest rates and the fact that no collateral may be required. The resulting advantages for Sparkassen and Landesbanken, especially

---

[3] There are two specific state guarantees, Gewahrtragerhaftung and Anstalt. Gewahrtragerhaftung was created in 1931, because it was thought that once the savings banks became independent undertakings, they would suffer a loss of credibility among customers and be at a disadvantage when they competed against private credit institutions. The term actually refers to the 'liability imposed by law or statute on a public authority or a public law association to the creditors of a legally independent credit institution set up or maintained by the public law authority or association for all the credit institution's liabilities' and is expressly stated in all the savings bank legislation. Anstalt is the term used to describe the obligation of the public authority, which established the credit institution to maintain the institution in such a way that it is capable of fulfilling its function. This feature of savings bank legislation appeared much later; it was introduced in the 1983 Savings Bank Act of the state of Rhineland-Palatine and was later adopted by all the other Länder. For WestLB and the savings banks of North Rhine–Westphalia, it did not appear until 1995.

in the area of raising funds and deposit protection, obviously distorts competition in the EU. This is the case presented to the European Commission by the European Federation of Banks. They argued that the special position of the Landesbanken distorts competition among credit institutions in the EU as the possibility of 'buying money cheaply' is an ever more important factor in terms of a bank's earning position and a key factor in a bank's economic success. The guarantees not only apply to the Landesbanken, but also to the ability of the savings banks to offer loans on favourable terms to public authorities and institutions, thus squeezing the private banks, and indeed foreign banks, out of the market.

The defence offered by the savings banks was that their public mission extended both to current accounts and to the small and medium-sized business sector; to the fact that they are regarded as a 'building block of a balanced regional structure' and to their contribution to the development of rural areas. The link between the savings banks and the Landesbanken exists in order to provide access to the international markets for their business customers as well as providing the full range of financial services to their customers. They also argued that the institutional and guarantor liabilities do not constitute state aid, even though the guarantors are the local authorities either singly or in a group, the federal states and/or the regional savings bank associations. The Landesbanken raise most of the capital they need internally and the savings banks generated their current equity capital from their own profits during their many years in business. Despite this obligation, the savings banks argued that they must remain profitable. The guarantee would only come into play if the debts were greater that their assets and the creditors' claims could not be met even after the liquidation of all its assets. The fact that the guarantee would only come into being as a last resort is the point. It is what gives these public sector banks a competitive edge.

The Banking Federation of the EU argued that the savings banks no longer needed such protection since they have developed far beyond the modest functions of a savings bank. The wide range of activities of the Landesbanken, in particular, has already been noted. WestLB in particular offers as wide a range of services as any of the major private banks and has become a major player in the German, European and international markets, growing at above average rates in the late 1990s. The same considerations also apply to Stadtsparkasse Koln, which specialises in corporate finance, including mergers and acquisitions, asset management for wealthy private customers and the provision of risk capital. However, the point is not that these banks are successful, but that their activities are supported by the state guarantees.

In May 2001 the European Commission announced its decision, namely that it found against the existence of such guarantees on the grounds that they distorted competition. It proposed that the guarantees should be removed, and after considerable debate and discussion with the savings banks, the German government liabilities incurred as at 18 July 2001 would be supported by both guarantees until 2005; however, liabilities already outstanding at that time and maturing before 2016 will continue to benefit from 'grandfathering' from the Gewahrtragerhaftung only, provided the debt does not mature beyond 2015. The process of phasing out the guarantees will begin in

2005, and the final abolition of the guarantees could well bring about changes in the ratings. Moody's draws a distinction between guaranteed and non-guaranteed debt; in the case of guaranteed debt it will depend on the timeliness of payment, and in the case of non-guaranteed debt it will depend on possible ownership support, be it public or private, and on the future financial strength of the bank itself.

THE IMPACT OF THE EC

The public sector banks are making preparations for their future after the end of the state guarantees. Eventually, perhaps sometime ahead, the Landesbanken will lose their AAA ratings and their funding advantages. Having relied on low-margin corporate lending, the higher funding costs will depress their earnings, in some cases significantly. Some analysts take the view that up to a third of the Landesbank sector's pre-tax earnings could be at risk because of higher funding costs. Having relied on low-margin corporate lending, which accounted for over 60% of revenues in 2000, the higher funding costs will depress their earnings, in some cases significantly. Some analysts take the view that up to a third of the Landesbank sector's pre-tax earnings could be at risk because of higher funding costs. The loss of the guarantees means that these banks will have to operate as profit maximisers, which will mean restructuring businesses and cutting costs, and perhaps turn to investment banking instead. Building up investment banking franchises, even for medium-sized corporate clients is an expensive business, and could lead to further loss of earnings. Another way forward might be to seek to increase profitability through cost-cutting mergers or by linking up back offices. WestLB has already taken the decision to develop a new structure to meet the EC's objections. The future model involves splitting off the public sector activities, including the Pfandbriefe business, from the bank's commercial activities, which will then be transferred to a wholly-owned private law subsidiary. The chairman, Jurgen Sengara, argued that 'this will enable us to focus on our core competencies, which we will consistently develop and expand'.

Later in 2002 the public finance activities will form part of NRW's new Landesbank. The bank's commercial activities are being consolidated under a new joint stock company, named WestLB AG. These activities account for 80% of the bank's revenue, and this means that almost all of WestLB will eventually be privatised, although the state bank will initially own all of WestLB. The state parliament is expected to approve the plan, known as the Spaltungsmodell, by 1 September, after which WestLB will be split up retroactively from 1 January 2003. The bank had long moved away from its traditional role of supporting the Sparkassen, but it has become a global player in investment banking, large-scale corporate lending, asset-backed securities and derivatives. The sale of the bank, however, is unlikely to take place until 2005, when the state guarantees run out.

Other Landesbanken could also seek to exploit their long-standing relation-ships with the Sparkassen and develop models of 'vertical integration', giving the

Landesbanken access to a large and stable retail deposit base. That course of action would not be without difficulties, partly because many Sparkassen consider that their own business is both more profitable and financially stronger than that of the Landesbanken. They are in the process of pooling resources in corporate finance and product development in a move that would enable them to circumvent the Landesbanken, which have traditionally provided them with central banking services, and thus reducing their reliance on the Landesbanken. The Landesbanken would then lose another source of cheap funding, namely, access to the savings banks' vast branch network, where small savings deposits provide the cheapest form of funding. Interest rates on such deposits are very low.

Other possibilities may be considered. The chairman of HVB Group, Germany's second largest bank, invited the public sector banks to consider cooperation with the private banks, but at the time he made the offer, in 1999, no one took it up. The time is ripe and some of the Landesbanken may now be ready to consider such moves. The loss of guarantees means that these banks will have to act as 'profit maximisers', which will mean restructuring businesses and cutting costs as well as reducing their dependence on lending, which accounted for over 60% of revenues in 2000.

The position of the savings banks may not be as secure as it first appears, despite their large share of various segments of the retail market. Deposits at savings banks have steadily declined over the last decade: households held DM 392 billion at the end of 1999 in deposits compared with DM 529 billion at the end of 1990, a drop of 26%. The large private banks have seen such liabilities more than halved to DM 34 billion compared with DM 79 billion over the same period. This reduction is due to the rapid rise in households' interest and investment in securities. Of the total DM 6,700 billion wealth held by households in financial assets at the end of 1999, 42% was in the form of securities and 46% in insurance and pension savings, compared with 6.5% in deposit-based savings. That marks a major shift over the past decade, when in 1992 just 24% was invested in securities, 24% in pensions and insurance, and 45% in bank deposits. The savings banks have responded to these trends by setting up their own mutual funds and offering their customers multichannel access as well as internet banking. Nevertheless, the competitive position of the savings banks may not be as advantageous as might first appear, partly because of the trends in savings and investment and partly because they are in a 'less advantageous position, unsubsidised and without a guarantee'. As one commercial banker put it, 'They will lose the advantage of refinancing at a cheap rate'.

Some of the Sparkassen, notably Bremen, Cologne's two savings banks, Frankfurt, Hamburg, Hanover, Munich and Wiesbaden, are looking at cooperation in a three-stage plan: first sharing experiences, followed by cooperation on technical matters, and finally joint ventures. The priorities for technical cooperation include corporate finance, risk control, human resources and public offerings. Such syndicates of Sparkassen could then offer competition in areas which are now dominated by the commercial banks and Landesbanken. The savings banks could then also bypass their traditional suppliers of central banking services, the Landesbanken. Other Sparkassen are seeking their own stand-alone ratings, a first step towards raising their own funds in the capital markets and again reducing their reliance on Landesbanken.

Having won the battle, the commercial banks are still in the process of assessing the implications. Leading bankers have widely differing views of the pace of change. One expects a 'tremendous change within the next two to three years. The importance of the state-owned banks will be sharply reduced. There will be great opportunities for private banks'. Another added, 'Acquiring a Landesbank is worth more than a thousand clicks'. The decision is a 'turning point for the future of the banking system'.

One of the leading bankers considered that a 'further possible step would be privatisation, but it is difficult to imagine that happening for the next ten years. The Landesbanken might change their status and ownership, and then they might well be a target for mergers and acquisitions'. As for the Sparkassen, 'a large Sparkassen might well be a target for an acquisition or an agreed merger with a commercial bank. . . . Indeed the strategy might well be to look at the ten largest savings banks in the ten largest cities and buy them with their own shares. The aim would be to buy the business strategy, but not necessarily the client base as they may not be the kind of clientele we want to have'.

The battle is on for the future of retail banking in Germany. It is the only leading European country in which the banking system has not yet undergone a fundamental change during the last decade or so. It is true that consolidation has taken place, especially over the past five years, with on average 169 mergers and acquisitions per year between 1995 and 2000. That has generally been within each sector, such as mergers of cooperative banks. Following the EC's decision, the scope for mergers and acquisitions has opened up.

THE IMPACT OF TAX REFORMS

In December 1999 the government finally announced its decision to remove the 53% capital gains tax on disposals of shareholdings by German banks and companies. The Bundestag eventually passed the Tax Reform Act at the beginning of July 2000 and it was approved by the Bundestag and the Bundesrat in July 2000 to take effect in January 2002. The capital gains from the sale of shareholdings between corporations, including shares in foreign corporations, will generally be exempted from tax. This will bring about dramatic changes in the whole structure of the German economy as well as the banking system.

It could free up at least €250 billion in capital tied up in cross-shareholdings, which could reduce the role of banks and insurance companies in setting the strategic direction of German industry. It could encourage companies to invest more in their own core business. The leading banks have already made it clear that their aim will be to sell their shareholdings as soon as possible. Deutsche Bank, whose stakes are worth about €20 billion, has already said, 'We will separate ourselves from all of our stock market listed holdings. It will just depend on the price we are offered'. Deutsche

Bank owns shares in 18 major companies, such Allianz, Continental, Munich Re, Phoenix, WMF and 12% of DaimlerChrysler, perhaps the most sought-after stock. Commerzbank owns stakes in six companies, including a 4.7% stake in Deutsche Börse, and Dresdner Bank owns shares in 15 companies, including Munich Re, Allianz, Deutsche Börse and BMW. HVB owns shares in Allianz, Munich Re and Brau und Brunnen. Some of these shareholdings were regarded as a protection by a large shareholder for smaller companies or as a means of extending sales and influence by the banks. The banks clearly plan to invest in providing banking services, but the tax reforms will also provide the leading German banks with vast capital resources for further domestic or cross-border mergers and acquisitions. An analysis provided by Commerzbank suggests that the potential for change is enormous—the financial services companies own 25% of the German market, whose total capitalisation is some €1,200 billion.

All told, the tax reforms would also allow hidden reserves to be realised without incurring high tax charges, more active portfolio management and the use of funds for business development and new investment. Once again the speed of change is unclear, given the uncertain state of the markets during 2001 and at the beginning of 2002.

A further tax reform to mention in this context is the so-called Riester Plan, that is, the introduction of a new private pension scheme designed to supplement the state system. It offers tax relief on contributions transferred to private pension plans from social security contributions. It is expected this reform will open up another vast pool of potential savings, estimated at some €30–40 billion by 2008, and such prospects are a partial explanation of the Dresdner–Allianz merger.

Over the last few years, a whole series of mergers and acquisitions were mooted but failed to materialise. ING successfully completed its bid for the bank BHF in August 1999, finally giving ING an entrée into the German banking market. The retail banking sector has proved to be much more difficult. The Deutsche Bank–Dresdner merger proposed in March 2000 failed to take place, and that was followed by the collapse of another proposed merger with Commerzbank. There was a winning deal in that year, the merger of Hypovereinsbank with Bank Austria, a deal which was discreetly conducted under the leadership of the two chairmen, Albrecht Schmidt and Gerhard Randa. This merger attracted a great deal of attention, as it was the first cross-border merger of any significance in the EU, creating the third largest bank in Europe in terms of assets, the fifth in terms of equity and the twelfth in terms of market capitalisation. Hypovereinsbank was well-founded in Bavaria with the bulk of its earnings (over 80%) and most of its branches (over 90%) there, and it was closer to Salzburg than Frankfurt anyway. The bank is now known as HVB Group.

Dresdner's double failure left it exposed to a takeover bid, which was finally resolved by the merger with Allianz in 2001, despite the chief executive's stated determination to keep the bank independent or at least to be 'in the driving seat'. That all changed when the merger was actually announced. Professor Bernd Fahrholz, who took over from Bernard Walter in May 2000 after the failed merger attempts, announced that the merger between Dresdner and Allianz is 'going to be a success story', opening 'new strategic perspectives and competitive advantages'. Referring to the introduction of private pension funds, he said 'We are demonstrating a leadership role in a newly emerging market'.

A combination of changes in the framework surrounding the German banking system will alter the landscape beyond recognition. The timescale is likely to be less than ten years, given the thoroughness and planning with which the prospects for change will be tackled. It is worth remembering that the Neuer Markt was launched in 1997 with just two companies, and by the end of 2000 some 338 companies were listed with a market cap of about €115 billion and by far the largest growth segment, 49% of the market cap of European growth markets, including 139 new listings, of which 133 were IPOs. These figures give some idea of the pace of change that is possible in Germany. There is no reason why changes in the banking structure should not take place at a similar speed, given the sophistication of the leading banks and the removal of obstacles. Developments in the banks' retail banking strategy should also be seen in the same context.

RETAIL BANKING STRATEGY

Savings Banks

The commercial banks may consider that their problems are over now that the public sector guarantees are going to be phased out. They have long taken the view that obstructive tax legislation and the public sector banking system have restricted consolidation and hampered competition. However, the Sparkassen may still present a formidable opposition. The only solution may well be to acquire large savings banks.

The savings banks have not been idle: the process of revamping branches is under way; about 450 branches out of over 700 have been established as investment advice centres; and the Sparkassen Financial Group is building up multichannel access for its customers, including full online services. On the other hand, the Sparkassen are in a strong position to exploit their branch network, the home of 50 million accounts. The commercial banks have long found it difficult to winkle customers away from the neighbourhood savings bank branch. The savings banks have another ace card in their hands—their favourable public rating. When Deloitte & Touche questioned German adults about which types of financial service provider offer the best service, rate and channel mix, Sparkassen were seen as the service most likely to deliver. Out of a sample of 500 adults with a bank account, 37% selected savings banks and 32% selected big banks. (That response is not a uniform response; in some areas, such as Berlin, there are local reasons why the savings banks do not have a good reputation.) Another significant feature is that less than 1 in 20 respondents thought that new entrants or e-banks could provide the best mix.[4]

---

[4] Deloitte Research, nationally representative survey of 500 German adults with bank accounts. Telephone interviews conducted in September 2001.

Commercial Banks

The obvious first move for the commercial banks, including the big banks, is to look for opportunities to merge and acquire banks and then to make the best use of the newly acquired capital from the sale of cross-shareholdings. The challenge for financial institutions, including banks, will be to decide how to make best use of the extra capital: return it to shareholders, invest it into new technologies, or spend it on acquisitions to get value-added returns. One of the leading banks has already made it plain that it 'will return some to shareholders and retain the rest for future acquisitions'. The long-term implications of such decisions have to be given careful thought, given the present uncertainty and volatility of the markets.

Technological Solutions

The big banks have already invested heavily in technology. Deutsche Bank's DB24 was the first stage of a multichannel re-engineering process, which fitted in well with so-called Martini banking (any time, any place, anywhere). Rolf Breuer, spokesman of the board of managing directors, said in June 2000 that 'in the concept of Deutsche Bank 24, we have brought movement into the German retail banking market, which is strongly influenced by the public sector banks. Deutsche Bank 24, as a full-scale bank, offers an ideal blend of geographically extensive branch bank with a high standard of advisory and service competence and the permanent accessibility of a modern direct bank.... We are constantly pursuing our strategy of opening a new chapter of performance, service quality and accessibility in retail banking business for our customers and the entire market. This also means we are relying on further expansion of online banking and broking.'

Online banking and broking suffered from depressed markets and volatility in 2001. But Deutsche Bank still has great ambitions for the DB24 model: 'We shall extend our Deutsche Bank 24 business model, which has already achieved excellent results in Germany to the rest of Europe, thus establishing the leading pan-European retail bank'. At one point, analysts concluded that Deutsche Bank has conceded the mass market in Germany to the Sparkassen, and was targeting the segment of European consumers with investible assets of €50,000. The bank already targets those with over €100,000 in its private banking division and estimates there are 16 million such individuals in Germany at present.

Other leading banks have adopted the same business models: 'We use a combination of bricks, clicks and telephone, but we do not know how broad it will become. It is important to get the timing right [in introducing new channels]; if you're late, you have to spend more than the early birds'. The same bank commented that 'our e-bank and direct brokerage has been a success story' but it later found this business was badly affected by the market. 'We recognise that we need to be in touch the customer outside branch opening hours. . . . Our clients prefer multichannel access, at least the clear majority do. Elderly customers still wish to use bank branches, but the young and the middle-aged have no problems with telephone or online banking or mobile telephones'.

'We're reducing branch networks, as the traffic in branches is much reduced. We thought e-banking would have an important role when opening hours are still restricted, but we have to admit that only about 10% of our clients are willing to use the internet, and then they often use it for additional access.' Another added that 'our data warehouse concept increases productivity and increases selling opportunities for our advisers dramatically. The database helps him to identify a list of all the selling possibilities and the probability of selling particular products to a customer with this client profile'.

'We regard at least some branches as embassies, but we also provide easy access by telephone to a personal adviser. . . . We have set up a sophisticated use of call centres so that it appears as if you are receiving a personal service through your bank branch. Our goal is a personal service. . . . We also aim to have a home page for each and every retail client. . . . We have to make this happen. It is highly complex and it is also expensive. . . . But to achieve this you need a critical mass. You have to have new clients, but how can you put the distribution capability with others, such as insurance companies.' Clearly some banks do wish to remain in charge of distribution rather than share clients with others, and to find more effective ways of serving the customer using technology to provide what appears to be a personal service without the presence of bank staff. At least the commercial banks have had one advantage—they did not have to close down large branch networks and they were readily able to establish multichannel networks.

The Customer

The banks are clearly aware that the needs and wishes of the customers are changing: 'What is driving the retail market? The client's attitudes and expectations have changed dramatically. We're not in the driving seat. If we don't respond to his needs, we'll lose him. On the technology side, that means ensuring higher transparency and lower margins,' according to one leading banker. They are more demanding, according to another: 'We have well-educated clients. It is easy enough to switch bank accounts. It is no longer a psychological hurdle to change banks, as the individual no longer has to visit the branch and ask to switch accounts in person. . . . It's getting more and more difficult to retain clients and retention is the issue'. As a result, 'it's still difficult to be profitable in retail banking; one's pricing power is limited. . . . 'We cannot make a profit out of current accounts. All banks can charge for current accounts and there are different models for charging and people pay for the kind of current account they want'.

Leading bankers are aware that they can no longer rely on customer loyalty and they need to meet the customer's financial needs. It is not always clear that they have found a suitable means of identifying the customer needs. Much is said about customer segmentation but bankers do not have the data to accurately calculate consumer profitability and their potential lifetime value to the bank. Few banks indicated that they had a suitable means of building customer profiles. One bank suggested that the current method of assessment—the amount of investible income available—is inadequate and that a variety of criteria are needed: income, age, sex, permanent address and behavioural aspects such as credit card use. Then cross-selling depends on the use of one product as an anchor, perhaps a current account or a mortgage, and building on that. There is clearly greater scope for developing models of customer segmentation and customer relationship models.

Solutions

The banks have responded to what they take to be customer wishes: access to banking and financial services at convenient times and in a convenient manner. They have turned their attention to cross-selling, recognising that 'the client is looking for an intelligent solution, not just deposit-based savings. Less than 30% of the savings are not on the balance sheet. It has been transferred to mutual fund products and other comparable assets, a process which is speeding up, as more people want an equity-based investment'. Another leading bank said, 'We have transformed ourselves from a traditional retail bank. We have spent the last five years providing each and every product to personal clients from loans and securities to investment banking products. . . . Our basic idea is to draw on our core know-how and experience, including investment banking and equity experience, and if the know-how is to be used, we need a retail banking and distribution network'.

The issue which has dominated the big banks' approach to cross-selling is the nature of the link with insurance companies. Various routes have been chosen: the merger of Allianz and Dresdner, Deutsche Bank's purchase of US fund manager Zurich Scudder as part of a deal with Zurich Financial Services. Hypovereinsbank bought Bank Austria in 2000, giving it a significant presence in Austria and Poland, and followed this by forging close ties with Munich Re, Germany's second largest primary insurer.

The Allianz and Dresdner merger has created the fourth largest financial group, and Europe's largest bancassurer. 'The partnership with Dresdner Bank is our joint answer to the challenges of the future,' according to Henning Schulte-Noelle, the chief executive. The aim is to become a 'fully integrated financial services supermarket with the insurance company controlling the bank' and so to overcome the weak profitability of the German banks' domestic retail activities, which still face intense competition and a high cost base. Having resisted the notion of buying a bank for so long, the fact that Allianz then bought Dresdner, a bank which analysts viewed as having a weak strategy, suggests a sense of urgency in finding a domestic partner. The move can be seen as a response to the twin pressures of the capital tax reform, allowing the sale and freeing up of capital, and the opportunities of the German pension reform. According to one leading banker, Allianz concluded that 'to gain a share in the long-term savings market, it needed to buy a bank'. Having acquired Dresdner, Allianz sees itself as being in a strong position. 'To put it in a nutshell, together with Dresdner Bank, we are second to none in the German market for retirement provision and asset management,' according to Dr Schulte-Noelle.

Bernd Fahrholz, chief executive, pointed out that 'the Riester reform creates a very attractive business field. We see considerable growth and earnings potential from the growth in pension savings. We expect two-digit growth yearly because of the pension reform. We, that is, Allianz and Dresdner Bank, will participate above average in this growth and take the lead in the market for pensions'. The initial process of integration was completed in autumn 2001, including integration of the sales forces. Allianz already deals with about 17.8 million customers in Germany, Dresdner with 6 million, and the sales force will be deployed in both the bank branches and agency offices, with a transfer of banking skills to the agency offices and insurance skills to the bank branches. Allianz expects that optimising all banking and insurance sales will bring in €630 million by 2006. In addition the merger creates one of the five largest asset managers in the world, Dresdner Asset Management Group, which manages more than €1 billion and has access to 50 million customers worldwide. Local sales will be organised in Germany, and Allianz's insurance sales force could be well placed to sell Dresdner's banking and mutual fund products. In addition, Allianz is taking the first step towards 'open architecture' by considering the sale of the products of other companies in order to 'maximise the value of its purchase'.

The other leading banks have taken the partnership route. Deutsche Bank acquired Zurich Scudder, and claims this places it in the 'bulge bracket in asset management', the fourth asset manager globally. In return, Zurich Financial Services will be the exclusive provider of all insurance products for Deutsche Bank in Germany (and Italy, Spain and Portugal). The strategic alliance with Deutsche Bank provides important distribution opportunities for Zurich and enables Deutsche Bank to offer a wider choice of integrated solutions for customers. According to Rolf Breuer, this is all part of the bank's 'aggressive expansion strategy', which 'includes private banking and asset management'. Herbert Walter, chief executive of DB24, described the way in which DB24 will contribute to the sales process: 'We can win three-quarters of a million of our own clients for the Riester pension products easily [since] we are aiming at a 6–7% market share for Riester products'. That would be about 18 million people, about 70% of those who are eligible to buy them. Of the 18 million potential purchasers, Walter expects 13 million to buy them through banks and insurance companies and 5 million through company pension schemes.

Commerzbank and HVB have also just set up their joint ventures. The European Commission approved the joint venture between Commerzbank and AMB, a German insurance company, which is part of the Assicurazioni Generali group. Under the agreement, Commerzbank agencies will distribute AMB's insurance and life insurance products, while Commerzbank's banking products will be sold through the

AMB network. Munich Re and HVB opted for a strategic union, underpinned by cross-shareholdings. Albrecht Schmidt, chairman of Hypovereinsbank, described the fundamental nature of the changes taking place in the market: 'The European financial services industry is in the throes of a radical transformation. . . . That means we also need a powerful partner in the field of bancassurance, and we have an excellent partner in this respect in the Munich Re group'.

All these relationships and acquisitions took place during 2001, so it is too early to estimate whether or not they have lived up to the expectations of their chairmen and chief executives. They all constitute a major advance in the development of stronger bancassurance models in Germany, and they speed up the development of the one-stop shop. They are all designed to take advantage of the highly significant structural and strategic changes taking place in Germany. The strength of the companies acquired could also assist at least one of the leading banks to look beyond the borders of Germany in the EU.

6
Italy: Fast-Track Banking

This chapter looks first at Italy as one of the banking systems which emerged from an overregulated, state-owned and inefficient banking system to establish modern and forward-looking banking groups in a few years. The other similar country is Spain. The banking system in Italy has probably undergone the most dramatic changes in the EU during the 1990s, moving from a largely state-owned banking system to one led by increasingly efficient private banks. The process of change during the last decade was very rapid. Competition among banks in Italy began in the 1980s as a result of the easing of restrictions on banking operations, including administrative limitations on the types of business banks could undertake, the size of loans they could grant, and the removal of geographical limits on a bank's activities.

DEVELOPMENTS IN THE 1990s

The First Steps

Known as the Amato-Carli Law, the Banking Law 1990 (Law 218) introduced a new legal framework for banking and the financial services industry and accelerated the pace of change. Until Law 218 was enacted, banks were almost stifled by the 1936 Banking Law, which severely restricted the services particular categories of banks could provide, and the existing structures were not conducive to profitability. The Amato-Carli Law, named after the prime minister at the time, Snr Amato, allowed for the privatisation of the state-owned banking system and reform of the system. It was particularly aimed at the privatisation of the nine public sector banks, which then accounted for more than half the banking system's assets. Change there was urgently required as the state-owned banks were notoriously inefficient, overstaffed and run by senior managers selected on the grounds of political patronage rather than competence. Italian banks were undercapitalised, costly with an average cost/income ratio of 70.1%, and underbranched with 16,000 bank branches serving an average of 3,700 people, compared with the then average of 1,800 people in Spain, Germany, France and the UK. The average deposit at a branch was €26 million, much higher than comparable branches in Germany ($14 million) and France ($12 million).

The Amato-Carli Law made provision for the sale of 49% of the shares to the public, but allowed the government to retain 51% of the shares. The government had set its sights on the privatisation of four large banks, Banca Commerciale Italiana, Credito Italiano, Banca di Roma and Banca Nazionale, controlled by the IRI, the state industrial holding company. By 1992 the Banca di Roma holding company had been established, comprising three Rome-based public sector banks: Banca di Roma, Banca di Santo Spirito and Cassa di Risparmio di Roma. The completion of the merger made Banca di Roma the largest banking group with 1,100 branches nationwide. Giuseppe Greco, then managing director of Banca di Roma, predicted that in the wake of deregulation, the Italian financial services market would 'comprise a few prime nationwide multifunctional banking groups of international standing'. That would be matched by a 'large number of smaller banks with closely knit branch networks in their own regional areas'. The Italian banking system indeed moved in that direction in the years that followed.

A further decree, Decree 385, implementing the first and second EU banking directives, became effective from 1 January 1994. Article 10 provides a wide and fully comprehensive definition of banking activities, including the conduct of securities business. Banks were allowed to conduct transactions on the stock exchanges from 1996 onwards, thus ending the exclusive role of the SIMs, the securities intermediation companies. The 1990 law encouraged banks to adopt a structure similar to holding companies, where non-financial services are carried out through separate subsidiaries, subject to the control of centralised management. Almost every bank adopted the structure proposed in Law 218 when the tax benefits for so doing came into being at the end of 1995. The pace of privatisation was still too slow for the government and the regulators, and also for industry. Confinindustria, which had long argued that the inefficiencies in Italian banking threatened the viability of Italian manufacturing, was impatient with the lack of progress. This was especially relevant with regard to lending policies which had more to do with politics and personal relationships than with the balance sheet or any fundamental analysis.

Moody's Investors Service noted that 'the depth of loan quality problems has been exacerbated by generally unsophisticated credit approval, review and monitoring systems'. The report also pointed out that the Association of Italian Bankers also drew attention to 'unsystematic ad hoc lending criteria, a superficial due diligence approach, insufficient awareness of the risks of cross-group borrowing and undisciplined loan-monitoring procedures'.[1] At that time, in 1996, 80% of total revenues were generated from lending and very little from commission or other fee-based income.

In June 1996 the then treasury, budget and economic planning minister informed the annual meeting of the Association of Italian Bankers that the 'major banks directly or

---

[1] Moody's Investors Services, 1996, *Italy: The Banking System Outlook*, p. 6.

indirectly controlled by the state have been sold'. The finance ministry keeps control only of BNL Group and Mediocredito Centrale. Credito Italiano (now Unicredito) and Banca Commerciale Italiana (now Banca Intesa BCI) were privatised in 1993 and 1994, respectively, although both were already quoted on the stock exchange, but still under indirect state control. In July 1996 the finance minister announced that the government had disposed of its remaining stake in Istituto Mobilaire Italiano (IMI), a Rome-based investment bank and financial services group, but in fact it was sold to a group of public sector banks. At that stage, Italian banks still suffered from low capitalisation at a time when other European banks had strengthened theirs in response to the Basel Accord 1988. Their capital bases had actually declined because of poor earnings retention and ambitious acquisition strategies. At that stage, bancassurance, custody services, payment systems, asset management and foreign exchange dealing were not viewed as potential sources of profit.

By the mid 1990s, the Italian banking system was still fragmented and the return on capital was far lower than other leading countries, with its earning capacity limited by the growing volume of non-performing loans, the narrow range of services provided to enterprises and households, and high labour costs. Staff costs absorbed 44% of the revenues, 7% more than the average for German, French, British and Spanish banks. Hence in 1997 the supervisory authorities pressed the banks to seek an agreement of the trade unions to curb their unit labour costs (the level of unionisation was 40%) and make better use of the professional skills of their staff on the understanding that government support would be available. Banks had been grossly overstaffed with higher pay for bank staff than other industries.

The initiative enabled the banks to limit the forthcoming increases in unit labour costs and make better use of the professional skills of their staff. The rise in these costs was reduced to an annual average of 1.2% in nominal terms between 1997 and 2000 together with a payment of L2.6 billion to encourage the departure of 21,900 employees. Employment declined by 3% in the banking industry as a whole: it fell by 10% in the largest banks and 3% in the smaller banks. Labour productivity increased at an annual average rate of 6%, and 8% for the largest banks. This was an important step forward, given the notorious inefficiency of Italian banks. It did produce results; by 1999 the ratio of staff costs to revenues was much closer to the average for France, Germany and Spain.

Between 1990 and 1997 the advantages of the new laws and competitive pressures accelerated the process of consolidation. The average number of mergers and acquisitions rose from 12% in the early 1990s to between 27 and 39 a year in 1997, including mutual banks. For the non-mutual banks, a total of 112 mergers and acquisitions were concluded by the end of 1997, involving 4–7% of banks and 5–7% of total assets. The process of privatisation of the public sector banks continued throughout the 1990s, and by 1997 the banks controlled by the state, local authorities and foundations accounted for 25% of the total assets of the banking system compared with 68% at the end of 1992. By 1999 that share had been reduced to 17%.

The process of consolidation has continued apace. By the end of 1999 some 79 registered banking groups consisted of 267 banks and controlled 89% of the system's assets. On average there were 11 companies in each group, two more than in 1992. In the same year, the concentration of the banking system, measured on the basis of the market share of the five largest groups, has reached 51%, similar to France. Between 1995 and 2000, bank mergers and acquisitions accounted for nearly 40% of all M&A activity by value. Over the whole decade there were 508 mergers and acquisitions. In 157 cases the banks taken over have retained their corporate identities. With operating structures becoming more and more integrated, this made it possible for acquiring banks to take full advantage of the local roots they acquired. The number of banks declined from 1,176 to 862 over the ten years, and banking groups have grown considerably in importance. The Bank of Italy has played an active role in encouraging these processes, recognising the extent of the change required to develop an efficient and competitive banking system.[2]

Further Consolidation?

By 2001 the governor of the Bank of Italy seemed to be satisfied that the process of consolidation was complete, at least as far as the large banks were concerned. By the end of 2000 the concentration of the banking system, measured on the basis of the market share of the five largest groups, had reached 51%, in line with the figure for France and higher than the figure for Germany. He was reported as making his opposition clear at a conference in Trieste, saying that 'mergers between large banks may pose competition problems, particularly to the detriment of the consumer and small companies' and that 'these would not necessarily be moves in the direction of stability'. Three years would seem to be a 'reasonable' period in which to allow the industry to consolidate the mergers and acquisitions which had taken place during that period. The governor has the power to intervene if he considers the stability of the Italian financial system to be at risk, and approval for takeovers of a banking institution has to be given by the central bank.[3] More than that, the 1993 Banking Law expressly refers to the competitiveness of the banking system as one of the objectives of supervisory activity. That power is limited in one respect. Foreign intermediaries are substantial shareholders in Italy's leading banks and hold sizeable interests in the five largest banking groups. The central bank's ability to curb foreign banks or financial institutions from taking more than a 5% share in Italian banks was brought to an end by the decision of the European Commission in 1999.

Consolidation led to the establishment of five large banking groups: Banca Intesa BCI, following the acquisition of Banca Commerciale Italiana in 1999; Unicredito Italiano, which came into being in 1998 when Credito Italiano and Rolo Banca merged several regional savings banks, and two other savings banks joined the group; San

---

[2] 'Competition, growth and the banking system', address by the governor of the Bank of Italy, October 2000. 'Innovation and growth in the Italian banking system', June 2000. Two speeches by Antonio Fazio, governor of the Bank of Italy.
[3] Quoted in *European Banker*, 22 February 2001, p. 3.

Paolo IMI; Banca di Roma; and Banca Monte dei Paschi di Siena (BMPS). All five are listed in the top 50 of *The Banker's* list of the top 300 European banks in terms of both capital and assets.[4] That year did see some further consolidation: San Paolo IMI absorbed Banca Cardine, an 800-branch bank, a non-listed institution giving the bank a strong presence in a wealthy region and allowing it to rebalance its geographical market and revenue mix.

Banca Nazionale del Lavore (BNL) missed out on the opportunity to merge with Banca Cardine, a merger which Davide Croffe, managing director of BNL, claimed would have been a 'merger between equals'. In fact, a merger between BNL and BMPS might serve both banks well and would create a strong banking institution in central Italy. Davide Croffe had made it clear that, contrary to the stated views of the governor of the Bank of Italy, 'the process [of consolidation] will continue. Banks need to grow to reach critical mass. . . . The new Basel rules and increased attention to risk are drivers for concentration. As in any other sector, market share is important'.[5]

With no immediate prospects for further mergers between the large banking groups, Italian banks engaged in acquisitions in Central and Eastern Europe with the blessing of the central bank. He informed the shareholders at the bank's annual general meeting, 'The biggest Italian banks are taking significant positions in important sectors of activity in European markets. By asserting themselves in other countries, they can widen their services and increase their revenue sources'. Unicredito purchased a 53% stake in Pekao, a Polish retail bank with over 800 branches and an 18% share in deposits, and followed it by the purchase of a 63% interest in Splitska Banka, a medium-sized Croatian bank with an 8% share in deposits. In October 2000 Unicredito acquired 93% of Bulgaria's Bulbank, with 105 branches and 26% share of deposits, and an 88% share of Slovakia's Pol'nobanka. The completion of the acquisition of Croatia's Zagrebacka, which has a 30% market share in Bosnia-Herzegovina, will make it the largest bank in the region.

Intesa is following the same strategy with its 1999 purchase of a 63% stake in PBZ, a Zagreb bank with substantial shares in retail and corporate lending. That bank has a wholly-owned subsidiary in Hungary, CIB, which is the third largest bank there. In 2001 Intesa BCI also bought a stake in Dogus, a Turkish group, on the grounds that 'Turkey is an important market of 60 million people. The time to invest is when prices are low, although you do not leap in without risk analysis'. They also won the bidding for VUB, the second largest bank in Slovakia. BNL also has a 134-branch subsidiary in Argentina, and San Paolo IMI owns a profitable French subsidiary, Banque Sanpaolo, which focuses on wealth management for private clients. All the banks realise that the overseas investments should show results.

Welcome as it may be from the viewpoint of the central bank, the extension of the activities of Italian banks is much more limited than in other member states. Their

[4] *The Banker*, September 2001, p. 117.
[5] Quoted in *The Banker*, December 2001, p. 23

share of total international activity of banks reporting to the Bank for International Settlements is about 5%, compared with German and French banks at 16% and 10% respectively. The activity of their foreign networks is on a particularly small scale. The strategy for the leading banks, constrained in their domestic market, is to build up their customer and capital base.

The Role of the Foundations

The existence of the foundations is a unique feature of the Italian banking system. They were established under the Amato-Carli Law when the state-owned banks were required to spin off their banking activities into joint stock corporations. Ownership of the shares was placed in the hands of the charitable foundations. These are non-profit-making bodies whose goal is to promote public and social interests with particular regard for the development of scientific research, education, the arts, social welfare and other charitable concerns. The boards of the foundations consist of local and central government appointees and the funds derived from their shares in the banks must be used for the charitable purposes defined in the act: their objectives must be quite different from the commercial objectives that may be expected of a privately owned bank. They were designed to play an important role in the privatisation process in that they were intended to provide a stable group of shareholders for the newly privatised banks. They cannot be involved in the management of banks, and members of their governing bodies may not hold positions in the banks in which they have an interest; rules on the incompatibilities must be observed.

The foundations tended to be concerned that the local or regional identity of the bank would be lost and that new owners would weaken local ties. They frequently presented a formidable obstacle to any transfer of ownership, since in the early 1990s the shareholdings in the banks accounted for 90% of the foundations' assets on average. Their contribution to the local communities and/or to scientific research also endeared them to the local community; for example, Compagnia di San Paolo has put €25 million into cancer research, and Milan's Fondazione Caripio assists the elderly in the Lombardy region and helps the La Scala opera house.

A further obstacle was the market value of the shares owned by the foundations. The reason for this is that when the transformation into joint stock companies took place, the banks took advantage of the untaxed revaluation of their assets, so many of the foundations had investments with high book values, whereas the average dividend yield earned by the foundations on their banking shares was only 1.7%. In 1994 Lamberto Dini, the then finance minister, issued a directive requiring all foundations to diversify their portfolios, allowing them five years (until 1999) to reduce revenues from bank interest to less than 50% of total revenues. A year later, little progress had been made—the foundations still controlled over half of all Italian banks.

In a speech to the Association of Italian Bankers in June 2000, the governor stated firmly that 'the foundations must continue to dispose of their holdings in banks, thereby fostering the formation of stable groups of core shareholders'. By 2000 the foundations still held large stakes in San Paolo IMI, BMPS, Unicredito and Banca Intesa BCI, whose second largest shareholder after Crédit Agricole is Fondazione Caripio, with assets of L13 trillion. Some banks have begun to divest themselves of the shareholdings of the foundation; BMPS sought a partial listing on the stock exchange in 1999. The role of the foundations is declining progressively but it is a slow process. ACRI, the association representing the foundations' interests, estimates that at the beginning of 2001 the foundations had L69 trillion of assets. Substantial though the figure may be, the market share of banks controlled by the state or foundations fell from 68% at the end of 1992 to 17% in 1999 and then to 12% in 2000.

Law 153/99, the legislative decree of April 1999, and Law 461/98 were designed to encourage the foundations to relinquish control of the banks they currently own. Banking foundations which disposed of their assets in this way would be granted the status of non-commercial entities and would be exempted from capital gains tax on the sale of their shares, provided they gave up control of their banking subsidiaries. For the banks, the concessions consist of a reduction from 37% to 12.5% tax rate on part of the revenue for the merger deals. If the foundations themselves have not completed the sales by 2004, the Bank of Italy, as the supervisory authority, will handle the sales. However, the minister of finance announced the suspension of fiscal incentives for banking foundations and credit institutions, pending a formal investigation by the European Commission over concerns that the measures may constitute unlawful state aid.

However, the foundations are still in a position to influence bank decisions and to render the banks susceptible to political interference. Not all leading bankers consider that the foundations politically influence the bank, nor do they divert the bank from its commercial objectives: 'The foundations are stable shareholders supporting the management. Their target is to increase the value of their stock. They are supportive. If they decrease their investment in the capital of the bank, then this will bring about great changes in the structure of the bank's shareholdings, leaving the bank more vulnerable to foreign takeovers. I have had no problems at all with the foundations in the development of the banking strategy'.

He did admit, however, that 'we need a clear definition of what the foundations are and what they will be'. The leading banker concerned would be very capable of managing his relationships with the foundations, ensuring their support for his strategies and was clearly successful in that task. His views were reinforced by another leading banker, who pointed out that 'it is very difficult for the foundations to maintain their influence in banks,' especially as their share of bank equity decreases.

The Banca Popolare

The whole process of privatisation excludes the cooperative sector, which still retains a 26% share of total deposits, enjoying high margins from retail customers in the wealthy industrial northern cities and regions of Milan, Verona, Novara, Bergamo and Mantua.

The savings banks, or *popolari*, came under pressure in 2001 to give up restrictive ownership rules with the aim of opening up the sector to competition and to force the pace of restructuring. In general, the *popolari* give one vote to each shareholder regardless of the size of the holding. These long-standing restrictions are designed to ensure the control of a particular bank remains in the hands of management and local businesses. Some of the banks, for example Banca Popolare di Brescia (Bipop), have converted into a joint stock company, but the majority have rejected change. Mergers and acquisitions have taken place within the sector. Not all the proposed mergers succeed, due to the wide range of members who have to agree to the deal. For example, a merger between Banca Popolare di Bergamo and Banca Popolare di Verona failed because the two sides could not agree on the location of the head office and the selection of the chief executive. Both banks had to purchase smaller banks which they did not want, and probably at too high a price.

The possibility of reform was raised by the Finance Minister in summer 2001. Tax incentives could be used to encourage the *popolari* to demutualise, but at the time of writing no action has been taken. Some of the *popolari* are already considering conversion into joint stock companies, and in other cases trade unions are opposed to such moves on the grounds that the elimination of the *popolari* banks would be a 'gift to powerful financial groups and speculators'. Since 92 of the cooperatives have 4,750 branches in some of the wealthiest areas of Italy, such as Lombardy and Piedmont, the issue of conversion is becoming highly significant. They also represent some 20% of the entire banking network.

The argument in favour of encouraging demutualisation is that the Italian banking system will continue to be weak and fragmented unless change occurs. However, large and successful cooperatives may not be convinced of the need to change their status. They have the advantages of being firmly rooted in their local areas and of posessing loyal clients, many of whom are small and medium-sized businesses. They are not necessarily set in old-fashioned methods of banking; for example, Banca Popolare di Lodi has linked up with CGNU to sell insurance policies; it recently launched a joint venture with BSCH to sell a wide range of products and services and established a new multichannel bank, Bipielle.Net, with 600 financial consultants and 100 financial boutiques. They would, however, prove attractive targets for mergers, if they were only joint stock companies.

Bancassurance

Under Italian law, banks can acquire control of insurance companies, and insurance companies can take control of banks. Cross-shareholdings between banks and insurance companies are now typical of Italy's financial services industry, as elsewhere in Europe. Bancassurance involves some of the country's largest intermediaries, including five of the ten leading life insurance companies. In September 2000, banks owned interests in 72 Italian insurance companies, of which 34 are engaged in life policies and 24 in general insurance and life insurance; some smaller banks are controlled by insurance companies. Cross-selling of insurance products is permitted as long as the products are standardised, but it must be carried out under agreements that clearly define the contractual liabilities and the risks associated with the products being sold.

The extent of bancassurance is shown by its share of total life premium income, which rose from 5% in the early 1990s to 50% in 1999. In that year, a Bank of Italy survey showed life premium income from new policies sold by the banking system amounted to L41 trillion. About two-thirds of the premium income was generated by large banks that accounted for 56% of deposits and bonds. About 84% of the premium income came from policies issued by insurance companies in which banks own an interest. The rest referred to policies sold exclusively under distribution arrangements.

Conclusion

Within the space of ten years, the Italian banking system was transformed into a modern banking system from a centrally controlled, inefficient, bureaucratic, and often locally based system. That is an achievement, even if Italian banks are still not as strong as their counterparts in other member states. It was also essential for Italy to move forward in this way, since the establishment of the single market and the emergence of international financial markets requires standards of organisation and size which would simply have been incompatible with Italy's former banking system.

The mergers and acquisitions have narrowed the gap between Italy and the other member states, but may not be sufficient to ensure the organisational structure and minimum efficient size necessary to compete in the wider markets. Efficient forms of ownership have not yet emerged from the ten years of consolidation. Italian banks still depend for their competitive advantages on their strong local roots and retail business, and for their income on non-traditional banking services. It is in this context that the banking strategies of the leading banks should be seen.

BANKING STRATEGIES

Organisation and Efficiency

The process of consolidation and reorganisation of the banks between the years 1990 and 2000, one of the fastest in Europe, helped to bring about bank efficiency and increased competitiveness in the markets. The newly privatised banks were encouraged to follow a federal model, with the various banks involved brought under a single holding company and part of the back-office activities transferred to a central function. At the beginning of the consolidation process, this model had certain advantages allowing the newly merged bank to overcome local resistance and to strengthen the traditional elements of the retail business. It allowed the member banks of the group considerable freedom and autonomy. As time goes on, there is a real question that the model will continue to work, especially against the background of the complex web of cross-shareholdings and the role of the foundations.

It has created problems. One leading banker pointed out that Italian 'banks still face a problem of integration'. They either follow a federal model or a divisional model. The bank 'used the federal model, because we thought it was the only way'. It is still 'not a fully integrated banking group, although the group has the same computer system, risk management system and EDP [electronic data processing]'. However, the bank plans to complete the full integration of the bank, which involves three large banks, including unification of information technology by 2003. 'The creation of a divisional structure is the only way to integrate the bank, as it did not fit the federal model. . . . Nowhere else in Europe is there an example of such restructuring,' he claimed.

Another leading banker defined his strategy as 'moving on from the federal model, which has generated very good results up till now, but now we have to move towards a multi-specialist business model. This will enable us to focus on customer relations, market coverage and human resources, which have been and are vital elements of our strategy'.

Merging banks did not have the opportunity to consider which was the most appropriate business model in terms of their strategic goals and objectives. As one banker indicated, banks went along with the model because that was the form that privatisation took—the holding company model allowed for the introduction of the foundations. In the years since 1990, the impact of technology, the demands of the market and of banking supervision all point in the direction of a multifunctional or integrated bank. Clearly the bank has to have an integrated computer system that can manage and inform all the relationships with the retail customers. Prudential supervision increasingly requires banks to have a coherent risk management system, covering the activities of the banking group as a whole. Italian banks have not had the opportunity of creating integrated, multi-specialist groups.

Mergers and acquisitions directed from the very beginning at creating such a model have encountered difficulties as well, and the application of such models might have disadvantages in terms of the geographical base, which cannot be overcome just by buying a stake in a local bank or some other compromise. But whatever the organisational difficulties involved, the opportunity costs of the failure to move towards these or similar models could damage the competitive standing of the bank. Some leading bankers recognise that as they move towards new structures and move away from the foundations and the federal structure, this is the only way forward.

Multichannels and Technology

The banks have invested extensively in technology, telecommunications systems and the internet over the past ten years. Investment in data processing systems, calculated on a constant quality basis, rose at an average annual rate of 12.5% in the 1990s. At the end of 2000, the stock of IT capital per employee was more than four times that available in 1990. Labour productivity increased by 6% per year between 1995 and 2000, and about two-thirds of the growth is attributed to technological progress and the remaining third from the increase in capital per employee.[6]

Leading bankers have already adopted the multichannel approach, but with a clear emphasis on the personal touch: 'We have applied the multichannel approach across all entities. That is a fundamental to our approach. I do not believe in the use of the internet only. Of course, we have to train the customer to use the right channel for the right transaction. If we do that, it allows us to reduce the structure of costs and improve the quality of service to the customer'. But the same banker insists that 'the human touch is still fundamental' and 'it must be used for the right things—for advice, for example'. It is all part of the appropriate approach to selling in Italy: 'The front office is much more important; the customer identifies much more with the front-office employees than with the bank itself; if you slim the company, you risk losing the client. The clients also identify with the individual leading the bank than with the bank itself. All our market research bears this out'.

Another leading banker welcomed the multichannel approach: 'It is very much a winning concept. Transactions are ideal for the internet; these could be conducted entirely on the internet. Banks are going to be central to internet development,' but that will be balanced by 'personal communication'. 'The Italians do not want to be treated by machines, even ones which can guide choices through decision trees. They want the human contact and they want advice. That is very much part of the culture in Italy.'

Cross-selling and Customer Segmentation

Italian banks have one important advantage in that the Italians have always had a high propensity to save. It has declined over recent years, but nevertheless it is still much higher than in some other leading member states, such as Germany and the UK. In 1999 the proportion of disposable income saved was 11.2% compared with 16.6% in 1993. The decline is due to a long period of weak growth in disposable income. The continuing fall has been mitigated by the widespread expectation of smaller pensions, which seems to have encouraged people to increase their savings in financial assets.

The decline in real interest rates, the reduction in the supply of government securities and the expansion in asset management all led to a switch in the nature of savings. It presents a challenge for fund managers; as one banker put it: 'The Italians are very demanding when it comes to savings. They were used to very high returns on government bonds with no perceived risk'.

---

[6] Antonio Fazio, 2001, *Progress in the Italian Banking System*, Bank of Italy.

As far as the banks are concerned, 'mutual funds have led to an increase in prof-itability, in large part due to the transformation of direct deposits in mutual funds. We are able to charge high fees for asset management. We are now beginning to sell third-party funds through our networks and our internet platform offers a fund supermarket. Unfortunately, sales are slower than we thought they would be a year ago'.

Another noted a new trend: 'There is a huge switch from mutual funds to pension savings. Mutual funds are now regarded as short-term and speculative propositions, which are not the best use of the tool we have provided'. This bank had moved its fund management operation to Dublin and encouraged their Italian clients to invest in pan-European equities, a move which proved to be successful. Only about 200 companies are listed on the Italian stock exchanges, so that enabled the Italian investor to select from over 5,000 stocks in the wider Europe: 'It is perceived by Italian investors as a big market opportunity. They have more complete portfolios so they are happy'. Pension funds were introduced in Italy in 1998 but had attracted just under 1 million contributors by the end of 1999. Their growth is stimulated by a further decree in 2000 which improved the levels of tax relief on contributions. At present, even though competition is intense, the banks play a central role in the development of investment funds and portfolio management accounts. The mutual fund business has grown dramatically and is now the fourth largest in the world, after the US, Japan and France.

The 1998 Consolidated Law on Financial Intermediation created asset management companies; these are not independent of banks but separate companies with banking and insurance groups. By December 2000 the assets of investment funds reached L880 trillion, with assets invested in money market and bond funds, but increasingly in equities. The redirection of savings from deposits to mutual funds has been to the banks' advantage in terms of profitability and for offering services to the customer. They present no threat to the banks, since as one banker said, smiling happily, 'We own them all'.

The success of cross-selling insurance policies is shown by the increase in their share of total life premium income, which rose from 5% at the beginning of the 1990s to 50% in 1999. About 84% of the premium income came from policies issued by insurance companies in which the banks own an interest; the remainder referred to policies sold under exclusive distribution agreements. Investment in life insurance policies and mutual funds can contribute to as much as 45–55% of the banks' income. Overall, banks have been able to recoup profitability by expanding the supply of services. Income from asset management and securities custody accounts reached L12 trillion in 1999 and the rising trend has continued, even with the short-term increases in net interest income which occurred in 2000.

The need for customer segmentation is recognised: 'We must have the capability to segment the customer base in a proper way to cross-sell the right products. . . . You could, for example [having identified the mass market], develop a mass market based on a plastic card, but not on the internet, and you could increase the value of that by cross-selling other products, including investment products, in packaged products, which are easy to understand'. As yet, that idea has not been implemented. Another banker explained: 'We shall segment the market by the end of the year as far as the mass market is concerned. We have already identified private banking and corporate banking with specialised staff using the required technology. The reorganisation has already given very good results: we have the right people in the right place and the right products and improved efficiency in terms of cost and income'. Corporate banking does offer considerable scope for extending the customer base, given the high proportion of small to medium-sized firms in Italy and the fact that they usually have banking relationships with six or seven banks. Capturing such a company would mean extending the corporate market and the possibility of personal savings and investments as well.

There is seemingly less focus on the mass market: 'We must concentrate on clients creating the most business volume, and the great mass of the people are not interesting in that respect. We shall deal with their transactions and it is not very costly to do so. We have to dedicate our channels to clients who are worth it'. It is perhaps inevitable that the focus should be on identifying the high-net-worth clients or the more affluent, given that Northern Italy contains some of the wealthiest areas in Europe, but it also suggests that customer segmentation could be more sophisticated.

Profitable Banks

The return to profitability on the part of Italian banks was made possible primarily by a change in the structure of income. In 1999 net interest income had been nearly 3.3% of total assets, and by 1998 that had fallen to 2.1% with an especially marked decline between 1995 and 1998. Fees and commissions in Italy, as elsewhere, have contributed substantially to the increase in profitability. The average returns on equity are improving, at least as far as the largest banks are concerned. For the three largest banks, they reached 10% in 1998 and increased to 15% in 1999, about 2% above the average for banking groups in Euroland.

The leading banks have tackled the problems of mergers and acquisitions in a much more difficult period of transition than other member states have faced. Strategies for cutting costs have focused mainly on staff reductions and the application of technology, requiring much increased expenditure to make up for the past and to prepare for the future. The consolidation of the strong profit performance achieved so far will require further increases in income from services, especially those with high value added, and cost-cutting measures. 'We have to recognise,' said one leading banker, 'that we cannot create value through cost savings. Another 10% is nothing. We have to work on growth factors and increase our return on equity and reduce the cost of equity. . . . The focus has to be entrepreneurial. The goal of the holding company is to identify new business lines and create synergies with the existing business.' Another leading banker aims at a 'return on equity of over 20% in 2003 as compared with 13.5% in 2000, and a cost/income ratio of 50% compared with 64% in the same years. That would require a series of measures, including full integration [where amalgamations had left senior management intact] and streamlining banking services and the sale of competing insurance products'. Such measures are a long way from the lumbering, bureaucratically run, overstaffed banks of the early 1990s.

7
Spain: Off to a Flying Start

The Spanish banking system was tightly regulated and largely closed to foreign competition during the 1960s and 1970s. Innovation was stifled by detailed and heavy regulation, including administratively fixed interest rates, compulsory investment and reserve requirements, entry restrictions in geographical markets, and asymmetry between the commercial and savings banks. Banks were able to obtain deposits at very low interest rates, and in return they were expected to finance public expenditure cheaply through investment requirements. They did not have to compete over interest rates, since these were regulated.

EARLY DEREGULATION

The process of deregulation began in the 1970s, when the authorities began to worry about the solvency of the banking system, following the oil price shock of 1973. The first step was taken in 1974. Banks were allowed to open branches and new banks were authorised; the reserve requirements were reduced and interest rates were liberalised (for operations of more than two years' maturity). In 1977 interest rates of more than one year's maturity were all freed from administrative controls, part of the process of allowing all banks to engage in the same range of activities throughout the country. This did not apply to savings banks, which were still restricted to their own geographical areas. It took another ten years for all interest rates and service charges to be freed from controls. In 1986 Spain joined the EU, and immediately volunteered to abandon the requirement that foreign banks should only hold public assets; it agreed that all the remaining restrictions would be removed by 1992. Foreign banks were able to enter the Spanish market on equal terms, although in general they found it difficult to break into the market. From 1985 onwards Spain applied strict solvency requirements and one of the highest capital requirements in the world on all financial intermediaries; it applied the Basel Accord and the EU capital regulation in 1992.

Mutual funds were introduced in 1991, the beginning of the growth of investment in the funds.

Changing the reserve requirements in 1990 enabled the banks to compete for new deposits without incurring the cash reserve requirements of 5%. The elimination of credit controls at the same time as high interest rates sparked off a deposit war. This war was also a contributory factor to the changing face of retail banking in Spain. Both the government and the central bank were concerned that Spanish banks may not be large enough to compete in the global market or even the European market.

TWO MAIN CATEGORIES OF BANK

Spain has three types of banking institutions: private (commercial banks), savings banks and credit cooperatives; credit cooperatives account for 3% of total assets. The changes in the regulatory framework did benefit both the savings banks and the commercial banks.

The Savings Banks

Savings banks were originally created as not-for-profit, mutually owned, social benefit institutions, but they gradually lost many of the characteristics which made them different from the commercial banks. They have extended their range of operations during the 1990s, so they now compete with commercial banks in almost every line of business: mortgages, consumer credit, corporate syndication, mutual and pension fund management, and stockbroking. There are currently 48 savings banks in Spain, but the 12 largest, that is, those with more than €8 billion on their balance sheets, account for about 70% of the sector's assets. La Caixa and Caja Madrid, the leading banks in this sector, together account for 35% of the assets. Clearly there is a wide disparity of interests among the savings banks, given the dominance in the association of a small number of large banks, who would be in a position to challenge the leading commercial banks if they could grow through acquisition.

The savings banks are not public limited companies, and like savings banks in other parts of the EU, they direct funds into community projects—the 'social dividend'. Since it is still a legal requirement for banks to allocate such profits after making contributions to the reserves and paying corporation tax, it is still an important aspect of the activities of savings banks.

In 2000, according to the figures released by the Spanish Association of Savings Banks (CECA), they provided a 'social dividend' of Pta 144.2 billion, 26% of their net profits. The savings banks are free to distribute up to 50% of their annual post-tax profits to such projects, but the average has tended to be about 25% over recent years. Such distributions have helped to maintain a loyal customer base, as they fund many educational, health, cultural and sports projects.

They are also governed by a general assembly, the equivalent of an annual meeting of shareholders, which is composed of depositors, representatives of local authorities, the staff of the savings bank and its founding institution. Savings banks are only allowed to merge with other savings banks within the same region, since that is the only process of concentration the rules allow. If all the savings banks in each region were to merge, the number of savings banks would be reduced to 17, one for each of the regions or autonomous communities. This approach is being promoted by some regional governments, which would retain the large disparities between the size of the banks in each region. The interest taken by some regional government indicates the extent to which the future of the savings banks is a political hot potato.

The same rules apply to all savings banks, and CECA allows only one vote to each *caja*, no matter what its size. The sector itself takes in a wide range of banks; some are very small and others are large and profitable. Most of the banks have progressed from their origins as locally based, quasi-charitable institutions and are in a position to challenge the large commercial banks.

Some of the mergers prevented by the existing rules would lead to much larger savings banks with a far stronger capital base. For example, if La Caixa, which has total assets of €68.3 billion, were to absorb Caixa de Catalunya, it would have about €90 billion on its balance sheet, double Caja Madrid's current total. This would increase to nearly €110 billion if La Caixa acquired the other eight small savings banks domiciled in Catalonia. On the other hand, if the five savings banks in the southern region of Andalucia were to merge under the name of Caja Andalucia—a name already registered by the regional government—their combined assets would be only €27 billion, less than half the anticipated balance sheet strength of Caja Madrid in 2003.

Development Post Liberalisation

Savings banks initially gained market share through the process of liberalisation of the 1970s and 1980s. At first they seemed able to take advantage of the newfound freedoms. Between 1986 and 1993 the banks grew rapidly through a series of mergers and the extension of their branch networks for the convenience of the customer. The value of accounts in both sectors grew more quickly than the number of accounts, and both experienced growth rates of over 2%. However, the productivity of the best-practice savings banks increased rapidly at first but then declined, whereas the productivity of the average savings banks began to converge with that of the best-practice savings banks. The commercial banks were unable to keep up with the improving performance of the best-practice savings banks. Managerial inefficiency was a serious problem in the commercial banking sector.

The savings banks were unable to retain their initial advantage, although they seem to have had a more efficient organisational structure. They have, however, opened over 4,000 new branches since 1990 and the total reached 18,295 by the end of 2000. The number of branches could have an adverse effect on profitability, although that has not yet happened. Average efficiency ratios fell to 56.7% by March 2001 from 65.7% at the end of December 2000. Some savings banks are much more efficient than the average; Caja Madrid, for example, achieved 40.5% in 2001. Although they are less efficient than the commercial banks, they compare well with other banking systems in Europe.

The savings banks have sought to adapt to a changing economic and banking environment over the past decade or more, and increased their market share in deposit and credit business, but at a cost. They primarily serve the retail customer through mortgages and loans as well as credit accounts, and have moved into asset management and other fee- and commission-based business. These institutions are now active in financing major public and private projects by subscribing to and purchasing fixed-income securities, and have recently increased their equity investments in industry through privatisations, which have increased by 265% over the past five years. For example, Caja Madrid bought a 10.5% stake in Indra, the elctronics group, and 10% of Iberia, the national airline, out of privatisations in 2000. Other large savings banks, such as Banaja and Caixa Galicia, followed suit. As a result, the governor of the central bank, Jaime Caruana, warned them that such investments increased their risk profile and that they must have sufficient financial and management capacity and suitable reserves in case of a stock market collapse. He warned them that such shares carry 'additional responsibilities' and that if they 'exceed certain limits and reach relatively important proportions, they go against the savings banks' objectives and their very nature'.[1] They require the savings banks to issue hybrid instruments, 'which does not seem very natural for an entity which has the character of a foundation'.

However, the limitations imposed by their inability to raise outside capital as mutual institutions became more significant during the 1990s, outweigh any advantages they may have enjoyed from not having to pay dividends to stockholders. Their inability to raise capital hindered expansion in the 1990s and into the twenty-first century, and the legal structure of the savings banks prohibits cross-regional mergers or purchases of savings banks. They are not prevented from purchasing private banks, and early in 2000 Caja Madrid bought the 82-branch network of Bank Jover, a subsidiary in Spain of Crédit Lyonnais, located in Catalonia and the Balearic Islands, the two growth areas in which Caja Madrid wishes to focus its efforts. In other words, Caja Madrid grasped the only opportunity of expansion open to it, given that it is the only registered savings bank in Madrid and cannot merge with any other savings bank outside Madrid. Other large savings banks will continue to grow by acquiring small and subsidiary private networks.

Reforms Ahead?

In 2000 the savings banks decided to issue shares, in a move which could bring about the privatisation of the fifty or so confederated savings banks. Like commercial banks,

---

[1] Speech to the annual meeting of the Spanish Association of Savings Banks, June 2001.

they have the option of raising funds through wholly-owned subsidiaries, which issue preference shares on their behalf. These shares are considered to be tier 1 capital by the regulatory authorities, available for use to assist solvency levels as risky assets increase. There is no legal limit on the use of these shares as high-leverage instruments, but the Bank of Spain recommends a 30% limit for savings banks.

Caixa Galicia, one of the top five savings banks, took the first step by approving the issuance of up to Pta 25 billion in non-voting shares, which would be available to bank customers and employees. Others followed suit and issued subordinated debt (€210 billion) and non-voting preference shares (€2.7 billion) between 1999 and 2000. Spain is following Norway—where 21 out of the 132 savings banks have launched share issues without putting their mutual status at risk—but with the advantage of enabling banks to submit themselves to market scrutiny, thus improving their efficiency. Share ownership by any one share owner is capped at 10%. The large savings banks are facing huge outlays of capital to pay for investments in e-commerce and technology. They need to develop an efficient system of customer segmentation and concentrate on joint marketing in order to reduce costs. It has been estimated that, given their top-heavy cost structures, the average *caja* faces the same level of expenditure on running 150 regional branches as BBVA, Spain's largest bank, spends on its network of some 3,000 branches.

There is growing domestic and international pressure for the *cajas* to open up to private capital, partly because savings banks have used their positions to purchase small private banks when they cannot themselves be acquired. Both the International Monetary Fund (IMF) and the Organisation for Economic Cooperation and Development (OECD) have recommended privatising the sector. The Circulo de Empresarios, the business confederation, argues that the *cajas*, representing half of Spain's financial system, should have a clear structure of ownership and should be freed from political control. The latter claim is based on the fact that the boards of the savings banks consist of local councillors, reflecting the balance of political power in each region. They claim that the boards use the banks as a source of soft loans to local enterprises and that they provide support to officials appointed to privatised companies.

The Bank of Spain supports the consolidation of the savings bank sector to achieve the target of one *caja* for each of the 17 autonomous regions. Even that would not solve the problem in some regions, where the merged savings banks would still be too small to sustain sufficient investment to be efficient and viable. The central bank in the shape of the deputy governor, Miguel Martin, recently called for the regional governments to ensure that the *cajas* did not become a 'battlefield' and a tool for achieving politcal objectives. The finance minister, Rodrigo Rato, called for 'the most professional degree of management possible' and for permission to allow the savings banks to merge outside their own regions. The radical steps of demutualisation and a consequent sale to the private sector are unlikely to be taken before the current government's term expires in 2004.

However, it is likely that more limited reforms will be introduced in the near future. In summer 2001 the Spanish government held informal talks with the opposition Socialist Party to agree rule changes for the savings banks. The reforms have three objectives: limiting the presence of the political parties on the board of a bank; regulating shareholdings as a means of increasing the banks' assets; and generating cooperation and collaboration between savings banks. The main objective is to limit the growing political influence on the savings banks. The European Commission takes the view that the extent of the political representation on the boards of savings banks converts the credit they receive into state aid. The necessity of limiting political influence on the banks through the reforms proposed by the government has won the support of the director general of CECA, Juan Quintas. These are the only changes which are likely to take place, given the political unwillingness for more radical reform before the next election. That has not been enough to allay the fears of the banks and their customers. The savings banks have identified three main risks to the sector: privatisation, the possibility of becoming a bank, and disintegration as a financial group stemming from territorial expansion and a consequent increase in competition between former partners. The first fear is unlikely to be realised for many years, and even the possibility of territorial expansion will be limited.

Commercial Banks

There are 158 registered private banks in Spain, of which 105 are domestic banks, 34 are branches of foreign banks with headquarters in the EU and 19 have headquarters outside the EU; they have some 17,500 branches. From the 12 large banks in existence in the late 1980s, the process of consolidation led to the creation of two major nation-wide banking groups. Including the two largest savings banks and Banco Popular, they account for more than half the banking system's total loans and deposits. They do, however, face competition from regional banks with strong market shares in their home regions.

   The transformation of the banking system between 1987 and 1991 was accelerated by the prospect of the single market and the liberalisation of capital. Banco Bilbao Vizcaya (BBV) was created in 1989 from the merger of the Bank of Bilbao and the Bank of Vizcaya. It was followed by the merger of Banco Central and Banco Central Hispano to form BCH, the largest bank in Spain with respect to deposits.

   Then came the Bank of Spain's intervention in the case of Banesto (Banco Español de Credito), the fifth largest bank. This led to the emergence of a new banking group, created by Banco Santander's winning bid for a controlling stake in Banesto against bids from BBV and Argentaria. The Bank of Spain had already mounted a speedy rescue operation once the hidden losses in its balance sheet had been exposed. Banco Santander immediately began to reduce Banesto's holdings and its international exposure in Argentina, Chile and Mexico as well as its real-estate holdings. Banesto acquired a new management, but one with considerable autonomy and focused on retail banking, as opposed to supporting the economic system through holding extensive stakes in industry. Banco Santander kept Banesto as a separate brand name rather than merging the bank into its own operations. Both Banco Santander and Banesto took the view that banks should retain interests in industrial companies but at the minimum level necessary to be considered as the bank for the companies concerned. Santander pursued an innovative marketing approach through the 1990s, which included strengthening its position in the insurance market by acting as a distribution channel (through the branches and telephone sales) for Genesis, a company owned jointly by Santander and Metlife.

As part of the privatisation process, Argentaria was created to group state-owned holdings into one single entity. The state retained a 50% holding in the bank until 1998, when the state sold its shares, and Argentaria merged with BBV in October 1999 to form Spain's largest bank, BBVA, and the second largest bank in Europe by market capitalisation. In January 1999 Banco Santander and Banco Central Hispano also reached an agreement to merge and form Banco Santander Central Hispano (BSCH), the second largest banking group in Spain.

The two leading banks have sought to strengthen their position with an eye to their long-term strategy in two quite different ways: first by forming alliances throughout Europe, and second by their acquisitions in Latin America.

Strategic Alliances

BSCH and BBVA, Spain's two world-class banks, have carefully positioned themselves to be at the centre of any forthcoming pan-European consolidation. Pedro Uriarte put it well when he was chief executive of BBVA, 'You have to be at the ball, when the dancing starts, or you risk being left without a partner'.[2] Angel Corcostegui, chief executive of BSCH, is much more cautious: 'We are still far from having pan-European markets. In wholesale banking perhaps: that is where economies of scale are tremendous, and it is what is driving the consolidation in financial services. But in retail banking, the cross-border synergies are not obvious and the obstacles are huge.... Nobody knows how the future of European banking will look, what combination of entities or formulas will be successful. The only thing I know is that, to survive, you will have to be big. And BSCH has achieved that'.[3] Not only has it achieved size, but the bank has also ensured that it is well placed to take advantage of any moves towards pan-European banks.

First of all, BSCH announced a strategic alliance in 2000 with Société Générale: BSCH has taken a 7% stake in Société Générale and Société Générale has taken a 3% stake in BSCH. The alliance also involves setting up joint ventures in the areas of asset management, specialised financial services, wholesale and investment banking, retail banking, and internet banking and brokerage. Cross-shareholdings in the Royal Bank of Scotland (RBS), Commerzbank and San Paolo IMI soon followed. Both Société Générale and RBS are in the debt of BSCH, because BSCH assisted RBS in

---

[2] Quoted in *The Banker*, March 2000, p. 42.
[3] Quoted in the *Financial Times*, 22 November 2000, p. 7.

its bid for NatWest, and Société Générale appreciated the possibility of BSCH being its white knight during the 'battle of the banks' in 1999. Furthermore, the alliance between BSCH and Société Générale in investment banking and asset management has already prodcuced tangible benefits: €75 million for the two groups in 2000 and an estimated €92 million in 2001. However, by the end of the year, BSCH had sold most of its holding in Société Générale and may well sell the remaining 1.5%. Nor did the bank rule out selling its 4.5% stake in Commerzbank on the grounds that it is not a strategic investment and that there is no point in tying up capital unnecesarily.

BBVA does not have quite such extensive links, but it does own 3.75% of Crédit Lyonnais and recently increased its holding in BNL to 15%. BBVA also has Telefónica as an industrial partner, and since it is the largest shareholder, it was able to turn this into a formal alliance and set up a range of joint ventures to develop business-to-business portals and enable financial services products to be accessed over a mobile telephone. Such an approach is typical of Spanish banks. The financial groups use their industrial holdings in energy and telecommunications to ensure they remain essential partners for all transactions on the internet. Other European banks lack that privileged status in the eyes of so many industrial groups. Even so, the proposed merger with Unicredito came to nothing in 2000, in the face of opposition from the Italian government and the central bank. Both banks have close links with Portugal, where BSCH has a 12% share of the Portuguese market following the acquisition of Banco Totta and Acores in 1999.

Latin American Excursions

The two leading Spanish banks have made extensive investments in Latin America, which is a very significant part of their strategy to increase the client base and attain greater diversification in economic areas with high growth potential. Other European banks have followed suit, but few have shown the intensity of the Spanish banks over the last decade. Between 1996 and 1999 the consolidated financial assets of the Spanish banking system increased by 62%. Latin America has obviously been one of the main destinations for Spanish bank financing and one of the key areas for the development of Spanish international banking activity. By the end of 1999 more than one-quarter of the total Spanish financing to foreign countries was to Latin America. Spain was the second largest supplier of funds to the region, with 14% of the total, exceeded only by 22% of the US banking system. Argentina was the largest beneficiary, with 41% of the total flows to the region, followed by Mexico (15%) and then Peru and Brazil (10%).

Expansion in the form of acquisitions began cautiously in 1995 and speeded up between 1996 and 1999 as opportunities increased owing to the privatisation programmes and the withdrawal of US banks during this period. BBVA and BSCH seized the chance to acquire branch networks and build up the retail banking base.

Their objective was not only to grow in size, but also to improve the management of the banks acquired by controlling them and integrating the banking structures there with the banks in Spain. The strategy was somewhat different in each case: BSCH purchased investment banks and BBVA concentrated on purchasing small shareholdings, gradually increasing the stakes over time and forming partnerships with local banks.

Pension fund business is the other target for the two Spanish banks. Argentaria had focused on buying into the pension fund business in the region prior to its merger with BBV, and in June 1999 BBV had acquired a 41.2% stake in Provida of Chile, a pension fund management company, and increased its stake to 100% from 64% in Consolidar, Argentina's largest pension fund manager. By the end of that year, BBVA had a 30% market share in the Latin American pension fund business. Further Latin American acquisitions followed a year later: the takeover of the Mexican bank, Bancomer, which dominates the Mexican market with a 30% share, made it the largest financial institution in Latin America, financing it with a €3.3 billion equity sale. BBVA acquired Banespa in Brazil, the country's fifth largest bank. In 2000 some 20% of its profits came from Latin America, rising to 35% in 2001. Pension funds have provided a useful source of profits for the Spanish banks, given that most Latin American countries have adopted the Chilean model of private pension plans. Brazil, which is responsible for 70% of Latin America's gross domestic product (GDP), is the priority for BSCH. In January 2000 BSCH bought Banco Meridional, the leading bank in the state of Rio Grande du Sol, as part of its strategy of concentrating on the richest seven states in the south-east of the country. The aim is to achieve 10% market share, more than double the share achieved in 1999. BSCH had also purchased banks in Peru and Colombia for the same reason.

There are several reasons for pursuing this strategy. Privatisation, which began in 1990, provided opportunities for purchase. In 1994 some 36% of Argentina's banking assets were owned by the state, and 30% in Venezuela; by 2000 the shares had fallen to 26% and 5%, respectively. The valuations made it possible to obtain a large market share with a lower cost than in the EU. Foreign banks were allowed to enter the market in the belief that they would bring in banking technology and know-how. Spanish banks in particular have much to offer, since they have had to deal with intense competition in the home markets and frequently unfavourable economic environments. Managers of Spanish banks have handled both banking crises and severe recessions. The strategy of the leading Spanish banks can also be seen as an opportunity to use the experience they have gained to improve the management and skills of the banks they have acquired. The high level of solvency enjoyed by the leading Spanish banks enables them to obtain licences, and indeed the solvency levels are thought to contribute to the stability of the financial system. Meanwhile the Bank of Spain imposes strict conditions on the banks, and their Latin American subsidiaries are consolidated with the Spanish banks in terms of the regulatory capital required. The shared language and culture are obviously important advantages.

The region has been dominated by extreme volatility over recent years, but the Spanish banks have a long-term strategy for development in Latin America and so far have been able to maintain their positions when other financial institutions have withdrawn from the region. They have achieved strategic control of major banking institutions, especially Bolivia, Argentina, Columbia and Venezuela. Such developments could be regarded as extremely risky, yet the Bank of Spain not only insists on a consolidated balance sheet, but also requires the banks to comply with solvency ratios significantly above international standards. BBVA and BSCH have higher capitalisation, providing a cushion for a higher exposure to risks. In autumn 2001 most analysts took the view that the two Spanish banks underestimated the full cost of the Argentina crisis, although it was agreed they would be able to handle even a worst-case scenario for Argentina. The banks themselves take the view that their subsidiaries are well capitalised: risk is under control; they are in the process of squeezing out costs; and the region is expected to be a source of profit growth even though lending in both countries has come to a halt. At the time of writing and given the extent of the economic and political disaster facing Argentina, it is difficult to see whether such long-term optimism is justified, but many analysts share their view that 'over the long term, Latin America will offer good returns'. However, the banks are reported to take the view that Argentina is just one rotten apple that will not spoil the barrel, but at the request of the central bank, both BSCH and BBVA have made provision of €1.7 billion and €1.34 billion out of their current profits against losses there.

If the Latin American problems can be overcome, then BSCH and BBVA, as two of the top banks in the EU, well-capitalised, modern and efficient banks, are well placed to plan a merger or an acquisition that would put one or other at the centre of a pan-European bank. Their strategy has been planned and carefully executed over several years.

Spain's Medium-Sized Banks

The three medium-sized commercial banks, Banco Popular, Bankinter and Banco Sabadell, have retained their independence and are successful banks. The first is one of the most profitable banks in Europe, geared entirely to the Spanish retail and small business market. It has added over 500,000 new customers over the past two years, and it specialises in cross-selling with excellent efficiency ratios, a return on equity of 20% per year since 1998, and a cost/income ratio of 43.3%. The bank launches a large number of sales campaigns each year, aimed at geographical, income and through affinity sales such as deals with specific professional groups. The bank applies the same principles to groups of small and medium-sized companies (SMEs), offering fund management for the families owning SMEs through a newly acquired fund management company (Iberagentes), which targets middle-income clients.

In spite of its higher levels of efficiency, the bank is always regarded as a takeover target. Its determined strategy of going for growth rapidly gained market share in loans and deposits, which increased by 24% in 1999 and 20% in 1999, followed by a further 16% in the first nine months of 2001. It currently has some 4 million clients and plans to double in size by 2003. The strategy is directed at gaining critical mass, possibly in preparation for a merger or the acceptance of an offer from a larger institution.

Although a relatively small bank, Bankinter is seen as one of the most creative and internet-aware banks. It has a loyal band of affluent customers to whom it was the first to offer telephone banking, followed by a wide range of services over the internet; and coupled with a high quality of service, it uses these techniques to sell on average five products per customer. Its strategy is based on encouraging its existing clients to transfer to the internet, rather than winning new clients with expensive deposits. The bank won plaudits for being the best internet bank with the best strategy, the highest internet penetration, the best quality of service and motivation of its employees. About 350 blue-chip companies, investment banks and multinationals use the bank's virtual branches, taking advantage of the self-service banking services. The total number of clients at the end of September 2001 was some 366,000, conducting 40% (17 million) of their transactions online. The changeover to becoming primarily an internet bank has been a costly exercise in which profit has been sacrificed to pay for the investment in technology. The investment accounted for some 20% of its costs in 2000 and a further 15% in 2001.

Banco Sabadell seeks to challenge the leading banks at least in some areas of business and has carefully positioned itself to do so. Its listing strategy was designed to capture market share from BSCH and BBVA, when it floated on the Madrid Stock Exchange in April 2001. Banco Sabadell acquired Banco Herrero in January 2001 and has a 15% share in La Caixa. These acquisitions have given Sabadell a branch network extending over most of Northern Spain. La Caixa and Banco Comercial Portugues (BCP) became core shareholders in 2000, jointly holding 23.5% of the shares and adding to the existing 40,000; no single shareholder owns more than 0.75% of the equity capital.

Banco Sabadell became a listed company on the Madrid and Barcelona stock exchanges in April 2001 with the aim of increasing liquidity for the present shareholders and to create a more accurate value reference for the shares and for the bank. This amounted to merely an application for listing because at that time the Sabadell group already had an adequate capital base and did not need to increase its share capital. It was also designed to protect the bank from large banks seeking to buy up the small regional banks, but since then the value of the shares has risen, which means the protective system has lost its value. The share capital raised equalled €102 million with the issue of 29.1 million new shares. Solbank, the former NatWest bank, was merged with Sabadell in 2000. The bank offers a wide range of retail banking services and has benefited from the growing awareness of the need for insurance and pensions-related savings. All the group's insurance and pensions-related business is handled through BanSabadell Vida (pension products) and BanSabadell Correduria (all classes of insurance), with sales continuing to increase.

Table 7.1 Top six banks in Spain by market share as at December 2000

	Value (€m)	Fraction of total banking assets
Banco Bilbao Vizcaya Argentaria	193,570	29.51%
Banco Santander Central Hispano	172,300	26.27%
Banco Español de Credito	46,925	7.15%
Banco Popular Español	22,471	3.43%
Bankinter	19,034	2.90%
Banco Sabadell	16,403	2.50%

Source: Association of Spanish Banks

BANKING STRATEGIES

Refining Customer Contact

'Margins are decreasing, and as a consequence, retail banking is a volume business, and market concentration follows from this trend,' said one banker firmly. Given that it is a 'volume business', how do Spanish banks seek to personalise the relationship with the customer? The first move was to offer multichannel access to the bank: branches, call centres and the internet. Branch closures have taken place for all the leading banks, but they have to recognise that Spanish customers still use branches and prefer a personal contact, because as one commentator put it, 'We did not understand the impact of the weather'. People spend much more time outside their homes in Southern Europe and 'the gregarious Spanish are keen supporters of neighbourhood banking'. However, the branch network is changing as the way of life changes, as one banker pointed out: 'Spanish people used to choose their bank because it was close to where they worked and/or lived. Once they had made this choice, they rarely changed to another institution. Spain is becoming increasingly suburban. This means that many urban dwellers are moving to new housing developments and adopting a different lifestyle. Often they need to find a new bank, and in their changed situation innovative banking may provide an attractive solution'.[4]

However, the branch is still seen as an important part of the multichannel approach: 'Bricks and clicks will be with us for at least ten years ahead'. Some banks 'set up small branches to act as sales points'. One large bank pointed out that it 'has been able to close branches and move customers from one branch to another with a certain degree of success, with a resulting loss of less than 2% of the business. But we still have one of the largest branch networks in Spain. . . . We do, however, practise a kind of segmentation at branch level and offer specialist branches for corporate, retail and private clients. and that is very successful'. As with many other banks, 'back-office activities have been centralised'. One senior banker commented, 'We have concluded

---

[4] Michael Rowe, Battling through the net. *Distribution Management Briefing*, November 2001, pp. 6–7. The journal is now called *Financial Services Distribution*.

that multichannel access is appropriate for the majority of customers. . . . But we note that a handshake is worth a thousand clicks'. Another medium-sized bank pointed out that the 'question of opening and closing branches is an obsolete one. We need a lot more branches, but we are also closing them. All we have to consider is where a new corporate operation should take place, some of which are specialised branches and others are urban branch offices, designed to provide advice to retail customers, who always want a face they know'.

Another leading banker intimated that 'loyalty is a key factor in attacking the customer base. We do this through the branches using financial advisers. This is much more effective than direct selling'. This is in spite of the fact that the bank closed a large number of branches as a result of a merger and reduced staff, but it did enable the bank to maximise the value of the merger very rapidly. The same bank provides a multichannel approach through multi-sector alliances to provide mobile phone payments, e-commerce, credit cards and e-banking.

It is vital to use the branch for its proper purpose—establishing and retaining the customer by offering advice about products. One banker said, 'Just think how many branch managers every morning spend their time processing bank transfers that are completely lacking in any value added. To my mind, their job is to provide specific advice on specific and complex issues that cannot be handled by telephone or internet banking'.[5] It is doubtful that many successful banks allow managers to undertake such work, having centralised back-office functions and transferred them away from branch staff. The branch still has a role to play and no one can be complacent about the competition.

Customer Relationships and Selling

'We specialise in dealing with customer relationships. Indeed, we are a customer relations management driven bank. That is the key to our future success. We are in the process of segmenting the customer base and identifying who our customers are, using a single IT platform and a single date warehouse. We are using our system to develop a single view of the customer, and have categorised our customers into nine segments for the purpose of cross-selling.'

Another bank segments the market into six groups, including private banking for customers with Pta 50 million or more, an intermediate market and then for those with Pta 100 million or more available for asset management. Both are distinguished from the mass affluent on the one hand and the high-net-worth individuals on the other. He recognised that his products are becoming more and more commoditised, but suggested there is scope for individual management of funds: 'We do manage individual portfolios and we are not confined to our own products or our own funds. . . . [We have] developed a large number of funds and can offer the customer investments ranging from zero risk to high risk'.

[5] Honore Jiminez del Valle, quoted in *The Banker*, November 2000, p. 32.

The same bank 'focuses on the ordinary retail customer, who does not have very creative ideas, but we seek to keep him as a loyal customer, provide attractive products and keep in touch with the customers by telephone, often one call per week. We have a very good database and are expert at data mining, so that we know all about our customers, so that we are in a position to offer them appropriate products. We have made more progress with cross-selling. The advantage is the technology, especially the application of advanced techniques; segmentation is the answer in terms of management and market information. The result is that we sell 2 to 3 products per customer with a new target of 2.5 to 3.5'.

The banks sell mutual funds and life insurance products. As with other banking systems, banks have faced a decline in their interest rate margins for the past ten years, due to the decline in nominal interest rates and increased competition. Investment in deposit accounts competes with mutual funds, but the banks have virtually full control of the mutual funds, offering a wide range to their customers and occasionally mutual funds provided by other companies with whom they have formed a partnership. Fee income from pension funds and personal pension plans is also increasing.

Spanish banks proudly claim that they 'own' their clients, which does not mean that they view the issue of customer retention lightly. As one banker expressed it, personalised attention to customers is 'vital, combined with high levels of investment in technology'. To succeed, a bank has to make full use of its assets, including branding, and to know when it is possible to change the brand, and also when to change the approach. Another said that the 'multi-brand strategy has allowed the bank to increase market share in every product at a time when the market share was growing very fast. . . . Now the market is not growing quite so fast, so it's the perfect time to launch the new brand name without losing market share'. Flexibility in the use of the brand name and an awareness of the importance of keeping track of new developments are the key to success. A leading banker stressed the importance of flexibility for his own bank, but it applies across the board: 'We are doing banking in a different way now than we were ten years ago and we will be doing it differently again in ten years' time. It's important that the human capital of the group is prepared for that change'. Few have referred to the importance of human capital in maintaining and developing customer relationships, given that this is the basis of cross-selling.

One Spanish bank was prepared to share a detailed analysis of its client segmentation. The first step of adding value to customer data is to segment the client base, which involves detailed records of every client's transactions with the bank. This is due to a built-in IT system on a single platform, which covers all products with which the bank reaches the customer through whichever channel. Describing the approach adopted in his bank, a senior manager said, 'We divide customers into the 87% who are the current franchise and the 13% who are the future; that is, teenagers and minors. The current franchise is then divided again according to product usage or financial needs'.

Basic customers (30%) are those who have basic products and services, such as direct debit accounts or high-yield savings accounts. Transactional customers (15%)

are those who actively use credit cards as well as basic customer services. Investment demand customers include savers (17%) who typically own the basic products and additionally hold a time deposit or a guaranteed mutual fund; sophisticated customers (3%) are risk-taking clients who are likely to own mutual funds and pension funds. The investor is the least risk-averse client and also tends to have stocks or high-yield products. The lending demand customers include borrowers (14%) who in addition to transaction services hold a mortgage or consumer loan. Affluent customers (3%) have the borrower package plus high-risk investment products.

The total size of the customer's business with the bank is analysed in terms of these seven groups—the six from the previous paragraph plus teenagers and minors— and according to age. The older customers do most business with the bank and the difference in outstanding balance between the eldest and the youngest age group is 7 times. The difference in average balance between the first and seventh customer category is 97 times, meaning that the bank's own customer segmentation model provides many more opportunities for product and pricing differentiation.

The bank recognises that high-value customers are rare and hard to attract through mass marketing, which means that it is important to recognise potential high-value clients from existing and potential customers and to offer the right range of products at the right time so that the value of the relationship can be maximised. It is important to retain customers and ensure there is no reduction in the balances which the client keeps with the bank, because declining balances destroy value. Hence the bank creates a strategy for dealing with each and every customer.

By tracking customer behaviour, the bank identified a four-part client management cycle from acquisition to the first year, then value management and finally retention. For example, consider the following trends among a group of customers to whom the bank has successfully cross-sold certain products:

- 13% of the group purchased a mortgage and then accounted for 60% of credit card cross-selling and 14% of pension cross-selling.
- 9% of the customers placed money in a savings account and then bought 22% of pensions cross-sold and 5% of credit cards.
- 71% of customers first opened another form of deposit account and then took out 50% of pension policies sold and opened 27% of credit card accounts.
- 7% of new customers set up a transactional relationship with the bank and then accounted for 8% of credit card cross-selling and 14% of new pensions.

Having estimated the share of the wallet the bank expects to gain from a new customer, the risk aversion of the customer and the likely preferred product mix, the bank selects the appropriate strategy for dealing with the customer from one of eight strategies. Product and channel management is a key element of this strategy—deciding which products to sell to which customers, based on the channel through which they came to the bank, while simultaneously targeting specific customers with the products the bank wishes to sell. The final stage of the client management process is an evolving model, whereby customers are divided into those to be targeted via mass marketing and those to be offered a solution-based service: 'All the while, the bank must perform the careful juggling act of maximising channel efficiency, which is the critical element of retail banking profitability'.

Using the Internet

Most of the leading banks do not intend to introduce a stand-alone internet bank at this time. One leading banker indicated that 'it is complicated to link the internet with bank branches. We have a traditional approach to banking. We give satisfaction to the customer, and when the customer demands it, the technology is there'. All the banks have internet subsidiaries, but most are not ready to replace the other channels, such as bank branches, by the internet alone. Some are definitely more sceptical about the value of the internet at this time than they were a year or two ago. One said, 'The internet is a cost if it does not improve efficiency and give added value to the service to the customer . . . and one of the potential effects of new technologies in the banking sector is to increase price competition, which represents a clear threat to the margins'. Another bank has its own internet subsidiary, but recognises that the internet bank may take some of the bank's own customers; nevertheless, 'it is better if we do it, rather than our competitors'. The internet is 'seen as one more channel in a mix of strategies' and 'as an opportunity to overhaul procedures within the bank, of leveraging technology to make relations with customers more efficient'.

They do, however, operate separate internet-only subsidiaries as well as offering home banking services through their main retail branching network. Another medium-sized bank formed a joint venture with a Portuguese bank to launch an internet banking operation, following the successful introduction of its telephone and internet banking, which has been the key to the increase in its private banking operations'. For some bankers, the 'main objective of the internet channel is to remove from the bank's branch office transactions which are not good for cross-selling'.

Another bank has set up an e-banking subsidiary with a distinctive strategy of offering loans as opposed to seeking to attract deposits on the grounds that the costs of attracting a new customer to save with the bank are too high, some Pta 50,000, and then high interest rates have to be offered, which are unprofitable for the bank. Such customers are unlikely to remain if they can find higher interest rates elsewhere. The policy of this bank is to use the internet to provide mortgages and loans, as the internet is seen as a particularly appropriate medium for marketing and processing loans, a procedure which should not take more than three days for a car loan. The loan also gives opportunities for selling insurance-linked policies. The aim of this strategy is to encourage people to switch their bank accounts on the basis of the loan on the grounds that many people have a deposit in one account but retain their current account with their main bank.

Although all the banks have incorporated internet banking in one form or another, the impact of e-banking is extremely limited. At present, internet penetration in Spain is about 15%, and of those only 1 in 4 undertake banking transactions online and only about 1% purchase products online. Many do not have an internet connection at home, and use the office computer instead with limited access allowed for personal use by their employers. Bankinter has the largest share, 25% of internet banking and only a 5% share in traditional banking. The market for internet banking, especially profitable internet banking, is generally more limited than expected, particularly in Spain.

Leading Spanish bankers are committed to the retail market, and their strategy for success in this field is clear: 'We will become enablers, facilitating the life of our retail clients, and of our corporate clients'. Another added, 'In the future in Europe, only those banks that can operate with a very low cost base and offer the very best quality of service will be able to compete'.

8
Scandinavia: A Silver Lining

In many ways the Nordic banking system can be regarded as a single banking system dominated by a small number of leading banks which operate throughout the region. With the Nordic countries as the base, the major banks have adopted a programme of expansion, especially in the Nordic and Baltic states rather than into other EU member states, apart from some notable exceptions. The potential customer base in Scandinavia is only 15 million people, divided between four regions and four currencies. Moving outside that market is the only way to expand, given the levels of concentration and the size of the market.

THE BANKING CRISIS

The banking crisis of the early 1990s, which affected most of the banks in the region, brought about a major restructuring of the banking sector. The cause of the crisis was a combination of rapid deregulation and sudden changes in the economic circumstances. In Sweden, for example, the latter half of the 1980s saw rapid deregulation of the banking system, including the freedom for banks to set their own limits on lending, instead of conforming to limits set by the government. Banks were exposed to currency risk as well, as they were able to increase their lending in foreign currencies. The banks responded to their newfound freedom by seeking market share in an overheated economy and rising real-estate prices and granting loans without sufficient risk assessment and controls. The real-estate prices bubble was burst at the beginning of the 1990s by an interest rate shock, caused partly by an international rise in real interest rates and partly by an expectation of continued inflation in Sweden. The banks were soon affected by non-performing loans, and the temporary rescue operations, following severe problems at Nordbanken and Forsta Sparbanken in 1991.

The risk of a total collapse of the banking system, with serious consequences for the payments system and credit supply, led to urgent action on the part of the government.

An emergency package was revealed in September 1992, which is now regarded as a textbook example of managing a crisis.

First of all, a general government guarantee was issued for the repayment of all claims on the Swedish banking sector and for most of the rest of the financial services sector. This step was thought to be essential to prevent the lenders from panicking and calling in the bank loans in the international interbank market. This was accompanied by a rescue operation in the form of the Bank Support Authority, created to support the banks in distress, but according to clearly defined principles. The banks requesting support had to submit themselves to a comprehensive review of their operations and any injection of public funds was on terms as close to commercial terms as possible. The government's guarantee did not extend to the bank shareholders. Finally, the support operation was conducted in as transparent a way as possible, partly as a way of retaining international confidence in the Swedish banking system. This approach to managing the crisis meant that none of the Swedish banks became bankrupt during the crisis nor were they taken into public ownership. The problems which might have arisen from the total collapse of a bank or its insolvency were handled through a temporary law, which in principle entitled the Bank Support Authority to take over the running of a bank through the compulsory takeover of a bank's shares if its capital adequacy ratio fell below 2%, but the authority did not need to use it.

The Swedish banking sector recovered comparatively quickly; the acute phase of the crisis was over by autumn 1993, and by 1997 Moody's Investors Service could report that the system had recovered from the banking crisis of the early 1990s as a result of a stronger economy and the banks' successful efforts to introduce more successful provisioning policies and more rigorous risk management procedures. The report added that together these developments have restored the financial condition of Sweden's banking system. Both asset quality and the banks' profitability, capital and equity have improved and removed the need for government support mechanisms. Since the crisis, Swedish banks are carefully supervised by rigorous financial sector regulations, which have simultaneosly allowed the Swedish financial institutions sufficient flexibility to engage in new business and to offer innovative products. After a decade of legislative and regulatory action, Swedish banks were ready to move forward.

Norway also faced a serious banking crisis, which began in 1986, following the collapse in oil prices below $10 a barrel that year. Bank lending had soared when the financial services industry was deregulated in the mid 1980s and the Nordic economies were growing rapidly. The decision to open up the financial system more fully to market forces was not accompanied by proper incentives for prudent private lending and borrowing decisions. The sharp decline in oil prices brought about a severe recession, causing property and share prices to fall, and bankruptcies to reach record levels. Norway's banks, previously used to strict regulation and rationed credit, were unable to make the appropriate risk assessments.

The first sign of trouble emerged with the insolvency of several savings banks and when another medium-sized commercial bank was declared illiquid. That was only the beginning. Bank profits continued to decline throughout 1990 and 1991, reflecting the amount of non-performing loans and heavy capital losses on security holdings. The continuing slide in commercial real-estate prices finally reached a stage where it had to be recognised in the banks' published accounts. Finally in autumn 1991, Christiana, the second largest bank, announced that its bad debts had wiped out the bank's share capital, leading to a run on the bank, despite the announcement of the government's support for the banking system. Fokus Bank, the third largest bank declared itself insolvent a few weeks later. Initially, the government had left the practical handling of the problem banks to the two private sector deposit insurance schemes, but when these failed, the government had to take drastic measures. Two separate government funds were established, the Government Bank Insurance Fund and the Government Bank Investment Fund.

Christiana Bank was too important to be liquidated, so the government had to deal with the banks more directly. The Insurance Fund was allowed to provide core capital directly to failing banks and the Investment Fund was designed to increase the amount of long-term capital in the banking agency. These tools were used to great effect in the rescue operations: Den norske Bank (DnB) was given support from both funds in an agreement involving the purchase of RealKredit, a mortgage company. They also injected Nkr 5.1 billion and NKr 0.5 billion respectively into Christiana Bank and Fokus Bank in 1991, and yet more funds were provided to all three banks in 1992. A condition of the assistance to DnB was a write-off of ordinary share capital against losses realised for 1992. All this new funding was necessary so that the these institutions would be able to meet the Bank for International Settlement's capital adequacy standards in January 1993. Altogether the government had to spend NKr 30 billion, or about 4% of gross domestic product (GDP), in rescuing the banks between 1988 and 1992, using the private insurance funds and the central bank as the channels.

The steps taken did prevent a systemic collapse of the Norwegian banking system. The state's participation in the three largest commercial banks was through the ownership of Christiana bank, which reached 98% in 1991, and Fokus bank by the Government Bank Insurance Fund and through the Government Bank Investment Fund's majority stake in DnB. In the course of four years, the Norwegian financial system moved from being one of the lowest in terms of state ownership of banking assets in Europe to being one of the highest, and state bank lending rose to almost 20% in 1993. The Postal Savings Bank was reorganised into the Post Bank in 1993 and was given increased powers to extend credit on top of an already substantial share, 15% of the deposit market. It was already the fourth largest bank in Norway but its exclusive access to the network of post offices gives it a competitive edge over the privately owned bank.

As soon as the worst of the banking crisis was over, the government turned its attention to a process of privatisation. The banks recovered quite quickly and by 1993 they were back in profit, mainly because the past provisions for bad loans proved to have been overcautious as companies started repaying their loans. In addition, the carry forward of the loan losses sheltered profits from taxes. By early 1995 the government had recouped two-thirds of its initial outlay. The government sold all its shares in Fokus Bank and the Union Bank of Norway.

In early 1994 DnB was 87% state-owned and Christiania 69% after the state had pumped in a further NKr 22 billion to keep the banking sector afloat. In 1996 the state succeeded in reducing its holdings in DnB and Christiania Bank to 52% and 51% respectively, only to see its stake in DnB increase to 61% in 1999, when DnB was merged with Postbanken. In 2000 the government eventually sold its remaining 35% share in Christiania og Kreditkasse to the Finno-Swedish bank Nordea, formerly Merita Nordbanken. Nordea also bought out DnB's 10% share and now owns Christiania bank outright. Meanwhile the government plans to reduce its stake in DnB to about 33% from the level of 47% in 2001 in a move which will increase Norway's exposure to the dynamics of continual regional restructuring in the financial services sector.

In Norway the collapse of the banks was in some ways more devastating than in Sweden, and the ensuing state takeover and the retention of substantial state shares in the banks seems to have restricted their development and made them vulnerable to takeover. Eventually the government had to give way and allow the acquisition of Christiana Bank, leaving DnB as the remaining major Norwegian bank with 1.8 million retail customers, well over 500,000 business customers and a 25% market share as the principal bankers for Norwegian corporate customers. It is a universal bank, offering financial advice, investment products, life assurance and pensions. But Norway's banks are not in a position to develop much further, facing stiff competition as they do from other Nordic banks.

The Finnish banking system also faced a major banking crisis in the early 1990s. Most of the problems facing Finnish banks were due to their own mistakes, including an overextended use of credit at excessively low interest rates and inadequate collateral, a lax system of checking customer creditworthiness, risky investments in real estate and a wasteful use of resources. The crisis was similar to that in other Nordic countries. Sudden financial deregulation and the government's loose fiscal policy at the end of the 1980s were also major factors in the bank's woes.

To deal with the crisis and to restore confidence in the banking system, the central bank first provided Skopbank, the fourth largest commercial bank, with a Fmk 2 billion capital injection and a radical restructuring of the bank, which involved the creation of three separate holding companies to cover industry, shareholdings and real estate, and it wrote off outstanding loans. In 1992 the government had to take even more drastic action by creating a government bank guarantee fund totalling Fmk 20 billion and for government investments of Fmk 8 billion in certificates issued by the banks. The government also encouraged the consolidation of the banking sector through the mergers and amalgamations so that 41 of the country's regional savings banks were brought together in one organisation, the Savings Bank of Finland. Further provision had to be made to cover the resulting losses for Skopbank and other banks, amounting to Fmk 60 billion. All told, the extent of the public support amounted to some 7% of GDP. The severe crisis itself gave the banks a strong impetus to restructure, cut costs and generally improve efficiency.

By June 1995 the remaining part of Skopbank was sold by the State Guarantee Fund to Svenska Handelsbanken. This was followed by the merger of Kansallis-Osake-Pankki (KOP) with the Union Bank of Finland to form Merita Bank, which reduced the risk of either bank collapsing. KOP was in an especially fragile state, having suffered a loss of Fmk 1.8 billion, making its total losses equal to Fmk 10 billion between 1991 and 1995. It gave both banks the opportunity to cut costs by reducing branches and personnel. The new bank became one of the largest banks in the Nordic region and, of course, dwarfed competition in Finland. Indeed its dominance there is formidable, since it has over 3 million customers in a country with a population of 5 million, about 40% of private clients and a market share of 45% of deposits. Meanwhile Handelsbanken and Skandinaviska Enskilda Banken (SEB) began to move into the Finnish market.

Other significant mergers took place in Finland; in late 1997 the state-owned Posti-pankki and Finnish Export Credit were combined under a new holding company to form a new banking group, Leonia Bank, and SEB acquired the whole share capital of Ane Gyllenberg, a Finnish private bank specialising in stockbroking, asset manage-ment and fund management. In April 1998 Interbank Osapankki and Mandatum Bank merged to form Mandatum and then acquired a stockbroking firm, Finnish Protos. A new investment bank was created out of three such banks in the same year. Other mergers and acquisitions include Sampo, the insurance company, which took over Leonia Bank in 1999, and followed that by taking over Mandatum in 2000; Svenska Handelsbanken, Mitbank and Bergensbanken in 2000 and 2001. Altogether, the num-ber of banks in Finland fell from 654 in 1985 to 347 in 2000. It still has more than 300 cooperative banks and savings banks, but the cooperative banks work together closely with their central financial institutions and belong to the same group, the OKO Bank group.

Financial consolidation has resulted in the domination of the banking system by three major groups of deposit banks: Merita Nordbanken, now Nordea; OKO Bank, the cooperative bank group; and the 100% state-owned Leonia with a total of 1,242 branches. In addition there are two large commercial banks with national branch networks and five smaller ones, a further 40 savings banks and 294 cooperative banks with their own extensive branch networks.

Denmark remained largely unaffected by the banking crisis in the Nordic region, partly because the deregulation of the financial markets began in the 1970s, much earlier than in other Nordic countries, and consequently had more time to adjust to conditions in a deregulated market. Danish banks were more strongly capitalised at that time than other Nordic banks, because of regulations which had been in existence since the 1930s. They were in fact significantly overcapitalised when the Basel Accord was introduced in 1988, with an average capital ratio of 13% in 1990. When the Danish economy went into recession in 1987 and experienced very slow growth in the following four years, bank losses were substantial, and the banks set aside provisions of 1.9% of outstanding loans and guarantees in 1990. They did suffer during the recession of the late 1980s and early 1990s, but not nearly as much as the other Nordic banks.

The leading banks curbed their overseas activities and reduced the branch network. On the domestic front, they refocused their business strategies and reorganised their banks into separate business units. The two largest banks gradually expanded their businesses into mortgages and life insurance, and sought to improve fee income. By 2000 the Danish banks were still vulnerable to competition from the Swedish banks, Nordea, Handelsbanken and SEB, due to their highly competitive cost structures and strong earnings.

By the end of the decade, the two largest banking and financial services groups, Danske Bank and Unibank, used their strong balance sheet to buy up smaller rivals within Denmark and the Nordic region. In 1999 Unibank announced a merger with Tryg-Baltica, the leading non-life insurer, with the aim of becoming the seventh largest financial institution in the Nordic region. The Unidanmark group then acquired Vesta, a Norwegian insurance company, but was in turn taken over by Merita Nordbanken (now Nordea) in 2000. In 1998 RealKredit merged with BG Bank, the third largest commercial bank, to create another new banking giant. This was followed by an agreed takeover of Fokus Bank, in a move which frustrated a rival offer for Fokus from Sweden's Handelsbanken.

Denmark still has its large commercial banks, but hardly any medium-sized banks, and then a swathe of small regional banks. They have to charge higher rates of interest to be viable and often rely on customer loyalty and mortgage bond business to remain in business and retain customers. This part of the banking sector is very fragmented and it is hard to see how some banks will survive, but the possibilities of mergers and acquisitions are insufficiently attractive.

As a result of the restructuring brought about by the crises of the early 1990s in much of the Nordic region, it now has a range of efficient, well-capitalised banks. Capacity has been reduced, and profitability and solvency have been improved throughout a decade of restructuring and adjustment in the banking industry. Banks were compelled to handle a process of adjustment and the resulting mergers and acquisitions; affiliations between banks, securities firms, insurance companies, and the start-up of new niche banks. The whole Nordic banking sector has become highly concentrated; three large banks account for over 80% of the Nordic countries' bank assets. The largest bank in the Nordic region is Nordea (which included the Swedish bank Nordbanken, the Danish bank Unibank and the Norwegian bank Christiana Bank og Creditkasse) with a market share ranging from 15% to 40% of the banking market in the different Nordic countries. SEB has built up an extensive international business by acquiring several banks, including the German bank BfG. Svenska Handelsbanken expanded in the Nordic region partly through acquisitions, such as Stadshypotek, one of the leading mortgage credit banks, and SPP, a large life insurance company, and partly through establishing new branches. ForeningsSparbanken/Swedbank was formed in 1997 as a result of the merger between the former savings bank Sparbanken and the former cooperative agricultural bank Foreningsbanken; it now has an extensive branch network in Sweden. The bank has expanded internationally by taking stakes in or forming alliances with Nordic and Baltic banks. These four banks between them account for about 85% of the balance sheet total of the Swedish banking market.

Small commercial banks, niche banks, have some 5% of the market, offering internet and telephone banking for retail customers. Some 20 branches of foreign banks have about 6% of the market, but their focus is mainly on the corporate banking sector and stock market dealing.

There are still four leading banks in Sweden, since the proposed merger of Swedbank and SEB was abandoned by both parties once it became clear that the European Commission (EC) would refuse to allow the merger. One further acquisition was approved by the EC—Nordea was allowed to purchase Sweden's Postgirot Bank from Posten, the national postal service. This acquisition gives Nordea control of the country's largest payment system and access to 1.3 million banking customers, 70% of whom are not Nordea customers, and is intended to speed payments in the Nordic and Baltic region, helping to create an integrated market for financial services. The online system will be combined with Nordea's Solo internet bank. What this review shows is that the severe crisis of the early 1990s in fact brought about the development of strong and innovative banks. They have led the way in the application of technology to banking. The dark clouds had a silver lining.

BANKING STRATEGIES

The Nordic countries in general and Sweden in particular have taken the lead in internet banking services. They have been in the vanguard of applying technology to enable their customers to handle all their banking services online. As a result, these banks have a very high proportion of internet customers, compared with banks in most other countries, partly because they have invested vast sums in developing customer-friendly and efficient online services.

That is against a background in which 76% of Swedish households have at least one personal computer and 69% of households are connected to the internet; furthermore, Sweden and the other Nordic countries have the highest level of mobile phone usage. The first internet banking services were launched in 1996, initially only offering a limited range of services. Internet banking covers all age groups; in fact, one bank reported a customer aged 100 who used the internet for all transactions plus several customers in their nineties. The same bank reported a rapid increase in internet use by the 40–60 age group. By 2001 the most widely used services included the payment of bills, transfer of money between accounts, buying and selling securities and units in mutual funds as well as the sale of mortgage credits; bill payment is the most popular of these services.

The Swedish Bankers Association estimates that 30% of the banks' customers use the internet services provided by the banks regularly; for SEB, 55% of personal payments are made via the internet; for Handelsbanken, 43% of corporate customers use the internet for banking services; and for SBAB (a Swedish mortgage institution), 60% of the new mortgage lending is in response to online loan applicants.[1]

---

[1] 'Internet banking in Sweden', speech by Mrs Ulla Lundquist, managing director of the Swedish Bankers Association, April 2001.

Looking into the future, the Swedish Bankers Association considers that the next channel for online banking services is likely to be through interactive television. This is still in the testing stage in Sweden but it is expected to be fully developed in two to three years' time, and it is expected that 95% of the Swedish population will be able to use interactive digital TV within about five years. The larger screen could encourage customers to be more interactive and digital television will make it very easy for customers to contact their banks. Swedish banks had apparently reached the conclusion that internet banking had improved the efficiency of traditional banking services, increased competition in the financial markets, and increased customer satisfaction. New and more advanced services will be delivered through combining and integrating internet, mobile banking, automatic teller machines (ATMs), digital television, telephone banking and the branches.

Using the Branch Network

Partly because of mergers and acquisitions and the impact of technological development over the past few years, the number of branches has declined sharply. Branches are often used to provide advisory services and information about the bank's services, rather than transactions. Cash withdrawals take place through Swedish Post, supermarkets and petrol stations.

However, views on the role of the bank branch differ considerably. One banker said:

> We have a strong philosophy on the importance of the branch network, on the importance of a physical presence. We do not consider that there is any competition between the internet and the branch offices. We are not closing branches down, but of course we have reduced the staff and centralised back-office functions.
>
> We have decentralised the branch network, and have given each branch its own home page and local portals. We do not have a central marketing department, since almost all of our advertising is from the local branch. This is because we believe that the physical presence is important: banking is built on trust and confidence in real people, not virtual people. It is interesting, even if people do not visit the branch office very often, they know that if they do, they will see a real person, and one who is responsible for that individual customer, and with whom they have a real relationship of trust. The customer regards that stable relationship as important. We have noted a general shift from branch closures to bricks and clicks.

To emphasise the kernel of their approach to banking, he said 'All business is local, even with an international approach'.

The branches in this model are given a high degree of freedom, although they do not have a franchise, but 'all customers, private and corporate, whatever their size, are the responsibility of a local branch'. Each manager is responsible for the branch's performance, even for sensitive areas such as the credit portfolio. The central office has oversight 'but the portfolio is not managed as such. It is built up through the lending decisions of each branch'. That is justified because 'all our experience shows that credit losses particularly come when you work with customers from outside the area you work in'. Extreme competition between branches is prevented because tight geographical catchment areas apply. The unusual approach adopted by the bank allows for 'organic growth' by establishing branches in appropriate areas and by acquisition. It has also enabled the bank to have a higher return on equity and lower costs than the other leading banks. It has achieved an efficiency ratio of 50%, whereas the European average is just over 60%.

Internet Strategies

Two contradictory trends appear to be emerging. On the one hand, internet usage is continuing to grow. About 3.5 million banking customers in Sweden are currently internet banking customers of Swedish banks. Nordea has a total of 2.7 million internet customers, including some outside Sweden, and the group expects this figure to rise to 3.2 million in 2002. Swedbank has about 1 million private internet customers, and the bank claims this figure grows by about 5,000 per week. Nordea believes it is the largest internet bank worldwide, recording SKr 88 million worth of internet payments in 2001. The same bank also reported that the number of logons and payments reached an all-time high, a 40% increase on the previous year. In their efforts to capture and keep e-bank customers, Nordea and indeed Danske Bank have ventured into business areas which are remote from banking, such as web shopping. The customers of both banks have enabled their customers to use their bank websites to purchase a wide range of goods. These are designed to provide secure payment services for online shoppers. Payment for goods is then deducted from a customer's account and transferred to the vendor; the bank does not charge for the service.

As part of the attempt to create compact pan-Nordic financial services groups, banks sought not only mergers and acquisitions, but also extending the use of e-banking to cut costs. In addition there has been a steady flow of new entrants to the sector, such as Coop Bank, an online e-bank formed; the state telecom company Telia; retail chain KF; and KF's rival ICA, which set up its own bank in May 2001. Coop Bank was launched in January 2002, thus gaining immediate access to MedMera loyalty store card holders.

However, despite having the highest penetration of online customers, including electronic payment systems, some banks are beginning to wonder just how profitable these services are. Most customers have generally reserved internet services for simple financial transactions, such as transferring money from one account to another and paying bills. Mobile banking, with customers using their mobile handset to conduct transactions, has proved to be less popular than anticipated. All the banks have found it difficult to use online distribution to increase revenues by selling more complex financial products. Internet banking is not likely to decline, but banks are looking to other sources of income instead of relying simply on cutting costs.

One bank, which had cut about a third of its branches in the belief that people did not visit them anymore, is reviewing its strategy: 'We overestimated the cost benefits of online banking,' said one leading banker. 'We have perhaps focused too much on internet banking and we need to refocus on our branch network. Branches closed and although the numbers affected were small, we did lose touch. By pushing e-banking, customers felt that they were not welcome at our branches.... As a bank, we talked too much about e-banking'. As a result, the bank is looking at its branch network as the key to cross-selling, customer satisfaction and profitability.

This bank has decided to give more responsibility to managers of the local branch network: 'We need to strengthen the role of bank offices, while improving cooperation between various divisions in the markets.... We shall give more attention to our branches, building new branches and offering self-service, but with greater emphasis on advice. We started to offer large mutual funds operations a year ago, for our upmarket customers, allowing them to select from a range of funds and commission levels.... We started this advisory service a year or so ago, and we expect this to become more and more focused over time. We have to keep the levels of advice and service under review. We do not plan to limit the customer to one particular channel, nor are we likely to change the multichannel approach'.

Reflections on internet developments may shift the emphasis to other channels: 'The physical presence of the bank branch will be an important factor in the future. That is why we retain a large retail network. Our customers still think that there is the security of the bank nearby, if anything goes wrong. They also appreciate the social aspect of visiting a branch.... We also ensure that the customer has a full relationship with the bank through accounts, loans, asset management, credit cards so that we can help them with the management of their affairs. We have built up effective technology to handle our customer relations management, so that we can directly mail our customers with marketing material they really need, partly based on an analysis of card usage. We think we do not waste our marketing material, but now it is just a question of time before we use the system more efficiently'.

As with other banks, internet services are provided; indeed, for this bank, the 'increased use of technology has been driven by the customer. It has been self-promoting and has required very little marketing'. As far as this bank is concerned, 'Our bank is a one-stop shop, and the advantage of the internet for us is that the internet increases the "stickiness" of the relationship with the customer. It increases the number of products they purchase. The internet customer purchases 7 products, whereas the average customer purchases 3.8 products. That is partly because the internet customers are more affluent, and partly because the use of e-banking has encouraged more purchases'.

As 2001 went on, the fall in the stock markets hit Swedish banks quite hard, leading to a decline in net commission income, partly due to lower transaction fees. Fees from online broking also fell sharply, hitting both banks and independent brokers, both of whom had invested heavily to cope with the previous demand: 'People who are able to use the internet tend to trade in shares more often, so you have more share transactions, but at the same time there are lower charges when you trade on the internet'. Banks claim that they are simply offering their customers more choices, but this might simply add another layer of costs. The banks protest that it is much cheaper for them if customers transact payments online rather than in the branch, but as they pass on the cost reductions to their customers, the net gain may be small.

There are now question marks over the value of such intensive and expensive investment in technology, especially as 'size is increasingly important with IT spending'. No one expects internet banking to decline, but its impact on bank profitability is less obvious. What is interesting is that these doubts have arisen in Sweden at exactly the time when Sweden is on the brink of exciting technological developments. There are two important elements in these doubts: (1) the continuing importance of the branch network and the personal relationship between the customer and the bank, a significant factor in retaining customers and increasing sales; and (2) the importance of trust in the banking relationship. That should give bankers pause for thought. They should spend time considering why the relationship of trust is so valuable.

9
Netherlands: An Early Consolidator

This chapter and the next cover the Dutch and the British banking systems, where the developments in the banking system followed similar lines and at an earlier stage than the rest of Europe. Banks have not been regulated in the detailed and burdensome ways experienced in other member states of the EU throughout the 1990s. They have been free to develop along commercial lines and the shape of the banking system was, broadly speaking, determined in the late 1980s and early 1990s, rather than over the last five years or so.

The Dutch banking system is now dominated by four banks, which altogether have 98% of the retail market, leaving the rest to be shared by several small cooperative banks. However, the current structure reflects changes in the banking system, such as the deregulation of interest rates in 1981, and the liberalisation of capital flows and the consolidation in the market which began in earnest in 1990 after restrictive legislation was lifted in 1989; this led to the establishment of three large conglomerates: ABN-AMRO, ING and Rabobank. These three banks also have the lion's share in bank lending at about 75%. Between 1981 and 1989, regulatory barriers prevented banks and insurance companies from owning more than 5% of each other. The change in legislation in 1989 legitimised existing alliances, leading to the formation of financial services conglomerates. Unlike other leading member states in the EU, there have been no major developments in banking in the Netherlands during the 1990s. The leading banks have had a stable background in which to operate in terms of regulation, where restrictions on the ability of banks to open branches and to sell a range of products were removed in the 1970s.

THE MAJOR BANKS

The original bank, Nederlandsche Handel-Maatschappij, was founded in 1824 with the aim of reviving trade between the Netherlands and the Dutch East Indies. The present bank was formed out of the merger first between De Twentsche Bank to form Algemene Bank (ABN) in 1964, and at the same time, the Amsterdamsche Bank and the Rotterdamsche Bank merged to form the Amsterdam-Rotterdam Bank (AMRO). These two banks merged in 1991 to form the ABN-AMRO Bank. However, the bank did not join in the mergers of insurance companies and banks, preferring to set up its own life and non-life operations. Given the purpose of establishing the bank in the first place, it is hardly surprising that the bank operates globally and is ranked eighth in Europe and seventeenth in the world, based on tier 1 capital.[1] The bank has over 3,000 branches, a staff of over 100,000 and total assets of €597.7 billion.

It is one of the largest European-based wholesale banking businesses, working for major international corporations and institutions with about 10,000 clients and a presence in a wide range of countries. In 2001 ABN-AMRO announced a new strategy of concentrating on countries in which it has a leading position, and therefore withdrew from 11 countries, including its activities in Panama, Chile, Venezuela, Kenya and Argentina. The bank's aim is now to rank among the major players in Europe and not worldwide. Its new service concept was launched in February 2001 through its Consumer and Commercial Clients Business Unit, which will focus on the consumer market, small and medium-sized enterprises (SMEs), large companies, and institutions in the private and public sectors. The new service concept will have different distribution methods for various banking products, with the emphasis on personal client contact through advisory centres.

ING originated in 1991 from the merger between Nationale Nederlanden and NMB Group following the amalgamation of the insurance company Nationale Nederlanden with Postbank and Nederlandsche Middenstandsbank in 1989 with ING Group as its statutory name. When ING was formed, Nationale Nederlanden was the Netherlands' largest insurer and NMB Postbank was the country's third largest bank. ING distributes through direct marketing involving Postbank; ING branches; independent brokers, tied agents and sales staff. It has been selling investment funds to Postbank customers since 1993. It has grown very rapidly since then, having acquired Barings Bank in 1995, the US insurer Equitable of Iowa Companies in 1997, Brussels Lambert in 1998 and the German bank BHF in 1999, followed by the US insurance company ReliaStar in 2000. As far as its Netherlands operations are concerned, the merger of insurance and banking has worked out well but left the company with a large number of staff, adding to its expense base. ING has the same brand name for all its products, and an increasing proportion of the sales through its bank branches and its network of post offices.

Of the three, Rabobank Group is perhaps the most unusual, consisting as it does of approximately 400 independent local cooperatives (Rabobanks), which together have some 700,000 members. The local Rabobanks jointly own the supralocal organisation Rabobank Nederland, which is responsible for managing the group's interests. The specialised businesses of the group—asset management, insurance, leasing, private

---

[1] *The Banker*, July 2001, p. 31.

banking, venture capital, and corporate and investment banking—are largely conducted by Rabobank Nederland through its subsidiaries.

As with other continental European cooperatives, there are no legal procedures for demutualisation, although in theory all the member banks could change the legal structure with the approval of the central bank. Another alternative would be to adopt the same approach as Crédit Agricole—restructure and then allow the central organisation to list on the stock exchange. In practice, though, Rabobank sought to merge its corporate and investment banking activities with the Germany bank DG, another cooperative bank, but called it off in November 2000. At the time, Rabobank claimed this was due to the complexity of the operation and legal, fiscal, compliance and IT problems. The link-up was also opposed by two of Germany's regional cooperative banks, Frankfurt-based GZ and Dusseldorf-based WGZ, which together have a substantial stake in DG. DG had set its sights on becoming the leading mittelstand bank in Europe's cooperative sector. However, the failure of this merger puts cross-border developments of this kind in the cooperative sector on hold for the time being at least, or perhaps indefinitely.

The current ownership structure inhibits its potential for further acquisitions and merger. Its opportunities to raise capital are limited, although the bank has issued member certificates from time to time; these certificates are purchased by members and employees of Rabobank. The last offer, October 2001, raised €1.5 billion for certificates which attracted a dividend of 6.06% initially and in general offered a better rate than the return on Dutch government bonds. The member certificates can be traded on an internal market maintained by the Rabobank group.

Rabobank has made it clear that it does not wish to cease being a cooperative; indeed cooperative status is regarded as a competitive weapon of great importance. However, the bank does not wish to 'confine itself to the Netherlands' and wants to 'make that leap to Europe as part of a leading European retail group'. The bank is open to partners that do not operate as cooperatives, a broadening of the strategy and a wider search for alliances. That is difficult for a cooperative, certainly in terms of acquisitions. The failed merger was significant more generally for the cooperative sector in continental Europe, and the possibility of closer cross-border ties between banks in this sector seems to have faded into the distance. In Rabobank's case the difficulties of creating value through cross-border mergers involving large retail banks had proved insurmountable. Even in the Netherlands, mergers have proved difficult; the proposed merger between Achmea—a conglomerate of insurance, privatised social care and retail banking services—and Rabobank did not succeed, although it would have fitted with Rabobank's strategy.

The bank has achieved the status of an international bank, despite the limitations of its mutual status. The group is represented in 38 countries and it includes a large number of subsidiaries such as Robeco, acquired in 1993 and then Europe's largest asset manager; Interpolis, an insurance company acquired in 1990; Gilde Investment; and Rabobank International, originally set up to create new business units and to generate share capital to pay for acquisitions. It had to cut back sharply on its activities in 2000 in the face of intense competition, and now concentrates on traditional structured finance and capital market credits. The bank currently has 40% of the savings market in the Netherlands, with 36% held by local Rabobanks. Clients are also able to save through the bank's internet savings option and some 70,000 clients use this, with over €1 billion in deposits, nearly 2% of the total balance held on all savings accounts with banks.

The fourth player in the Netherlands is Fortis Bank Nederland. Fortis Bank, now based in Belgium, was formed when AMEV, a large Dutch insurer, and VSB, a Dutch bank, combined operations in 1990, followed by a further merger with AG Group, a major Belgian insurer, to create the first cross-border merger in the financial sector. Its banking operations were strengthened by the takeover of several savings banks, followed by the acquisition of the Dutch merchant bank MeesPierson, extending and strengthening its banking operations, especially in private, corporate and investment banking. In 2000 Fortis also announced its merger with ASR Verzekeringsgroep, ASR and AMEV Nederland, which was completed in April 2001. The group was enabled to extend its insurance sales through insurance intermediaries as the second largest insurer in the Netherlands. The Fortis group, with a market capitalisation of more than €40 billion, is approximately the same size as ABN-AMRO.

ROOM FOR MANOEUVRE

Dutch bankers and authorities maintain that the banking system is highly competitive, although the antitrust body in the Netherlands, Nederlandse mededingingsautoriteit, is currently investigating claims that there has been a banking cartel for some time, based on the similarity of margins found in the mortgage business. Others argue that this results from each bank keeping a keen eye on the other banks' products; if one of the banks lowers or raises the interest rate on its mortgage products, then the others will soon follow suit. Free banking is the norm in the Netherlands and interest rate margins have declined, as has happened throughout the EU, leaving fee income and cost-cutting as the only sources of increased profits.

The banks' interest income continues to stagnate, and the drop in prices and activities on the capital markets has worked through to a lower income from commission, decreasing total revenues. Operating expenses rose as banks made higher provision for loan losses (changes in the value of claims) as a result of weaker economic activity.

In the Netherlands itself, the banks have to compete to acquire retail accounts in difficult circumstances, since transactional services are free and overheads have already been cut by a branch closure programme; the number of branches per 1,000 inhabitants is lower than in most member states. The rapid increase in automatic teller machines (ATMs), telephone banking and internet banking is seen as a suitable alternative to branches. Much time, effort and resources have been spent on establishing an efficient giro-based payments system, which has led to the elimination of cheques. With little room for manouevre in the Netherlands itself, all the leading banks have spent the last decade or more in establishing themselves as global players. There has, however, been some retrenchment over recent months as the top three banks have disposed of assets and operations in various parts of the world.

The banks have little scope for expansion in the Netherlands itself. Any merger or acquisition on the part of the three leading banks would be ruled out by the European Commission. The view in the Netherlands is that this discriminates against smaller EU member states, since it makes it difficult for the retail banks to build up a sufficiently strong customer base to enable them to acquire a bank in another EU member state. The current rules, it is argued, effectively prevent cross-border mergers originating from one of the smaller countries, and also ignore the development of the means of distribution (the internet and e-business), which are not confined to national boundaries. The Dutch banks will continue to argue for changes in the competition rules, but in the meantime, the leading banks may well pursue expansion in the EU.

BANKING STRATEGIES

The Dutch banks operate in a particularly difficult context of a limited market in which banking transactions are free, backed up by an efficient and cost-effective payments infrastructure. Competition for retail customers is intense, but there is no scope for obtaining more customers in the Netherlands by acquisition. Not surprisingly, Dutch banks look outside the Netherlands to extend their customer base. Looking at UK and Dutch banks over the 1990s, one study noted that 'the preference of external actions [i.e. mergers, acquisitions, joint ventures and alliances] over internal actions [i.e. starting up new businesses, closing offices, and launching new products] is marked, with twice as many external actions over internal actions'.[2]

A branch closure programme, linked with cost-cutting, has been under way for much of the last decade, and the number of branches has been reduced considerably over the past two years; the number of branches per capita is now much lower than most of the member states in the EU. In the words of one Dutch observer, there has been 'little development in Dutch banking in the 1990s', apart from internet banking. The ATM network was introduced in the Netherlands in 1985, but the debit card network, EFTPOS (electronic funds transfer at point of sale), was not brought in until 1990. The Netherlands has a variety of ways to conduct remote banking, including telephone banking, internet banking, and using the personal computer to link with the bank and manage one's account. In fact, the country was one of the first to adopt telephone banking, with Postbank (now part of ING) leading the way in 1993; this followed its introduction of Girotel (PC banking) in 1986. Rabobank was the first to offer internet banking in 1997.

---

[2] H.W. Volberda, F. van den Bosch, B. Flier and E. Gedajlovic, 2001, Following the herd or not? Patterns of renewal in the Netherlands and the UK. *Long Range Planning*, vol. 34, p. 221.

Against this background, it is difficult for a bank to develop an effective strategy. One banker describes his strategy as seeing the branch as 'part of a multidistribution approach, supported by the internet and with the support of the call centre. The only way to attract a customer as a potential long-term customer is to build a trust relationship. . . . People tend to do business with a face they know and trust for the more important matters in life. That is intrinsically human'.

This is why we 'reinforce the use of the internet with the call centre, but for mortgages, where people often stretch themselves, or a substantial investment portfolio, people prefer to talk to their bank managers. That is why we retain a physical distribution network, but not at every corner of the street'. The bank concerned embarked on a substantial cost-cutting programme during 2001, which involved the number of branches being reduced to about 500 bank shops and 80 advisory branches. Spread throughout the country, the advisory branches are staffed by experts who provide clients with customised financial advice. The bank shops or branches would meet customers' daily banking needs. Bank shops and advisory branches are designed to reinforce the personal client contact, and clients can access the bank's services through other distribution channels such as the computer, telephone, multifunctional cash machines and the internet.

The remaining branches are offices for fund managers and advisers. The internet is used for standard products, but the bank branches provide a 'natural constituency of customers to whom we can sell products provided the products are competitive and advisers are professionally trained to handle the sales process. It has been a huge effort, and so far has only had partial success. We now offer life and pensions products, and the growth in our sales has been phenomenal, reaching a market share of 9% by 2000 from a 1% share in 1995, and it is now beginning to be profitable. Our financial advisers sell our products but can also sell outside the franchise, and distribute the products of other financial institutions'. This is part of the development of 'open architecture' whereby, in their determination to maintain or increase fee and commission income, some banks are seeking to sell the products of other companies and offer their customers a wide choice of investment funds or even insurance products. In the Netherlands, in particular, there is no scope for competition over the basic account and payment services, so for this bank 'the relationship with the customer is the source of revenue'.

This is how it describes its strategy: 'To keep the transactional costs down, and encourage our customers to use the cheapest medium'. It has led to the branch closure programme, but it does not think it necessary to outsource the bank office, as it has enough scale to run that itself: 'We must sell more products . . . [which needs] more targeting, more fine tuning of the customer base. . . . We have a good information system and a data management system at middle-management level with up-to-date client profiles. . . . We have invested €300 million in a new system, which will also provide call centres with a client profile and record all the customer's transactions, enabling us to segment the market'. The reorganisation is expected to provide substantial annual net cost savings from 2004 and also increase sales.

Another bank has a wide range of branches through its subsidiary as well as its own branches. The bank offers a multichannel approach with particular emphasis on the internet, its speciality. However, 'for complicated products, a face is necessary. We cannot do without people, not now or in the foreseeable future. The importance of the personal contact remains, even if the products are not complicated. In the case of savings and pensions, it is very difficult to decide on the future and it depends on what assumptions you make and the implications of the decision you make. Customers want the personal contact. We have highly trained and expensive advisers, and we find that people are prepared to pay for advice, but not for information. . . . We provide information, which is of course free, . . . [and] we will develop more sophisticated search machines. Voice recognition is yet to come, and we shall provide more complex information and hence added value'.

The bank still has a substantial branch network but, as with other branches, it has 'gradually reduced the branch network and will stay at the current level. The function of some branches will be reduced, so that they are only open for cash withdrawal'. Cheques were abolished in the Netherlands and all payments are by bank giro and direct debit. The bank usually enjoys high fee and commission income, but that fell to under 50% in 2001, as 'net interest income increased in a reversal of the trend of the last ten years towards disintermediation. The reasons for that were that credit became less important owing to increasing access to the capital markets. We responded by separating the role of an investment bank from asset management and became both an investment bank and an asset manager. The current downturn in the stock market has made people more risk averse. They are going for wealth protection and a higher capital yield than in the past. The process of disintermediation will be reversed temporarily. . . . [The] universal bank has to have a flexible approach to its customers, and respond quickly to changing customer requirements'.

Another banker described the three basic criteria for evaluating the bank's performance: customer value, employee value and financial performance, leading to targets for the performance of each branch for its 'retail' business, targets which cannot be easily defined. It is a 'business of change, because the needs and lifestyles of customers alter constantly', and it demands 'constant communication with customers' to respond to their needs. The bank has long absorbed developments in information and communications technology, as is the case with all the Dutch banks. Indeed the banker regards the new technology as presenting a challenge rather than a threat: 'The price of financial products is important, but it is certainly not the only factor customers take into account when they are selecting a financial services provider'. The quality of advice is vital, and so are the reputation and the image of financial services providers.

The leading banks in the Netherlands have adopted similar strategies for expansion; mergers, acquisitions, joint ventures and alliances are inevitable elements of any effort to increase profitability. Indeed that has often been more important than expanding the current range of activities, rationalising the product range, making cost savings, or supplementing their repertoire with insurance products or internet banking. Given the varied nature of the Netherlands' three leading banks—one cooperative bank, one insurance company which merged with the third largest bank, and one bank which set up its own insurance operations—it is interesting that all three are universal banks. According to an article in *Long Range Planning*, the similarity is partly due to the extremely limited size of the market in which the banks are confined, but it may also be due to an 'industry-specific common mindset' or a 'shared managerial schema'.[3]

Based on a study of the strategies of the leading Dutch banks between 1990 and 1997, the article first analyses strategies in terms of external actions, exploitative actions and exploration actions. External actions include mergers and acquisitions, joint ventures and alliances. Exploitative actions are renewal actions that elaborate on the current range of activities and fall within the current geographical area, or actions that rationalise activities; they include cost savings, disposing of product ranges, sale of activities or increasing scale. Exploration actions are defined as renewal activities to the current repertoire of the organisation or actions that extend it, perhaps through the internet. It was noted that one bank, ING, did not quite fit the pattern, but since ING's branch network is the Postbank, which customers use for other purposes, this warrants a fuller development of the unique advantages it offers.

The study concludes that such 'herd behaviour' shown by similar balances of 'exploration/exploitative attributes of renewal actions' suggests that firms may share a 'common industry recipe'. It also notes that the strategies adopted differ from those of a set of UK banks during the same period. It is interesting to note that the authors appear unable to explain such similar strategies in a particular country, especially in view of the concluding comments: 'These differences [between the Dutch banks and the UK banks] may be the result of the distinct structures of the financial services sector in these countries, and their domestic economic cycles. ... The Dutch sector is much more concentrated than the British sector. If the Dutch companies want to grow, they need to go abroad: establishing a new branch network is not an attractive option because of the overbranched nature of many countries and because of considerations related to timing. Dutch firms have no option other than acquiring or merging with another firm'. In this context, references to 'herd behaviour' or a 'common industry recipe' seem to be redundant. The strategies adopted are a rational reaction to the context in which the banks operate.

---

[3] H.W. Volberda, F. van den Bosch, B. Flier and E. Gedajlovic, 2001, Following the herd or not? Patterns of renewal in the Netherlands and the UK. *Long Range Planning*, vol. 34, pp. 206–9.

10
UK: Another Early Consolidator

The development of banking in the UK over the last decade has been quite different from that of other EU member states. Banks do not face competition from a state-owned banking sector, and a rapid decline in the number of mutually owned building societies during the 1990s has left the commercial banks in a strong but not always unassailable position. Banks in the UK as elsewhere face increasing global competition in wholesale and retail banking and the substitution of the capital markets for banks, as companies increasingly have a choice between issuing debt and borrowing from banks. The process of opening up competition began in 1971 with the regulatory authorities' introduction of competition and credit control, which led the clearing banks to abandon their interest rate agreements and to more competition between different types of bank. It is the only case in which the government took action to break up a cartel rather than removing state-imposed restrictions on bank interest rates, indicating one of the many differences between the UK banking system and continental banking systems.

THE BANKING SYSTEM

Under the Banking Act 1987, all UK deposit-taking businesses had to be authorised by the Bank of England. This power was transferred to the Financial Services Authority (FSA) in 1997, the single regulator that was formally established by the Financial Services and Markets Act 2000.[1] The FSA is responsible for the prudential supervision of banks and building societies and for all the investment activities of banks. Deposit-taking is not subject to formal conduct of business regulation, but is

---

[1] The Chancellor of the Exchequer announced the transfer of the supervisory responsibilities of the Bank of England to the Financial Services Authority in May 1997. The subsequent legislation was introduced in Parliament in 1999, following an unprecedented scrutiny by a Joint Committee of the House of Lords and the House of Commons of the draft bill in the 1997–98 session of Parliament.

subject to the voluntary codes; the Banking Code, followed by the 130 retail banks and building societies; and the Business Banking Code, which extends the principles of the Banking Code to small business customers. These codes are supported by the British Bankers Association; the Building Societies Association and the Association for the Payment Clearing Services (APACS). The Banking Code Standard Board is responsible for monitoring bank and building society compliance with the Banking Code. Its rules cover the contractual relationship with the banks and building societies, and it administers the disciplinary procedures and penalties. It is funded by the banks and building societies through annual subscriptions but its board has a majority of directors who are independent of banking interests.

The supervision of certain aspects of bank lending in the UK is quite different from the approach to regulation in other EU member states. Lending activities in the provision of personal secured and unsecured loans up to £25,000 are regulated under the Consumer Credit Act 1974, the responsibility for which lies with the Office of Fair Trading, not with the FSA. The Act and regulations made under it cover the terms under which credit may be advertised and provided and also the enforcement of creditors' rights. Authorisation and supervision are their responsibility, and enforcement responsibilities lie with the local authority trading standards officers. Mortgage lending is not currently subject to conduct of business regulation, but comes under the Mortgage Code, a voluntary code supported by the Council of Mortgage Lenders. This will change in 2002, when residential mortgage lending (but not mortgage advice) will be regulated by the FSA. Consumer credit companies can therefore exist separately from banks and building societies and are not subject to the same prudential regulation. There is therefore greater scope for competition from new entrants or non-banks through the medium of consumer credit.

In the UK, the major competition with the banks comes from credit cards; these are not simply debit or payment cards, but offer revolving credit at an average interest rate of 15.2% in March 2001. The effect of the inroads into the market by non-banks can be seen from the figures. The share of credit cards held by the traditional banks fell from 82% in 1995 to 70% in 2000; this includes the shares of Sainsbury's Bank, a joint venture with the Bank of Scotland, now HBOS (1.1%); and the banking arm of Tesco, a joint venture with the Royal Bank of Scotland Group (2.1%). The share of the Big Four has declined from 73% to 61%. New entrants have been much more successful in the credit card market than in other aspects of personal banking, and the American credit card companies MBNA, HFC Group and Capital One have led the way. They have captured some 13% of the market, which also enables them to sell other financial services products, such as general insurance.

MERGERS AND ACQUISITIONS

The traditional banks—Barclays, HSBC, Lloyds TSB, RBS/NatWest, the Bank of Scotland and Clydesdale—can be traced back to the development of local banks and joint stock banks in the eighteenth and nineteenth centuries. Lloyds TSB, for example, has its origins in the firm of Taylors and Lloyds, which opened a private bank in Birmingham in 1765. Much more recently the bank has grown rapidly through acquiring the Cheltenham & Gloucester Building Society in 1995, the merger with TSB in the same year, followed by minority shares in Lloyds Abbey Life plc in 1996, and then the acquisition of Scottish Widows and the Chartered Trust Group plc in 2000. The TSB part of Lloyds developed from the trustee savings bank movement of the late nineteenth century.

Barclays can also trace its origins back to the late eighteenth century, to a gold-smith banker in Lombard Street, the current London headquarters of the bank. Such bankers provided funds for merchants, and by 1896 the private banking business in Lombard Street merged with about 20 banks to become Barclays or a Quaker bank (because of the religious connections of the founding families) in 1918. Much later Barclays acquired Martins Bank in 1969, and then acquired the Woolwich Building Society in 2000. Similarly, National Westminster Bank can trace its origins to the early London goldsmith banks of the late seventeenth century, but was formed in 1968 from the merger of the National Provincial Bank (established in 1833), the District Bank (established in 1829) and Westminster Bank. This was followed by the merger with the Royal Bank of Scotland in March 2000. HSBC Group is the most unusual bank out of the Big Four. It was established in 1865 in Hong Kong by a Scotsman, Thomas Sutherland, then a superintendent of the Peninsular and Oriental Steam Navigation Company, and it grew from there throughout Asia. The group can also claim that its roots go back to another goldsmith bank, William Wright, which later became part of the London City and Midland Bank. London City and Midland became a full member of the group in 1992.

The two Scottish banks have even older histories. The Bank of Scotland is unique in that it was established by an Act of Parliament in 1695 to develop Scotland's trade with England and the Low Countries. It was also the first bank in Europe to successfully issue paper currency, as early as the 1690s. Much later it played a key role in financing the development of the North Sea oil industry, established branches in the US and Russia, acquired the British Linen Bank in 1971, and merged with the Halifax in 2001.

The Royal Bank of Scotland (RBS) was formed by royal charter in 1727, developed a major presence in England by acquiring banks from the 1920s onwards, and under the Williams & Glyn's banner enjoyed an extensive presence in England and Wales. In 1985 Williams & Glyn's bank merged fully with RBS. RBS then acquired the National Westminster Bank in March 2000 and became the third largest bank in the UK. The term 'clearing banks' is applied to the four leading banks in the UK and to the two leading Scottish banks, referring to the fact that they are members of the national cheque clearing system, which includes the leading English high-street banks, the Scottish banks and their Northern Irish equivalents, together with several regional banks. Only the Scottish banks retain the right to issue banknotes. For the rest, the Bank of England is the sole issuer.

THE CURRENT STATE OF BANKING

As in several EU member states, the banking system is highly concentrated. The mergers and acquisitions took place between 1880 and 1917 and again during the 1960s, so that by 1970 the four familiar clearing banks emerged and they still dominate the landscape. They took further steps to widen their customer base, with the result that in 2000 the Big Four—Barclays, HSBC, Lloyds TSB and RBS/NatWest—were responsible for 72% of current accounts and 32% of loans, and even 61% of the credit card market (despite the wide range of credit cards in the market). The other banks lag behind and include National Australia Bank, whose branches are concentrated in the traditional areas of its UK subsidiaries in Scotland, Yorkshire and Northern Ireland; and the Bank of Scotland, which had just 2% of current accounts, 2.6% of lending and 4.3% of credit cards in 2000. However, in 2001 the Bank of Scotland merged with the Halifax, a former building society, and the resulting bank, known as HBOS, should have a higher market share of some 7% of the current account market, 5% of loans and almost 6% of the credit card market. The merger created the fifth largest bank in the UK market.

The National Australia Bank acquired Clydesdale, Yorkshire Bank and Northern Bank, all of which had previously been in the sole or joint ownership of other British banks between 1987 and 1990. That leaves the Alliance & Leicester (which took over Girobank in 1990), Abbey National and Nationwide. Nationwide is the largest mutual apart from the Cooperative Bank, which has its roots in the cooperative movement of the nineteenth century. The Alliance & Leicester has remained relatively small, with a market cap of £4 billion, and its share of the current account market has remained at about 3% in spite of the fact that its customers have access to 17,500 post offices for cheque and cash handling.

The Role of the Building Societies

The first building societies were formed about two hundred years ago when people got together to cooperate with each other in building their own houses. Members regularly contributed to the society and built houses together, and then each completed house was allotted by lottery to a member. The society was dissolved when everyone had a house. During the nineteenth century they became self-help, mutually owned deposit-taking and lending institutions, often locally based. Their number steadily continued to fall throughout the twentieth century, initially through a process of mergers: the number has declined from 1,723 in 1910 to 66 in 2001. The pace of change was accelerated by the introduction of the Building Societies Act in 1986, which allowed building societies to 'demutualise', provided that 75% of the members voted in favour and that at least 50% of those eligible to vote actually voted.

Following the 1986 act, building societies began to diversify from savings accounts and mortgages into personal current accounts and a wide range of other products, including investment and insurance products. Most of the larger societies converted from mutual status to PLC status or have been acquired. Abbey National was the first and is one of the three largest of the former building societies, which include the Alliance & Leicester and the Halifax. The Nationwide is easily the biggest of the remaining mutually owned building societies. That process, among other things, led a reduction in the number of branches. There are now 14,000 bank and building society branches in the UK, a number which has been declining steadily and has fallen from about 17,000 in 1995, but the Big Four still have about 60% of the total number of branches between them.

Unlike continental mutual banks, those with savings accounts or mortgages hold shares in the society; they are members and have certain rights, including the right to vote for members of the board of directors, to attend the annual general meeting and to receive copies of the certified accounts. The board of directors may put the proposal to the membership that the building society should demutualise in accordance with the regulations set out in the Act of Parliament. Each member of the society has a right to vote by post or by attendance at the annual general meeting or at a special general meeting. Members are compensated for their loss of membership. The amount of compensation is calculated according to a formula devised by each individual building society, and the individual policyholder may receive his compensation in the form of cash or as shares in the new public limited company.[2]

The largest ten building societies include the Nationwide, Britannia, Yorkshire, Portman and then some smaller societies such as the Coventry Building Society, Skipton, Chelsea, Leeds & Holbeck, West Bromwich and the Derbyshire Building Society. Others are even smaller and are also often entirely local. They are well regulated, first by the Building Societies Commission and now by the FSA, and they are well financed. If they wish to remain independent, they often have to resist the determination of their members to push through a proposal to demutualise, with their eyes fixed on the windfall profits. Between them they have assets of over £165 billion, some 18 million savings accounts valued at £110 billion, and some 2.6 million mortgages.

The argument about demutualisation still continues. The building societies claim that it costs 35% more to run a PLC than to remain as a mutual, almost entirely due to the requirement to pay dividends to shareholders. The Consumers' Association published the results of research it conducted in July 2001, which concluded that 'former building societies that have converted to banks generally offer poorer deals than those building societies which remain mutual. This is true of their mortgages, tax-free savings accounts, known as TESSAs, and branch-based instant savings accounts. Mutuals are a competitive alternative to banks, because their lower margins allow them to offer good interest rates for both savers and borrowers. Large windfall payments go some way to compensate for this, but any future windfalls are likely to be fairly modest and they could be eroded quickly by less competitive rates'. Such reflections are not always sufficient to prevent policyholders from voting in favour of demutualisation in order to obtain the cash, when they are offered the opportunity.

---

[2] Full details of the demutualisation process are set out in the appendix on page 139.

Some of the largest building societies did demutualise and have become mortgage banks. These include Abbey National, Alliance & Leicester, Birmingham Midshires, Bristol & West, Cheltenham & Gloucestor, Halifax, National Provincial, Northern Rock; the Woolwich and Bradford & Bingley were two of the last to demutualise. Few remain independent, just the Abbey National, the Alliance & Leicester and Bradford & Bingley. The Halifax agreed a merger with the Bank of Scotland in 2001.

Banking Services

Both the building societies and the banks offer a full range of banking and investment services to their retail customers. The distribution of products and services indicates that the banks have the major share of the market, and that the top four banks dominate every market. The traditional market for building societies was the mortgage market, but the banks continue to dominate this market, as they have done since the mid 1990s. They account for 68% of the increase in mortgage lending in 2000 (after allowing for over £8.1 billion by banks in 2000). Building societies accounted for only 22%, with specialist lenders (some of which are bank subsidiaries) and others taking the rest. Following the building society conversions, the banking sector held 72% of all mortgage lending outstanding at the end of 2000, with over 11 million mortgage borrowers in the UK.

The banks also have about 75% of the unsecured lending market. Their share of this market has grown in recent years but in 2000 they captured the whole market as the specialist lenders saw their share disappear. The level of credit card borrowing declined but personal borrowing increased, with the cards being used to defer payment rather than borrow. Table 10.1 indicates the shift to credit cards as a growing source of consumer credit.

A 14% increase in the number of cards issued in 2000 brought the total in use to almost 50 million, with £40 million of credit outstanding at the year end. They are still regarded as a popular and convenient payment method and the number of transactions continues to increase. They were overtaken by the number of debit cards in 1997, which has continued to grow by 8% a year since then. Almost 50 million

Table 10.1 Net lending (£m) for consumer credit

	1995	1996	1997
Banks	6,099	9,516	14,718
Building societies	238	120	107
Insurance companies	39	4	−100
Other specialist lenders	1,992	2,165	−181
Retailers	−133	208	−285
Total net lending	8,234	12,013	14,258
Of which, credit cards	2,103	3,507	5,472

Source: *Banking Business*, vol. 18, p. 46, Table 4.06

Table 10.2   Market shares and concentration in personal banking markets, Great Britain 2000

	PCAs	Savings accounts	Mortgages	Loans	Credit cards
Big Four banks					
Barclays	18.2	10.4	7.7	6.5	21.7
HSBC	13.8	4.9	2.4	6.0	9.3
Lloyds TSB	22.0	10.0	9.4	12.0	13.6
RBS/NatWest	18.1	5.8	4.3	7.7	16.8
Other banks					
Bank of Scotland	2.1	2.4	1.4	2.6	4.3
NAB	3.7	1.7	—	2.1	2.1
Existing and former building societies					
Alliance & Leicester	3.4	3.9	4.2	2.6	2.8
Abbey National	5.1	12.9	13.2	5.7	1.7
Halifax	4.9	17.8	20.0	2.4	3.3
Nationwide	2.9	10.6	8.1	1.4	—
Others	5.8	19.6	29.3	51.0	24.4

Source: Competition Commission, *Lloyds TSB Group plc and Abbey National plc: A Report on the Proposed Merger*, 10 July 2001, p. 87
Note: Bank of Scotland and Halifax merged in 2001 to become HBOS

debit cards are in circulation and they are used more extensively than credit cards, obviously as an alternative to cash, whereas credit cards are usually used to defer payment for goods and services.

In terms of personal current accounts, the Big Four banks dominate with 72% of this market. The banks can earn income from current accounts by charging fees and by paying or charging customers interest rates that are higher or lower than market interest rates. The income from personal current accounts for all banks and building societies was £5.3 billion in 2000, and income from all five personal banking products (current accounts, savings accounts, mortgages, loans and credit cards) was about £30 billion.[3] The banks, however, claim that personal current accounts are not very profitable, their value being found mainly in their contribution to overheads and the opportunities they create for selling other products. They generate less income per customer than mortgages or personal loans. New entrants, such as the supermarkets, have not offered personal current accounts, partly because of the marginal profits and the operational complexity, and partly because of customers' unwillingness to switch accounts. Prudential's internet bank, Egg, had a significant impact on the savings market, at least in its early days, yet it announced in February 2001 that it did not intend to enter the current account market, having examined the experience and performance of other internet providers such as Cahoot and Intelligent Finance (Table 10.2).

---

[3] Competition Commission, *Lloyds TSB Group plc and Abbey National plc: A Report on the Proposed Merger*, 10 July 2001, p. 87.

Social Exclusion

In the UK, as elsewhere, the current account is rapidly becoming essential for consumers. It offers people access to money transmission services, including automated credit transfers, direct debits, standing orders, debit cards and cheques. The current account is also a means of holding deposits for individuals since cash can be easily paid in and withdrawn; it is also a means of obtaining credit through an overdraft or an accompanying credit card. Most people have access to at least one current account; a survey conducted in 1999 by the Office of Fair Trading found that 86% of households had a current account, but the 14% figure of those without is higher than in any of the leading member states of the EU.

This was a matter of great concern to the government, partly because of its concerns about social exclusion, but also because it plans to pay all social security through current accounts and the possibility of presenting one's social security passbook at the post office in order to obtain cash will be withdrawn in 2005. Under pressure from the government, most banks offer basic bank accounts without the overdraft facility and chequebook; this means payment by direct debit and standing order, and sometimes a debit card (requiring online authorisation for all transactions). Basic accounts are suitable for those with difficulties in managing their finances. This may lead to a decrease in the number of households without bank accounts, but the problem remains for those with very modest incomes and the decline in the number of bank branches and post offices still means that many will find it difficult to open and sustain a bank account.

The government pursued its goal with the establishment of universal banking services when it reached an agreement with 11 banks, including the Big Four, to make their basic bank accounts accessible through post offices and straightforward to open for those without bank accounts. The banks have agreed to contribute about £40 million to a new card-based post office account which would accept credits only from government agencies and only via automated credit transfer and from which cash could be withdrawn via post offices with no transaction charges. Such an account might be suitable for benefit recipients who are not ready to open a basic bank account.

Competition and Concentration

The Competition Commission reviewed the banking system in 2001 when it was considering the proposed takeover of Abbey National by Lloyds TSB. It decided to prohibit the merger on the grounds that Abbey National is both actually and potentially important as an independent competitor in the various markets where its operations overlap with those of Lloyds TSB. The members of the commission regarded the personal current account market as one of the most significant markets from this viewpoint in which it is vital to have 'well-established rivals' to the 'entrenched position' of the Big Four.[4] Abbey National is seen as one of the two most successful suppliers (the other being HBOS) because it is 'reasonably innovative' and 'has to compete actively in order to maintain its position'. Its branch network would have disappeared, if it had been acquired by Lloyds TSB. Its importance would remain, however, even if it were to be acquired by another bank besides one of the Big Four.

The recommendation of the Competition Commission that the acquisition should be prohibited has effectively blocked what some now call the Big Six banks from increasing their profitability through domestic consolidation. The existing concentration in current accounts and the continuing arguments about the costs and barriers to entry in the SME sector have been called in to prevent further consolidation among the largest banks. It will focus the strategic attention of the four largest UK banks on overseas opportunities but the barriers to such consolidation within the EU are thought to remain. The prospect of acquisition by continental banks does not seem likely when these banks believe that the returns on equity in the UK are bound to fall because the market is so competitive, while the high level of sterling relative to the euro makes them expensive. Within the boundaries set by the Competition Commission, UK banks will have to consider their strategy. But as one leading banker put it, 'All that is left for us is to hoover up the smaller banks'.

BANKING STRATEGIES

Cross-selling

Cross-selling has always been a more difficult proposition for UK banks than for their continental counterparts, and there are three main reasons. First, the concept of universal banking was a more recent introduction into the financial services industry than in most other European countries. That was all changed with the Financial Services Act 1986 and the introduction of personal pension plans, which were introduced when the Social Security Act 1986 was implemented in 1988. The Act gave people the choice of opting out of the state pension scheme or the employer's occupational pension scheme. For the first time, banks, building societies and unit trusts were allowed to enter the pensions market alongside the insurance companies.

The role of the traditional bank manager disappeared—advising customers on deposits and lending, and more generally on the management of their financial affairs. The bank manager and his branch staff were expected to be salespeople, but many were ill-fitted for this role and found it uncomfortable. Banks were slow to learn how to adapt their branches to selling investment products for which adherence to conduct of business rules was required. They also faced competition from two other sources: the sales forces employed by the life offices and the independent financial advisers,

---

[4] Competition Commission, *Lloyds TSB Group plc and Abbey National plc: A Report on the Proposed Merger*, 10 July 2001, p. 37.

together with the 'polarisation' rules. The concept of polarisation was introduced as part of the implementation of the Financial Services Act 1986, which also established a regulatory framework covering the full range of investments, product providers and the securities markets. Polarisation applied to the retail market and required all those selling investment products to be either direct sales staff or tied agents, on the one hand, or independent financial advisers on the other. Tied agents and direct sales staff could only advise their customers on the purchase of products from one product provider. They were obliged to make it clear on their business cards and in their entire dealings with the customer that they were only offering the products of one company.

Independent financial advisers are obliged to give their customers 'best advice'; that is, they should analyse their customers' financial needs and recommend the product best suited to their customers' needs and objectives. They are expected to review all the products available on the market and be able to justify (to the regulators as well as the customer) the one which best fits their customer's needs. In the early 1990s, independent financial advisers tended to be small firms, but by the end of the decade the market was dominated by large firms of independent financial advisers, with better resources in terms of technology and research as well as better-trained professional advisers. The quality and professionalism of the direct sales forces, tied agents and independent financial advisers improved considerably towards the end of the 1990s, following a major pensions misselling scandal in which personal pensions were sold to those who were in good occupational schemes and did not require a personal pension. The regulators insisted that compensation should be paid and the costs to the industry were some £10 billion.

The third reason is that, over the decade, banks and building societies generally offered poor-quality insurance and investment products, which were recognised as such by many of their customers. Their initial response to the changing marketplace in the late 1980s and the 1990s was to set up their own insurance and asset management companies within the banking group, for which banks lacked the expertise and seemed to be unable to hire it. Some of the life offices established by the banks have since been closed, such as Barclays Life and NatWest Life. The result is that, although the banks had all the advantages in terms of name recognition and a physical presence, staff and resources, they were never able to achieve more than 30% market share of investment products. Some banks have a company in the group offering independent financial advice to which they often refer their own bank customers.

However, that changed in 2000 and 2001, when several banks adopted a different approach. They purchased well-established insurance companies or formed strategic alliances with them. Barclays and the Alliance & Leicester formed partnerships with Legal & General; Lloyds TSB bought Scottish Widows; and CGNU formed a bancassurance arrangement with RBS. The Bank of Scotland agreed a joint venture with Zurich Financial Services to provide banking services for Zurich's 4.5 million retail customers. The pressure is on, with UK banks required to make a success of their bancassurance strategies and to get full value from the sale of high-margin insurance products.

The banks had two reasons for changing their strategy: one was the introduction of the stakeholder pension, a low-cost pension introduced by the government and designed to encourage those on low or moderate incomes to save for their own pensions. The product went on the market in spring 2001, but despite the government's high hopes for extensive sales, they did not materialise by the end of that year, and most experts do not expect the market to develop much further. The other reason is that the polarisation regime is expected to change, so banks will be able to be multi-tied to a wide range of providers; in other words, an 'open architecture' regime is likely to be introduced during 2002 or early 2003. Banks are preparing for the new regime by purchasing or arranging alliances with life and pensions companies or by acquiring asset managers.

'Any further change in the polarisation rules,' said one leading banker, 'will enable us to develop more relationships with other product providers.' One of the insurers involved pointed out, 'We have achieved good growth both from our own independent financial adviser channel and through our partnerships, where the benefits are becoming apparent'. Another banker commented on the market developments: 'There is some quite interesting positioning going on. . . . Classically, the distributor has an advantage as they are closer to the customer'. The real issue for UK banks is whether they are sufficiently close to their customers to be able to turn that relationship to their advantage.

Managing the Customer Relationship

Peter Ellwood, chief executive of Lloyds TSB, sets his strategy in the context of intense competition 'in which new entrants, especially from overseas, are capable of winning a substantial share of new business in the UK. The main battle in the future will be about the ability of financial suppliers to demonstrate that they truly understand and can meet fully the different needs of their customers. . . . It will be about creating trust through knowledge, so that customers allow their supplier the privilege of looking after more of their financial affairs. . . . We must get much closer to our customers, really understand what our customers need, when they need it, and how they want it delivered'. Here is what they have done:

> We have placed our customer relationship management programme at the heart of our strategy. . . . [It] will give staff access to a customer's complete portfolio with us. When a customer contacts us, the member of staff handling the inquiry will be able to recall when and why the customer last contacted us and the range of products that the customer holds. . . . We will also be able to collect and monitor information about the customer's preferred ways of banking, whether by branch, telephone or internet. We have already seen an improvement in customer loyalty.

The bank believes that customers will benefit from improved quality of service, and the information sent to customers will be relevant to their specific individual needs: 'We know that our customers have 8 financial services products on average, but only

2.3 were bought from our bank. Our target is to increase this to 2.5 by the end of 2002'. The focus of these remarks appears to be on sales rather than service, borne out by the fact that the call centre staff are not empowered to resolve customers' problems, but have to refer them back to the branch. That is quite a low target by comparison with many continental banks, but above the UK average of 1.5.[5]

Another has taken a critical look at what banks in general are doing. Its critical analysis forms the basis of its own strategy. For so many banks, 'there is no clarity of strategy'. He went on, 'They know they should be doing something, but they are not sure why or how all the pieces fit together'. So much of what the banks are currently doing is connercted with cost saving as opposed to customer service; for example, branch distribution is augmented by the call centre, which has not saved much money and offers an indifferent service, plus an underutilised internet:

> There is too much customer data and too little information and everyone is looking for new customers. . . . Customer and proposition segmentation is becoming common, but it is superficial. Mass affluent customers are sometimes separately distinguished but they are offered limited propositions or service differentiation. . . . Customer services are too often a focus for cost savings and not added value.
>
> What we plan to do is to work back from the solution, rather than simply planning to apply the existing product range to our customers. . . . What we have developed is an 'integrated approach' with 'flexible products', which enables the customer to sweep money between the current account, savings and borrowings according to the parameters set by the customer. . . . Each customer may have up to 15 'pots' but for most customers 5 or 6 'pots' are sufficient. . . . Plain vanilla products are also available for customers. . . . We can describe the basis of our strategy as the recognition that customers are individuals.
>
> We have learned some lessons from the auto manufacturers. They have long focused on the challenge of meeting a variety of customer needs as efficiently and quickly as possible. Here the industry's response has long been the development of product platforms from which families of models can be developed with the reuse of components, electronics, elements of body design and engineering. The aim is to reduce costs and shorten the new product development cycle. What we have taken from that is that we have the same basic ingredients but we can provide individual solutions. Our aim is to create new models that share platforms and components but use different development teams to customise models to attract distinct customers. . . . Taking our cue from the car manufacturers, we must act as monoline product companies. . . . [We must use] shared product and distribution platforms [to offer] customised solutions.

The aim is to unite what the bank calls 'customised solutions' and customer relations management with the aim of creating a 'premium business' out of a 'commoditised business'. This strategy is designed to meet what the bank has identified as the salient customer trends, beginning from the obvious but no less valuable insight that customers want to be treated as individuals. In particular, customers want banks to give them 'what they need, not what the banks have to sell. They are aware of the broad financial requirements, which underpin lifestyle goals but want help. Their needs are becoming increasingly sophisticated, and they are growing wealthier with more

---

[5] *Management Today*, May 2001, p. 16.

complex medium- and long-term savings and borrowing needs. They are aware that this is the case as well'.

Customers are also much more 'demanding in terms of service and value'. What is interesting is that these are the words of a leading senior banker in charge of UK retail banking, almost the only banker who started by analysing the customers' views before developing the bank's strategy. The bank in question was indeed redeveloping its strategy after a bruising period in which an earlier branch closure programme had attracted much adverse public and media comment.

Another leading banker described his bank's strategy in the context of its determination to provide banking services of such quality that the bank will stand out clearly from its peers:

> We are confident that we are in a position to deliver such quality of service, since we have been in the process of replacing our systems over the past seven years. That process has now been completed. Not only is our system fully integrated, but we are the only bank with a fully integrated system. This is part of the reason for our increase in market share over the past ten years, and our market share continues to increase. When people decide to change their bank, a high proportion of those dissatisfied customers select our bank.
>
> We now have a powerful system in place, which enables staff to have access to all information at any point. We are able to use our customer relations management system and data mining to provide individually tailored solutions for individual customers. The customer's details can be called up on a screen and provide a solution for them, which deals with the individual's needs. But we are driven by customer's needs: we do not seek to sell to them. . . . What we have to do is to exploit the power of the system to broaden and deepen relationships. Even then, we cannot expect an explosion of growth in our market share. We have to rely on personal recommendation and the steady growth which results from that.

Although the UK market is apparently highly concentrated—indeed it is dominated by the Big Four—there is in fact 'plenty of competition. People are spoilt for choice; in fact, the extent of the choice simply causes confusion'. At present, banks and building societies, including internet banks, are competing for both personal and small business accounts by offering attractive rates of interest. Interestingly enough, surveys conducted by the Consumers' Association suggest that customers make their selection or remain with their existing current account provider on the basis of quality of service, but the banks focus on competing with each other over rates of interest.

As with every other bank, the aim is to use the new channels as a means of cross-selling: 'We have found that cross-selling through the internet is relatively easy, when we have 150,000 hits a day. We use prompts on our internet banking for which we now have 1 million customers, although most people do not confine themselves to one channel. . . . The call centre is another source of information about customers, so that we can build a new product into the process or a different solution'. As far as banks are concerned, there has been greater innovation in the process rather than the product, and the reason for this is that 'it is easier to start with the process'. Take the branch network: 'We cut back the branch network in the 1980s during a period of financial difficulties for the bank and do not intend to reduce it any further. The customers want a branch network, and we recognise that face-to-face contact is an important delivery channel, and an important means of building a close relationship with the customer'.

So the bank has focused on the branch network as one important means of delivery. To that has been added 'micromarketing'—an attempt to 'map products onto the customer on the basis of the propensity to buy certain products. It is then assumed that the same propensity applies to the whole country and for the same customer profile. It seems to be rather a blunt instrument'. Aggregation means looking at all aspects of the customer's current accounts, including standing orders and direct debits. However, the bank is not sure how much the customer wants this and the extent to which it may be an invasion of privacy: 'We know that other suppliers are still deciding how far they can go. . . . What we shall consider is how far this fits in with the culture of the bank'.

The chief executive is the 'champion' of the bank's policy of a clear divide between the bank and its competitors, a policy which he sold to all the bank's staff, winning their support for it. The policy is defined as 'treating the customer fairly and in line with the bank's culture. It means putting the customer first and treating the customer in the right way. Involving all the staff through training and an open style of management serves to build the staff's confidence in handling customers. . . . To facilitate the policy, we have a tightly designed "collective management" in which various functions are coordinated so that we can speed up strategic planning and development. We can bring new products to the market very quickly'. The bank has concluded that its policy is bearing fruit in terms of a growing customer base, and its continual programme of consumer research suggests that it creates satisfied customers.

It is fair to say that UK banks are beginning to re-establish customer relationships after a period during the early to mid 1990s, when staff were made redundant, staff turnover was high, and staff were moved frequently from one post to another. The context for this was a focus on short-term profit rather than long-term relationships. Towards the end of the 1990s, UK banks began to realise that retention of customers and high levels of customer satisfaction in the light of public criticism required management of the relationship with the customer. Maintaining a relationship between the customer and the bank, in terms of service quality and staff continuity, was again recognised as valuable. Not all banks have placed the emphasis on personal contact; some rely on information about the customer's account, loans and investments being readily available to the person the customer contacts, whether in the branch or at the call centre. Problems remain in that banks have broken down what were formerly more highly skilled roles into their constituent parts so that routine inquiries can be handled at the call centre.

Customer service is understood by the banks to be a matter of integrating the channels, ensuring the same standards of service to the customer across channels, acquiring and mining information about customers, so that each one can be offered the solution to his needs (for one bank) or be offered the appropriate products (for another bank). From the bank's viewpoint, the main value of this contact is that it enables the bank to sell more products to the customer or advise the customer on the solution to his financial needs and/or problems. It has become even more important for the banks to move into selling investment products.

In the UK, the proportion of those with over £50,000 of liquid assets is set to rise from 6% of the population to 8% by 2005. However, the rate of increase is slowing down. The number of people with more than £50,000 rose by half between 1995 and 2000 but it will rise by only one-third over the next five years. A further 12% have over £20,000 in liquid assets, but that will rise to 17% by 2005.[6] The managing director of Inscape, Abbey National's wealth management arm, commented on the report, saying that 'wealth is no longer the preserve of the privileged few ... to the extent that 2005 will see 1 in 10 of the adult population fall into the mass affluent group, wielding a combined worth of £660 billion'. That is the size of the market all the banks wish to tap.

The focus for the banks is entirely clear. The customer, however, has a different view of the way in which his needs should be met. In the UK, as elsewhere, the customer uses all the channels the bank provides and wants to access the bank's services any time and anywhere. In addition 'most people still want a real live bank manager who understands their particular needs, and it is this function that has largely disappeared'.[7] Banks may consider it impossible to replace that function exactly, but they will be judged by how effectively they substitute systems for managing customer relations and delivering personal contact.

APPENDIX: THE DEMUTUALISATION OF UK BUILDING SOCIETIES

This appendix describes the process of demutualisation of mutually owned building societies in the UK. The information was supplied by Terry Mathews, a former member of the Building Societies Commission. The appendix is included partly to explain the developments in the UK banking system during the last decade, but also because the process is not available in continental Europe. The successful use of this legal process depends on two factors: (1) that deposits and mortgages confer membership on the individual account holder, and (2) that it is possible to compensate individuals for loss of membership in what have become known as windfall payments, which have sometimes been very substantial. This legal process may not always be possible in continental Europe, as individual account holders are not necessarily members.

The Building Societies Act 1986, as amended by the Building Societies Act 1997 and the Financial Services Act 2000, provides that a building society may transfer

---

[6] Michael Wilmott and the Future Foundation, *The Emergence of the Mass Affluent*. Report commissioned by Inscape at Abbey National, March 2001.
[7] Lorna Bourke, *Sunday Telegraph*, 5 August 2001, p. 21.

the whole of its business to a commercial company, which must be a public limited company, registered in the UK or another European Economic Area (EEA) member state. A transfer may take one of the two following routes:

- To a company specially formed by the society for that purpose (known as a conversion)
- To an existing company (known as a takeover)

A transfer must be approved by two resolutions of the society's members: (1) a shareholding members' resolution passed by a 75% majority of voting on which, in the case of a conversion, at least 50% of the members' eligible to vote actually voted in favour, or in the case of a takeover, at least 50% of members eligible to vote voted in favour; and (2) a borrowing members' resolution passed by a simple majority of those voting (there are no voting turnout requirements).

The transfer resolutions must be passed by a poll at a special general meeting (postal votes are not permitted but proxy votes are permitted). All members eligible to vote must be sent a notice of the meeting, together with a transfer statement containing information to enable the members to decide how to vote. (The information sent to members has to be approved by the FSA in advance.) The information members receive must include the up-to-date financial information about the society, and in the case of a takeover, about the successor company; the range and relative importance of the society's activities and any changes to be made following the transfer; the proposed terms of the transfer, including any windfall distribution to members of cash or shares in the successor company; the directors of the society and the successor company and any interests they have in the transfer; the consequences of the transfer (e.g. in investment account terms) and staff (e.g. any branch closures).

If the transfer resolutions are passed, the society must apply to the FSA for confirmation of the transfer. On the other hand, the FSA must confirm a transfer unless it finds that some material information was not made available to the members in the transfer statement, that the vote does not represent the views of the members, that there is a risk the successor company will not become, or remain, authorised to accept deposits, or that some relevant requirement of the act or the society's rules was not fulfilled. If the FSA finds that any of these considerations apply, it is not bound to refuse confirmation provided it is satisfied that the society has corrected the deficiency, which may include calling a further general meeting. The FSA may also disregard immaterial defects in the procedure required by the act and the rules.

Notes

1. The building societies have transferred their business to commercial companies in 10 cases: 7 by conversion and 3 by takeover.

2. The members of a society are shareholding members, who have made deposits in accounts, designated as share accounts, which give them voting rights, and borrowing members, who have taken out mortgages secured on residential property.
3. The 1986 act was intended to restrict windfall payments (i.e. compensation for loss of membership) of at least two years' standing. However, the High Court found that the restriction on distribution of shares in the successor company did not hold where a flat-rate distribution was given free of charge to a specified class of persons (which could include borrowing members and non-members).

11
Looking to the Future

The previous chapters have looked at developments in banking across leading EU states and they have discussed several technologies. However, in looking into the future, there is clearly a need to consider technology in even more detail. The first section reviews the technology process within banks and how this directs innovation. The second section discusses the customer base and how this is likely to change over the coming years. The third section details the major technologies of recent years and how they will be developed in the near future. The fourth section considers what issues will have to be confronted if the available technologies are to be harnessed by the banks. The final section offers conclusions and draws out the major lessons to be learned.

THE TECHNOLOGY PROCESS AND INNOVATION

This section considers how technological developments take place within the banking sector. It begins with the notion of innovation and how it takes place between internal departments and the major suppliers of technology.

What is Innovation?

For most individuals, innovation is normally associated with the white heat of scientific breakthroughs, for example, gene technology and nanotechnology. This view of innovation runs alongside the increasing dominance of science and manufacturing in the daily lives of individuals over the past few centuries. However, innovations have slowly taken place across the history of mankind without eureka being shouted every second moment. For example, while the invention and continued innovation of the wheel was obviously fundamental to the development of society, the continued innovation of clothing may have been just as important in the early development of man.

Similarly, the continued developments and innovations in teaching methods may not have the same media potential as the development of steam power, but it would be difficult to argue which is the more important.

So what is innovation? Well, it will be defined here as the development of a product or process so it is better able to meet the needs and desires of society. This simple definition will capture most of what is needed for later discussions without having to go into long discussions as to what is meant by needs, desires and society. In the context of banking, innovation can take place in the processes of offering current banking products and in the development of new products or combinations of products. In terms of banking products, remember that they are just one element of an individual's financial needs, and innovation may take place via the combination of protection, investment and straightforward banking products.

The Lack of R&D Departments

Banking products have been in existence since at least Roman times and until recently they showed surprisingly little innovation in terms of products or processes. This long history of stability may be one explanation why banks do not traditionally have a defined R&D function. It is very interesting that the large clearing banks have had armies of individuals concerned with planning and strategy but not one individual concerned with R&D per se. A further reason for the lack of an internal R&D function may reflect the nature of banking products. At the core of any banking product lies the notion of trust, and this comes about by clients being familiar, over a long period of time, with robust products. So, in one sense, the nature of banking products operates against their very development.

Of course, the more cynical among us might argue that there has been little drive to innovate within the banking industry given the large and sustainable margins which have been made across the centuries. It is a simple fact that several countries within Europe had fairly stable banking systems (even allowing for the two world wars) until the mid 1980s. Part of the reason for this stability was the explicit or implicit pact—it depends on the country—between the banking system and government. The pact can be described as the government having a blind eye to the often cartel-like nature of the banking industry, in return for the industry offering a stable, secure and 'universal' service to the population.

For several countries across Europe, this 'partnership' between the banking sector and government was changed radically when deregulation was brought into force. Deregulation of the industry has led to increased competition among the various participants and this has generated the need to offer a more compelling customer proposition; that is, over recent decades there has been an increased need to innovate. However, although there has been an increased need to innovate, most banks had little competence to develop their products or processes, and this left the door open for the banks' suppliers to sell their ideas and developments. As an aside, one of the more interesting aspects of a number of the remaining internet banks has been their willingness to develop internal R&D competencies.

The Dominance of the Supplier

At the heart of banking there are two fundamental features. First there is the trust of the customer in the bank having the integrity to properly manage funds. This feature of trust is conditioned by the bank having robust and resilient systems and by the way the bank handles the relationship with the customer. These features will be discussed several times in this chapter. A second core feature of banking is data. The essential operation of a bank is being able to record who has banked what and where investments have been made—essentially a data issue. In times gone by, such processes were handled by hierarchies of bank employees and, in particular, by large pools of bank clerks. In this context, therefore, it is not surprising that the post-war development of the IT industry had a lot to offer in terms of being able to automate large chunks of the basic banking functions.

The IT suppliers therefore had an increasingly important role in terms of supplying and supporting some of the core functions of the bank. In essence, for a number of banks, a partnership developed with the IT supply chain and it was to these companies that the banks turned when developments were needed. From a supplier viewpoint, this was an ideal relationship in two senses. First, in supporting the core systems, they became knowledgeable about the operations and politics of a bank and how improvements might be made to the core systems. Second, there was a potentially willing audience in terms of any developments made by the IT company. To put the scale of such partnerships in context, it is not unusual for a single IT supplier to have an annual contract with a major clearing bank of over £100 million.

The lack of an internal R&D function, the data-dominated nature of banking and the ongoing relationship with IT suppliers have led to the situation where innovations within banks are often born within the supplier instead of within the banks themselves. This also has the advantage for the suppliers that any single development—and these are often expensive given the complex nature of banking products vis-à-vis the customer base—can be sold to a range of banks.

This should also benefit the banks by enabling them to share the development costs. The downside for the ban is that any potential advantage from the development will disappear as more banks take it on.

While several of the developments in basic customer processing have come from the IT suppliers, in more recent years the large consultancies have gained a foothold in the larger banks. They have been selling innovations and management thinking—total quality management (TQM), performance management, strategic thinking—and they have had a willing customer base given the increasing competition in the marketplace. Any innovation has a degree of risk attached to it, and it is always comforting to have an external agent to blame if things go wrong.

There are several reasons why external suppliers have dominated the R&D activities of banks but just one important consequence. Almost by definition, the IT suppliers only bring IT innovations to the bank, hence the recent emphasis on customer relationship management (CRM) software. So far this software has done little to enhance customer relationships and, in fact, the software should be called customer marketing software (see later). Similarly, the management consultants have only brought innovation in management thinking. There is clearly an obvious gap within innovation in banking, given the current nature of the R&D process—the lack of bankers in the R&D process means there has been a lack of innovation in banking products themselves.

Times are Changing

While IT suppliers and management consultants still play a major role in the ongoing innovation within banks, there are now signs that the banks themselves are starting to take control of their own destinies. It is difficult to fully establish why this has been the case but there are a couple of characteristics which spring to mind. First, several of the internet banks developed internal R&D functions and this seems to have led to more product innovation than seen elsewhere, or indeed previously. Second, the increased competition within banking has heightened the need for a quicker R&D process and this will often only be achieved if it is handled by an internal process. Indeed there is one reasonable-sized UK bank which will not even allow management consultants through the door because of their cost and their slowing down of much needed change. This changing emphasis bodes well for the banking industry.

Summary

This section has argued that innovation can take place within processes and within products. Indeed some of the more important innovations in mankind's history have been concerned with processes rather than high-profile product developments. After many centuries of stability, the banking industry has undergone periods of development since the Second World War. The early developments were concerned with the IT automation of basic banking processes, and these have been followed by innovations in banking management during recent decades. This reliance upon external agents for process innovation has left the industry without a real means of driving product innovation.

It would seem that there is an element of confusion in the above arguments. We have argued that process innovation can be just as important as product innovation but then we are basically noting that a major weakness in banking has been the lack of product innovation. There is, however, no confusion for the following reasons. Process innovations are important and the banking industry has benefited from them for several decades. This has been to the detriment of product innovation. Product innovation is needed to meet changes in society and its requirements for particular types of banking product.

As a final word, society is changing, and the IT suppliers have had a role in that—witness the increasingly dispersed nature of the family unit through enabling communications technology. Only the banks can truly respond to the changing needs for banking products, because they are the ones with the knowledge and understanding.

BANKING CUSTOMERS AND THE DYNAMICS OF CHANGE

This section looks at the nature of the customer base and how it is changing. Many of the technological developments to date have worked from the premise that the customer base has been fairly static in its make-up. While this may have been the case up to the late 1980s and early 1990s, there have been some fundamental shifts in the way society operates and these should have consequences for the way the banking system operates.

Customer Segmentation

Banks have traditionally segmented the retail customer base according to wealth and the corporate base according to size. In terms of the retail base, this led to basic banking services for the masses and private banking services for the more affluent. Interestingly, these two basic segments were often supplied by very different organisations. Basic banking for the masses was supplied by the high-street retail banks and banking for the wealthy was supplied by niche banks, such as Coutts. For many years, this distinction worked well but the banking sector started to realise there were an increasing number of individuals with wealth, who needed services similar to the traditionally wealthy; this new group of individual has been called the 'mass affluent'. Not surprisingly, given the potential opportunity to sell high-margin products to these types of customer, several banks have tried to offer services to this segment. To date, however, most such offerings have been less than successful and it is instructive to consider why.

The retail banks in the UK have primarily been concerned with offering basic banking services to the masses. What has been important here is the provision of low-cost, standardised products with a minimum level of individualised service. In contrast, the private banks have had a history of offering bespoke services to a small client base. Effectively, servicing a mass affluent segment causes problems for both types of bank. The retail banks have neither a history nor an understanding of what is involved in providing a banking service to a fairly wealthy individual. One aspect of being affluent is the expectation that you will be given the service you have paid for and that you will be treated differently from those who have not paid for the service. A good example of this is the way airlines treat the different categories of passenger.

Although first class, business class and domestic passengers all share the same plane, take off at the same time and land at the same time, it is only reasonable that the first-class passenger expects a different quality of service compared to the domestic passenger; after all, it is likely they will have paid up to five times more for the privilege. There are many facets to the way first-class passengers are treated differently, but the most obvious to all passengers is the queuing process at check-in. The first-class passenger wanders up to the first-class desk and normally gets served immediately, as would be expected given the cost of the flight. In contrast, the domestic passenger joins the long queue and wishes they could afford a bit more, looking enviously at the first-class passengers. Nonetheless, it is clearly apparent to all types of passenger that they are getting what they have paid for.

Contrast this with the way the high-street banks normally treat different types of customer in the branch. The banks have tried to tackle the mass affluent opportunity with the development of platinum and premium types of service. These offer a range of additional benefits, such as free currency conversion, but there is a cost; many banks charge £10–12 per month for the privilege of being a premium customer. Now, let us consider the situation of the premium customer in the branch. They walk through the doors and find themselves in a queue with everybody else. They think to themselves, 'I thought I was special. That is what the bank has told me anyway, and that is what I am paying for, so why am I standing in the same queue as the basic customer?' To add insult to injury, several of the banks have saved costs by automating the cheque clearing process and they have passed costs on to the customer by having them fill in the requisite forms. So, just imagine an individual with £0.5 million of wealth, an income of £150,000 and a paid-for premium banking service who is then asked to stand in a long queue trying to fill in banking forms on the palm of their hand. In essence, the retail banks have tried to seize the mass affluent market without fully understanding what it means to be wealthy and, moreover, without investing in the physical infrastructure to service wealthy customers.

The private banks have a different problem. While they are more than used to dealing with the vagaries of wealthy individuals, they do not have the branch outlets or often the systems to deal with large customer numbers. An obvious solution would be for the two types of bank to come together, with the retail bank supplying the necessary infrastructure and the private bank supplying the knowledge of how to deal with wealthy customers. Sadly, most such initiatives seemed to have failed because of the very different cultures needed to operate in the two types of bank.

The efficient delivery of products and services to the corporate sector is clearly important to the future success of individual banks. While the provision of services to medium-sized companies and above is specialised and fairly well defined, the banks have a lot more to do in providing services to small and medium-sized enterprises (SMEs). The problem with this sector, and it is very much like trying to service the mass affluent in terms of retail customers, is that a large number of small firms need a mixture of low-cost standardised products, coupled with specialist advice. Although there are several potential technological solutions to a range of SME financial issues (e.g. the real-time pricing of loan applications) few banks have really cracked the problem. This is a specialist topic and this chapter does not discuss it any further.

In summary, if the bank is to tackle successfully the segment of the mass affluent, it will need a fuller understanding of what is involved in servicing these customers on a grand scale. Although it is too early to tell, this is likely to involve an integrated mixture of online technologies with a good physical infrastructure.

The Major Dynamics

While societies have changed through time, there are suggestions that we are now in a period of fundamental change. This section looks at those that are most important.

One of the most fundamental changes facing society is the increasing longevity of the population. Over recent decades the lifespan of individuals has increased by more than five years and it is not unusual for individuals to live into their eighties. This was rarely the case until the early 1970s. While there are several potential explanations for these changes (and it seems that increasing longevity will continue), we will only consider here the consequences for the banking system. With an increasingly ageing population, there will be a need for attractive savings products, sustainable pension schemes and easy-to-access banking services. Furthermore, given that the wealthy tend to live longer, the ageing population will add to the mass affluent segment, with all the consequences for advice and specialist services. For the time being at least, it also has an impact on the need to retain the branch networks and even update the nature of banks for access by the more elderly. Interestingly, in recent years, bank refurbishment has moved more towards an emphasis on youth, rather than the elderly. A further point is that although individuals will be living longer, it does not mean their mental capacities will keep pace with their physical survival. At the moment, there are suggestions that there will be increasing populations of elderly people with declining mental capacity and this has clear consequences for how banking relationships will need to be developed with the individuals themselves and their families.

A further major consequence of the changing demographics is the need to change the way pensions are provided. It is a basic financial fact that it is difficult for 30 years of work to sustain 30 years plus of retirement. This has clear consequences for the types of savings products which will need to be made available in the coming years. Essentially, individuals will need to be able to plan for their later years and this should be enabled by advice, a range of products and the ability to track portfolios of investments.

A second major trend is the increasing tendency for individuals to live by themselves. In contrast to the need to plan for one's old age, there are some suggestions that the trend to live as an individual is affecting the traditional mid-life savings cycle, with individuals consuming more than their income in their middle years. It is too early to tell how these two forces will eventually balance out. Nonetheless, in the current context, this trend will need a response in terms of flexible consumer credit, etc. This issue is further compounded by another trend towards several short-term careers with periods of unemployment between jobs rather than the more traditional notion of a career for life.

The above trends are accompanied by the move towards single-parent families. There is a need to financially sustain a family on a single income, while potentially coping with several periods of unemployment and the likelihood that the individual will have to sustain themselves during a lengthy period of retirement. Of course, it may be the case that the only way of coping with an ageing population is to increase the retirement age to the late sixties or early seventies. In fact, if one looks at retirement ages before the twentieth century, the recent move towards early retirement in the late fifties or early sixties may well be seen as an aberration.

The final trend to be considered here is the increasing activity of women in the workplace. When this is coupled with the tendency for the female to bring up children (in one- or two-parent families), this will have an impact on the types of service that will need to be offered by the banking sector.

Summary

This section has considered the traditional segmentation of the customer base by banks and the likely major changes to be confronted by the banking sector. The early part highlighted the difficulties the banks have faced in responding to changes in the segmentation of the customer base. More specifically, the banking sector has struggled to respond to the development of the mass affluent segment and to the increasing needs of the SME sector. Part of the difficulty they have faced has been their inability to integrate newer channels of delivery with traditional branch networks so as to be able to offer the quality of service expected by these segments. The interesting point is that a lot of the products needed were already in existence and what was really needed was process innovation to offer the requisite level of customer service.

The second part highlighted several key trends facing society and the likely consequences for the banking sector. While these trends will involve the need for the banks to further innovate in terms of their processes—the harnessing of new technologies—there will be an equal need to innovate in terms of core banking products. This is the real challenge facing banks.

TECHNOLOGICAL DEVELOPMENTS

This section outlines the major technological developments that have taken place within banks and those that are likely to take place over the coming years.

Branch Networks

For most banks the key channel is still the branch network. There are several ways in which banks have upgraded their branches both physically and technologically; some have gone for the hi-tech look, some have gone for the coffee-shop feel, and some have taken the traditional style then modernised it. Some branches have become completely automated with the ability to withdraw and deposit cash without human intervention and the ability to review portfolios of protection and investment products. However, because of the need to sustain the pact between the government and the banking sector, most banks now realise that reducing the branch network is not a strategic option. Given the costs of operating a branch, even an automated branch, there is a clear need to understand how they can be used to sell more products and to better service the customer base.

In the UK there have been discussions concerning different banks sharing the same branches and the branches even acting as outlets for a range of other 'non-tied' financial products. In other words, the branch becomes a minimart for financial products. Taking this retailing concept one step further, most minimart retailers target themselves very carefully on the nature of the immediate market. For example, the minimart in a wealthy area may well stock a wide range of champagnes, while this is unlikely to be the case for minimarts located in poorer areas. Somewhat strangely, this notion of micromarketing to the immediate locality has not been picked up by the majority of banks. It still seems to be the case that the banks stock and provide the same range of products and services no matter what the location. This is a good example of customer data not being properly harnessed to the benefit of the bank. Later sections will discuss in more detail the need to fully integrate all channels in terms of products, services and customers.

Cash Machines

One of the most radical banking innovations in recent decades has been the ability to withdraw cash from automatic teller machines (ATMs)—holes in the wall—virtually anywhere across the globe. The significance of this development should not be underestimated. Although we now take it for granted that we can withdraw our 200 Singapore dollars from a cash machine in the Funan Centre, downtown Singapore, to do so is quite a feat of technology and banking process. Yet the take-up of cash deposits without human intervention has been significantly less than the take-up of cash withdrawals, but this is not surprising. It again comes down to being able to trust the bank and its systems. Part of the reason for the slower than anticipated take-up of 'automatic' cash deposits has been the number of errors committed on withdrawing cash. It seems to be part of the human psyche that it is bad enough having errors on withdrawal but it is unbearable to contemplate money being lost at the point of deposit.

Few banks have taken full advantage of the services that could be offered by an ATM. Given the infrastructure behind ATMs, it would be possible to undertake a range of services (such as being able to have a detailed inspection of bank statements, the status of current investments, etc.). Nonetheless, it seems likely that ATMs will continue to form the core of more advanced offerings in the future.

Contact Centres

After ATMs, the next big development was the ability to undertake banking transactions via the telephone. This gave the ability for busy individuals to undertake transactions and transfers to fit in with a busy working life. For example, until recently, several banks had quite restrictive opening hours for their branches and it was impossible to do much more than withdraw cash from a hole in the wall outside of restricted office hours. Therefore, several individuals struggled to manage their banking finances efficiently because of the restricted branch channel. The advent of the contact centre changed this enormously.

However, several banks have realised that it takes real skill to manage a customer interaction across a telephone wire. In a face-to-face contact, it is possible to assuage any fears through a whole range of human interactions—facial expressions, body language, etc.—which are not directly replicable through voice alone. Moreover, it is possible for customers to be more direct in their opinions when the relationship is distanced via a telephone wire. Given all of this, the most successful contact centres have spent a lot of time and effort developing cultures and processes which reinforce the empathetic qualities of their staff. The banks that have really come unstuck with this technology are those that have seen it merely as another channel being operated by existing staff.

Internet

The internet overcomes several problems of the branch and the contact centre. For several transactions it is important to see where the money is coming from and where it is going to. If trust was not an issue, this would be almost the ideal channel for banking transactions—assuming there is no need for the physical handling of cash—because both sides of a transaction could see it being actualised in real time. Also, this type of system can operate at any point of the globe and at any time. Moreover, if financial calculators were included, it would be possible to undertake transactions of this nature across currencies.

However, the dotcom collapse and several initial breaches of security have left large parts of the population not trusting this as a meaningful channel for banking transactions. Furthermore, a number of the internet services are poor and slow in operation, and so far their primary use has been for individuals to retrieve their account balances, with few real banking transactions being conducted across the net. Nonetheless, as web retailing increases and as confidence in its integrity improves, the net will become an increasingly important channel. However, one of the major constraints with the net as a banking channel is that in a lot of homes the PC is hogged by children doing homework, and a number of poorer households do not have access to the net from their homes.

Interactive Digital Television

Given the potential limitations of the net as a banking channel for households, interactive TV (iTV) has been seen by a number of banks, especially Swedish banks, as the appropriate medium for taking banking services into the homes of the masses. It has been noted, however, that the take-up of interactive digital television (iDTV) has been very patchy across Europe. Although the UK has one of the highest percentages of iDTV use, it still has a very low take-up of interactive banking services.

There are several reasons for poor take-up of interactive banking services. First, the interactivity was very slow and at times it felt it would have been quicker to use a carrier pigeon. This is down to a lack of investment by the banks in developing services specifically designed for this medium. Second, the TV companies have been charging exorbitant rates for the use of these channels. There are signs, however, that both of these reasons are now being overcome and we are likely to see more use of this medium in the near future.

Customer Relationship Management

One of the biggest developments over recent years has been the investment by banks in customer relationship management (CRM) software. One simple reason for this is that the banking processes were usually set up on an account basis and not on a customer basis. So, if an individual had three separate accounts with the bank, they would normally receive three sets of instructions, general information, etc. CRM offered the banks the potential of being able to see a customer as a customer rather than as a combination of individual banking accounts. It is easy to see the appeal of CRM software. For a start, it should enable different channels to see the customer in the same way.

But to date, CRM does not seem to have fulfilled its promise—it may be too early to fully appreciate the benefits which can be brought by such an investment. So far CRM seems to have been used to guide marketing not customer liaison, and even here it is not clear how useful it has been—pensioners have been sent details of student loans. A good example of this is that while a contact centre may be able to call up all the details needed on a customer, this rarely seems to be the case within bank branches. Would it not be good if the branch clerk could pull up on a screen all the relevant customer details so that they were able to offer a more specialised service? For example, as soon as a client's account number is entered, the bank clerk should know when the client has been on holiday, when they have bought a new car, when it has been serviced, etc., as this would allow a more meaningful discussion and a more informed relationship between the client and the bank. This type of service should be at the heart of CRM.

Account Bundling

In the past, most banks have provided separate products for the different needs of individuals. They might provide a current account product, a savings account product, a mortgage product, and so on. Given the difficulties with managing a range of financial products, one would think that a single product which incorporated all the features of the separate products would be attractive to customers. Such 'one' accounts have been tried by a number of banks but in general they have not been very well received by customers. The evidence to date suggests these accounts are only attractive to individuals who have enough money not to worry about budgeting the individual aspects of their lives. It is something to do with the way individuals mentally account for their financial activities that they seem to prefer a range of separate products, with each one focusing on a specific issue. Besides providing simplicity, customers seem to like to keep a current account separate from a savings account. Equally, we do know that individuals will often take out loans while having balances in both their current and savings accounts. This can be explained by the human need to have access to liquid funds while at the same time being able to purchase more substantial assets.

The example of account bundling should tell us all that there is a need to understand the preferences and proclivities of customers before launching new products. To date, it would seem that banks attempt to launch new products without them being properly underpinned by detailed or rigorous research. This may well reflect the absence of R&D functions within banks.

Account Aggregation

In a similar vein to account bundling, it would seem reasonable to expect individuals to respond positively to an online service which brought all their financial transactions (including the payment of utility bills, etc.) into a bespoke personal portal; this has been called account aggregation. To date, however, this service has not had many takers and there seem to be two primary reasons. First, to achieve account aggregation the customer has to give all relevant access details to another party. Not surprisingly, customers seem to have been wary about giving away such information. Second, even if the customer is willing to give all their financial details to a third party, the account aggregator, the individual organisations dealing with a single customer have been less than keen to allow a third party into their systems. Again, the reluctance by both customers and other organisations to take part in account aggregation is a reflection of a lack of trust, both in the integrity of the third party and the resilience of its systems.

Finally, if the bank is handling the majority of payments via direct debit or standing orders, then it is not readily apparent what the customer gains by account aggregation over and above being able to access their bank account online.

New Access Devices

Currently under development is the ability to undertake banking transactions via mobile telephony and hand-held devices. Somewhat sadly, the telecommunications and IT industries have slightly undermined customer confidence in these devices by the early launch of wireless application protocol (WAP). This technology promised the earth in terms of being able to access a whole range of services and offered little that could be classed as meaningful. The interface was too limited to allow customers to undertake any significant information retrieval or indeed transactions. Nonetheless, the new generation of hand-held devices have very much improved screens and the size of the bandwidth is now approaching the point where it should be possible to carry out transactions equivalent to those on a desktop machine.

Summary

This section has outlined some of the major developments in technology and banking products. There is quite a lot of mileage in making further use of existing technology investments, and current or future technologies have a great deal of promise if they are not oversold at inception. There is a clear need to understand how customers respond to different types of technology and to new types of product. Both of these issues can be resolved by banking innovations being more solidly underpinned by research conducted under the auspices of the banks themselves.

IMPLEMENTATION ISSUES

This section offers more detail on the challenges that need to be overcome if banks are to offer a high quality of service on a sustainable cost model.

Customer Segmentation and Expectations

Banks have struggled to deal with the mass affluent and SME segments. They will also struggle to respond positively to major trends in society unless time and effort is spent understanding the needs of the various customer segments and unless sufficient investment is made in the R&D process. Part of the R&D process will be involved with fully understanding the elements of the various customer needs and how customer expectations could be set and managed given available technologies. To date, a lot of the issues can be put down to a poor understanding of expectation management. For example, if banks wish to fully harness the mass affluent by offering bespoke financial products and specialised levels of customer service, then they have to invest in ensuring that the various channels offer a consistent level of service. It is no good creating notions of specialised services and then offering the basic 'one size fits all' service. This approach is guaranteed to anger the very segment they are attempting to cultivate.

Trust and Resilience

The core of any banking service is that the customer can trust the bank to undertake transactions as agreed in the upfront contract. Furthermore, the bank will have the systems to ensure transactions are undertaken in an efficient and secure manner. Given these conditions, it is imperative that any product or process developments are pursued such that the core banking processes are not jeopardised. It is pointless having a whizz-bang hand-held banking facility that allows all and sundry into a client's account. Channel integration and product proliferation make systems integrity ever more important.

Channel Integration and Legacy Systems

A key feature in meeting customer needs is that they are handled consistently across the various channels. In other words, the customer expects to be treated the same way by a branch, by a contact centre and by the internet services. Given the complexities of the existing core banking systems, this is one of the major challenges facing banks bringing on new processes and products. The issue of integration has been compounded by the number of mergers which have taken place across the banking sector over recent years. In fact, it may be argued that the defensive strategy of merger comes at the cost of undermining a more aggressive strategy of product or process innovation. This is because while it is difficult to achieve channel integration within an existing organisation, it is doubly difficult across a merged entity. Experience suggests that it takes more than three years to integrate organisations, and some merged banks have still not managed to integrate their IT systems five to six years on.

Summary

The main task facing banks in terms of future development is achieving consistency of service offering while meeting customer expectations in terms of individual product or process innovation. This is only likely to be achieved if the banks themselves take charge of the innovation process and move away from their reliance on external agents for development. However, this does not mean that the banks should ignore what the supply base can offer in terms of innovation, rather they themselves should lead the process and properly harness the various competencies and understanding.

CONCLUSIONS

The future of European Banking is promising if the banks themselves learn some of the lessons of the recent past. Technology continues to develop in ways that should benefit the various customer segments. Examples are the fully integrated hand-held device for the busy executive, and the well-supported branch with wheelchair facilities and networks to other services needed by the elderly. However, this chapter has argued that technology is only part of the issue. If customers are to be properly served, their needs have to be fully understood and integrated into the various product and process innovations, and this is only likely to happen if the banks themselves lead the innovation process. As well as leading the innovation process, the banks need to spend more time setting and managing the expectations of the various customer segments.

If the European banks invest the time in understanding the various customer segments and in properly harnessing their technology suppliers, then there is no reason why they cannot prosper in the future. However, for this to happen, their boards will need people who understand banking issues and the technology required to meet customer demands. To date, Europe has not been good in developing senior executives who combine these two knowledge sets. It is therefore a challenge for the banks and the business schools in Europe to develop programmes that will help to create the technologically advanced banking executives of the future.

12
Who Will Jump First?

Crystal balls seem to be in short supply among senior bankers. Hardly anyone would look further ahead than the next five years and almost all of those interviewed refused to speculate about what banking would be like at the end of the decade. Their horizons are limited to two or three years ahead, with the focus on the size of the bank and increasing, maintaining or extending market share and improving profitability. Technology is viewed as supporting or extending their own banking activities by enhancing the services provided and enabling cost-cutting. Internet banking was no longer seen as a replacement for traditional banking but as one channel among others. Technology is viewed as supporting or extending their own banking activities by enhancing the services provided and enabling cost-cutting. All the senior managers interviewed had adopted a multichannel approach, often with a subsidiary internet bank or brokerage. Senior bankers have all concluded that the personal touch is vital. Customers have clearly demonstrated that they want to deal with human beings when they have problems with their accounts or when they want advice about important financial decisions.

Looking into the future, most senior bankers see themselves as developing and extending their current strategies, which are focused on maintaining, developing and extending the customer base, building on that base to ensure its profitability. Continental banks, in particular, regard the retail customer base as being absolutely essential for their existence, and indeed the source of their profits, and they do not seem to treat the retail customer in a cavalier fashion, which has been a feature of UK banks in recent years. What provides the focus for their banking strategies is the relationship with the customer, and their success or failure in building on the foundation of the current account.

The effectiveness of the strategy may well depend on the bank's attitude to the current account holder. One leading banker commented that 'retail banking is mainly a distribution business'. If the bank regards retail banking as just a means of distributing products, then ultimately the strategy may not be successful, as its first objective will not be to build up a relationship of trust. The beginning of this book defined the bank as having a key role in enabling the customer to manage his account—in other words, to manage his financial affairs—and noted that this relationship was one of trust. If retail banking is regarded as simply a means of distribution, that relationship of trust may no longer have precedence and distribution may no longer be successful.

AIMING AT GROWTH

Banks have spent much of the time during the last decade in squeezing costs out of banking more or less successfully. The focus now is on improving the prospects for growth in a difficult economic environment and with more volatile stock markets. Clients are bombarded through every possible channel and are offered a wider range of products, which are either a bank's own products or other attractive products on the market. These are presented as 'best value' products, which the bank has selected for the benefit of its clients. A range of funds from leading fund managers may be offered.

Cross-selling alone will not achieve the growth the banks seek, however wide the range of products on offer and however carefully the market is segmented or the customer relationship is managed. The banks have sought to extend their customer base in a variety of ways. One route is to form alliances with non-bank companies to cross-sell non-financial products and to provide access to the customer base of other companies in order to offer them banking services or financial services products. Others have formed alliances with internet portals such as Yahoo! and AOL Europe for third-party distribution of their products, or with supermarkets. Others have sought mergers or alliances with telecommunications companies and may consider such relationships or acquisitions of utilities or construction companies. According to one banker, 'We move in a changing world. Everyone wants to sell more, take care of more customers and to increase the customer base'. Linking up with a telecommunications company 'provides a different customer base but one which overlaps and forms a base for marketing'. The bank in question is exploring other such relationships with a view to marketing packages of financial services in what it regards as 'exploring new territory' in a 'framework of converging industries'. In that regard, the bank is more innovative than many other banks interviewed.

The other steps banks have taken to extend or retain the customer base include forming alliances with asset managers, internet brokerages and insurance companies to sell their products. In addition, banks have resorted to the purchase of a range of companies which, although they only carry out a limited range of banking services, could build on their own customer base to become full-blown banks. Examples include the acquisition of consumer credit companies, asset managers, stand-alone internet banks, internet brokerages and other brokerages. These strategies have served to eliminate competition, sometimes before that competition presents a real challenge to the banks, as well as extending services to customers as a means of retaining or extending the customer base.

GROWTH THROUGH M&A

Banks have adopted two approaches: cross-shareholdings and mergers and acquisitions (M&A); cross-shareholding is more often adopted by continental European banks. Cross-shareholdings are rarely found between the dominant banks in each country; for example, there are none between the 'big banks' in Germany, but the large insurance companies have long-established shareholdings in the major banks. Such moves were restricted to insurance companies, since during the 1970s, when these purchases took place, only the large German insurance companies had sufficient capital to acquire the shares. There are, however, significant cross-shareholdings between leading banks in one or more member states. Some examples of cross-shareholdings are given in the appendix, so that the web of mutual interest between banks across EU member states can be seen. That will not reveal the whole picture, since the extent or existence of cross-shareholdings are not fully disclosed in all member states, even in the company's annual reports.

Some of the leading banks regard cross-shareholdings as a key element in their strategy of expansion across borders, which involves taking a stake in other banks. One bank in particular greatly values its major cross-shareholdings: 'It is of great value to us in a number of ways. First of all, there is a financial pay-off. The value of the banks has increased very much recently and the dividends have been valuable. Our cross-shareholdings place us in a unique position to act in the new pan-European banking future. We are not in these relationships for the short run. We hope to be able to take advantage of these relationships. At present, we are learning to work together and to share business. It is hard to see exactly where it will lead, but at the moment we have set ourselves limited goals. We aim to get to know each other and to develop shared projects'.

Another leading banker describes the aims in this way: 'The purpose is to obtain a financial return, and to develop a partnership with a particular line of business, such as developing joint management of mutual funds with one bank or consumer credit, which has excellent potential in Central and Eastern Europe. Part of the strategy is to take a minority stake in banks in Central and Eastern Europe, where banking standards are catching up. Here we can pursue a niche strategy and wait for one of the banks with the freedom and the chance to choose its patron. This is a long-term strategy, where one of the banks is likely to be the target of a takeover bid, and we can afford to wait for the right opportunity'.

Others do not dismiss the value of shareholdings as such but regard them as being of limited use. One such banker stated that 'we have a small cross-shareholding in two other banks in two other member states, but we are not sure that we shall expand through such means. We do not believe in such alliances, although they could be interesting in a certain specific area, but it is difficult to see the use in a global sense or in establishing a real European group'.

Others take a much more critical approach to cross-shareholdings and question their value for the banks concerned. These cross-shareholdings provide no 'clear representation of the bank which has acquired shareholdings in another bank, and provide no clear perspective on the ownership structure. The shares have not been acquired for normal commercial reasons; for example, that the return of equity of the shares of the bank acquired would justify the purchase. This should be justified in terms of a real financial interest, which should be coherent with the strategy and management of the purchasing bank. In fact, such acquisitions of blocks of shares are designed to provide access to information about what is happening inside the bank, and to have a stake should that bank merge with another'. It is also 'possible that such cross-shareholdings limit competition'.

Another rejects the notion of cross-shareholdings altogether: 'Only one cross-shareholding between banks has worked and that is the one between the Royal Bank of Scotland and BSCH, but the others are not working well at all. The only choice is to wholly merge, otherwise you cannot develop a common project. Sooner or later there will be European consolidation, and if I am involved in that, I shall not want a third-party involvement. I could lose business that way. Of course, there could be an engagement before the wedding! But that would only be the first step and that a merger would take place would have to be clear from the start, otherwise we would not work together'.

Many continental European banks are likely to maintain the cross-shareholdings they already have, while the process of domestic consolidation continues. As one banker expressed it, 'You cannot envisage being a significant player in the European market, unless you have a strong position in the domestic market'. That is part of the reason for the domestic consolidation which has taken place in the leading member states of the EU. In some member states, banks of sufficient size to be a challenger within the EU have already emerged; in others, the further consolidation has specific hurdles to overcome; and for the remaining countries, no further domestic consolidation is possible.

For France there are seven national banking groups, each with a sizeable market share and each of which has become more profitable over the past decade by removing administrative functions from the branch network, by refocusing units on sales and by cost-cutting exercises. The three listed banks have relatively low market shares in deposits and loans, so the key issue for each is how to generate more sales and increase market share.

Mergers are the only possibility for the mutually owned banks, hence the merger between Caisse des Depots et Consignations (CDC) and Caisse d'Epargne, completed in autumn 2001, and Crédit Agricole's decision to list the central management of Crédit Agricole, the Caisse Nationale de Crédit Agricole (CNCA), on the Paris Stock Exchange in December 2001. Although there is currently no legal process of demutualisation, observers in Paris take the view that if Crédit Agricole decided to demutualise, the government would provide enabling legislation, certainly after the presidential election in 2002. Caisse d'Epargne and CDC have indicated that mutual banks as well as publicly listed companies must play a role in European banking consolidation. But they fear they could be left behind if banks such as BNP Paribas and Société Générale use their shares to strengthen their alliances and acquire other banks in Euroland.

The possibility of further consolidation does not end there. The government still plans to sell its 10% stake in Crédit Lyonnais, with Crédit Agricole as the favourite to purchase. Crédit Agricole may have to face stiff competition from Société Générale and Allianz, each of which has a stake in Crédit Lyonnais. On the other hand, Crédit Agricole's Italian partner, Banca Intesa BCI, in which Crédit Agricole has a 16% stake, is also a major shareholder in Crédit Lyonnais. Meanwhile at least one of the three listed banks is 'obsessed with the possibility that that they may be swallowed up by another bank one day'. Further domestic consolidation in France is at the very least a possibility and in the case of Crédit Lyonnais very likely.

In Germany the process of domestic consolidation is still under way, as indicated by the purchase of Dresdner by Allianz. Commerzbank is generally regarded as being in a weak position with an insecure future. However, further changes may well come about as a result of the European Commission's decision that the guarantees for the Landesbanken counted as state aid and also as a result of the removal of capital gains tax (CGT) on the disposal of shares. The EC decision could put the Landesbanken into play, but leave the Sparkassen intact. The removal of CGT could provide the commercial banks with available capital to acquire other banks or even insurance companies.

In Italy further domestic consolidation may well take place, but the outcome will depend as much on the result of political decisions as on the determination of some leading banks to obtain critical mass. Antonio Fazio, governor of the Bank of Italy, announced in November 2001 that the time had come to launch the second phase of consolidation in the country's banking sector. This statement was taken as a hint that medium-sized banking institutions, such as BMPS and BNL should consider further mergers and acquisitions. It seemed to contradict his earlier statement in July 2001, when he claimed that the process was over and that even smaller banks such as BNL could manage on its own. However, merger talks are under way and it is expected that the merger will be completed by April 2002. He has certainly opposed major mergers: the merger of Unicredito with Banca Intesa was blocked in February 2001; and Unicredito's plans to merge with Commerzbank were rejected in autumn 2001, although it would also have been unpopular with the markets.

The governor has also made it plain that he would prefer larger banks to acquire smaller banks, and San Paolo IMI 'complied' when it agreed in October 2001 to merge with a group of regional retail banks, known as Banca Cardine. The bank is now the second largest bank after Unicredito Italiano, with €211 billion assets. Banca di Roma with its new chief executive, appointed in July 2001, following the hurried departure of its previous chief executive, Carlo Salvatori, announced a strategy to expand in the north by acquiring a bank. Its plans, however, have turned out to be seeking to buy the rest of Banco di Sicilia and selling Banca Mediterranea, plans which have run into local or union opposition. It has since merged with Bipop. Banca Popolare di Verona and Banca Popolare di Novara, two cooperative banks, have also agreed to merge. The governor also wants to see the consolidation of mergers that have already taken place but which have failed to combine networks and/or management structures and still operate through a variety of brands. However, as one banking analyst put it, 'Italian players still lack the critical mass... needed to compete in the European mergers and acquisitions area'.

The Bank of Italy has also made it clear that the role of the foundations must be reduced. Indeed, to comply with the Amato–Carli Law, the foundations should give up the control they exercise over Italian banks and insurance groups. Further reductions in the proportion of assets held by the foundations in the Italian banking sector have taken place. This fell from 52.8% in 1999 to 43.8% in 2000, less than half of their investments in the sector, which stood at 95% in 1994. By 2001 only 22 of the 89 foundations still retained majority stakes in their respective banks, with the highest proportion held by Fondazioni dei Paschi di Siena, the largest foundation and owner of 66% of BMPS, and the ninth largest, Fondazioni Cassa di Risparmio di Genova e Imperia, which owns 58.7% of Carige.

The Italian banking industry is still undergoing structural change, characterised by consolidation, decreased state involvement and modernisation of management practices. To optimise synergies, banking groups are streamlining their businesses with some group structures moving to a divisional model from a federal model. The focus can be on improving efficiency and profitability, while the industry is still protected to a large extent from the potential turmoil on global financial markets by the essentially domestic and retail nature of the banking business in Italy. While domestically large, the leading banks are still relatively smaller than most European competitors. Unicredito, Banca Intesa BCI and San Paolo IMI all rank between positions 14 and 17. Unless a much larger Italian bank comes into being in the very near future, there is little chance of any one of them competing in the market for pan-European banks.

In Spain the process of deregulation and consolidation has created two major global players, BBVA and BSCH. BBVA is second only to Deutsche Bank, with a market capitalisation of €52 billion, and has had a clear strategy of seeking a cross-border merger or acquisition in the EU. Francisco Gonzalez, now sole chairman of BBVA, is prepared to challenge those forces resisting the emergence of pan-European banks. 'National and regulatory dykes will not stop the tide of banking consolidation in Europe,' he claims.

The merger of Santander with BSC was finally completed in August 2001, when Emilio Botin became the sole chairman; the name BSCH was adopted at the same time. The name change was part of the cost-saving and rationalising measures which the bank carried out as part of the process of combining the two networks under a single denomination, with one specialising in retail banking and the other in corporate banking. BSCH has also established cross-shareholdings in other banks in the EU, including Commerzbank, Société Générale, the Royal Bank of Scotland and San Paolo IMI. These cross-shareholdings may ultimately put the bank at the head of a powerful grouping, taking advantage of the single currency. BSCH has other advantages. Its professional management has made it Europe's fourth most profitable bank.

Both banks have invested heavily in Latin America, investments which account for a third of BSCH's assets and profits. BBVA is also highly exposed to Latin America. The long-expected crisis in Argentina finally arrived in December 2001. BBVA stated that it had been preparing for months for a possible devaluation or a default on Argentina's debt of some €146 billion. In November BBVA announced special provisions of some €400 million for its operations in Argentina and points out that Argentina accounts for between 6% and 7% of its total income. BSCH is in a similar position. In the event, the Bank of Spain required the two banks to make provisions of €1.4 billion and €1.5 billion to cover their Argentinean exposure. Both banks would still expect and hope to be in a position to engage in cross-border mergers as soon as opportunities appear on the horizon. Their Latin American adventures may delay any potential moves in the very near future.

For the Netherlands, the Nordic countries and the UK, the possibility of further growth through domestic mergers and acquisitions is over. The Dutch banks have not sought further consolidation, knowing that the competition authorities would not grant permission for a merger between the two leading banks. Both banks are truly global banks.

The planned merger between SEB and ForeningsSparbanken was notified to the European Commission in June 2001, which began an in-depth investigation under the EU's merger regulation about concerns that the deal would create a dominant position in a number of retail banking markets, that is, households and small and medium-sized enterprises (SMEs). The EC issued a statement of objections in September 2001, which pointed out that the deal would have brought together two of the leading full-service banks, creating the largest provider of retail banking services to households and SMEs in Sweden, with market shares in number of markets in the range of 40–60%. The merged entity's large customer base together with its extensive network of over 1,000 branches would have placed it well ahead of its closest competitors in the Swedish market. The two banks withdrew their plans for the merger before the oral hearing in November 2001, but they were clearly disappointed. 'We would have been one of the top 25 banks in Europe and played an active role in the cross-border merger process. Now we cannot take that role,' stated Lars Thunell, chief executive of SEB. Indeed 'there cannot be any major bank mergers in Sweden now'.[1]

The scope left in other Nordic markets for large-scale domestic consolidation is also limited. In Denmark the acquisition of Real Danmark by Danske Bank in 2000 was probably the last takeover in the domestic market. In Finland, Sampo, the insurer, merged with Leonia Bank at the beginning of 2001 and thus created a rival to Nordea. Nordea is a four-nation universal bank created over three years from 1998.

[1] Quoted in the *Financial Times*, 12 November 2001, p. 14.

However, the EC judgement leaves the Nordic banks unable to build up a sufficiently strong domestic retail base from which to move into leading Europe with a pan-European retail bank. The UK is in a similar position following the Competition Commission's rejection of the proposed merger of Lloyds Bank plc with Abbey National.

Abbey National was first of all in merger talks with the Bank of Scotland in November 2000, and soon after that Lloyds TSB approached Abbey National with a view to a friendly takeover, which Abbey National rejected. In January 2001 Lloyds TSB again approached Abbey National with the terms of a conditional offer, which was also rejected. The matter was referred to the Competition Commission in February, and Abbey National broke off negotiations with the Bank of Scotland, citing uncertainty over the Lloyds bid as the reason. The merger was rejected on the grounds that it would raise Lloyds' share of the personal current account market from 22% to 27% and the share of the Big Four from 72% to 77%. The Competition Commission reckoned there would be little impact on the mortgage and savings markets, both of which are highly competitive.

But the market for the supply of banking services to SMEs is highly concentrated and dominated by the traditional banks, especially the four leading banks, which together have about 85% of the market. Lloyds TSB itself has about 16% of the market. There are high barriers to entry, and there has been little change in the suppliers' market shares. The Competition Commission is itself concerned that the structure and levels of prices charged by the traditional banks are similar. The government accepted the recommendation and the merger was refused. The leading UK banks cannot expand in a major way in their domestic market, leaving expansion in Euroland as the only possibility for them.

THE ROLE OF THE EUROPEAN COMMISSION

The banks in the smaller member states of the EU have complained about the definition of a geographic market and its centrality in the process of application of EU competition rules. Mario Monti, European Commissioner for Competition Policy, argues that the market definition is simply being used as a tool to identify situations in which there might be competition concerns. But by defining the market as a particular geographical area, when that market is a national market in a small country, it prevents companies from that country merging, because they would quickly reach dominance in the national market. It does not allow these companies to grow sufficiently to compete throughout the EU, still less globally. The problem does not arise in large member states, because companies could expand without reaching the level of dominance that would attract the attention of competition authorities. Monti argues that the 'Commission's objective in defining geographic markets is simply to identify the competitive constraints that the companies concerned will face'.

This issue came to the fore when SEB and ForeningsSparbanken abandoned their merger in September 2001. Some critics object to the application of the same rules throughout the EU that discriminate against companies in small member states by preventing them from merging domestically. The Swedish prime minister, Gorean Persson, argued that the 'present rules are disadvantageous to us, since we tend to dominate our market fraction to such a great extent'. Monte rejects this view on the grounds that it rests on the view that companies can only gain sufficient market size by dominating their national market, but they can grow by offering better services at competitive prices or by cross-border mergers. Banks feel that they cannot engage in cross-border mergers without a substantial share of the retail domestic market.

However, Monti does open up real possibilities for the future: 'Market definitions are not immutable and that they can change in time. The opening up to competition of markets as a result of EU liberalisation efforts or harmonisation directives will normally result in the widening of the scope of markets at some point in time [e.g. the telecommunications industry]. . . . The faster barriers fall and markets become integrated, the easier it will be for companies from smaller member states to consolidate, even domestically, without infringing competition rules'.[2] This, however, is precisely the point made by the smaller countries and their banks. The only disagreement is when the single market is indeed regarded as a single market, so that proposed mergers are assessed in that context.

Market definition is not the only criticism levelled at the EC; it also stands accused of cutting corners, bending the rules and exercising its powers in arbitrary, unpredictable and inconsistent ways. The EC is alleged to act as prosecutor, judge and jury in merger cases, and the recent decision to appoint 'hearing officers' to supervise the handling of cases and to introduce faster appeal procedures at the European Court has not satisfied the critics. The main concern of the critics is with the interpretation of the rules, in particular, what is the domain of 'dominance' and why not substitute 'substantial lessening of competition'? Following the publication of the Green Paper in November 2001, there is now a consultation process that will deal with this question, but it will not address all the procedural issues which exercise the minds of competition lawyers. It is difficult at this stage to know how far the result of the consultation process will encourage or inhibit the development of pan-European banks, but opening up the definition of the relevant 'market' may speed up the emergence of pan-European banks. The consultation process does not end until March 2002.

The EC does not regard itself as being a major obstacle to the development of pan-European banks, but it is concerned about the obstacles created by some of the central banks or the competition authorities. The policy of some central banks is to push towards domestic consolidation as opposed to cross-border mergers. The resistance to cross-border mergers is often concealed in the guise of regulatory concerns, allowing governments to play the national card: 'Globally, we need stronger banks, so we need to reduce all possible legal and contractual obstacles in the way of retail banking'. For example, in the development of e-commerce rules, we 'saw that the directive is the key to push national authorities to harmonise the contractual rules' and so from February 2002 they are obliged to accept the 'general good' rules of the market if

---

[2] Speech by Mario Monti at the EU Competition Policy Workshop on Market Definition, 5 October 5 2001.

the issuer of electronic services is in another country. Facilitating the emergence of cross-border e-commerce, especially in financial services, 'could be the trailblazer for pan-European banks'. The next step should be a 'single supervisory authority' for banks.

SHOULD THEY MERGE?

Banking analysts and academics generally take a sceptical view of mergers and acquisitions. There is an apparent paradox here: 'If bank consolidation is such a good thing to so many bankers and bank stockholders, why is there such an overwhelming body of evidence against its successful outcome?'[3] The focus for analysts is on cost savings and revenue synergies, with the cost savings being calculated on the basis of the present value of future savings based on the management's projections and discounting them at an appropriate rate of interest.

Revenue synergies are generally viewed as an extra benefit but much less reliable than cost savings. Many banks, especially in continental Europe, do not publicise their cost-savings targets, but that does not mean they are not a significant element in the merger strategy. Achieving revenue synergies through mergers is much more difficult to attain, given that most banks already offer a full range of retail and corporate banking products. Indeed there may be revenue losses due to a branch closure programme and the consequent loss of customers.

Merger cost savings are usually highlighted, but there are associated costs. These include the development of modified or new IT systems with the all too familiar budget overruns. The selection or integration of major systems is both complex and expensive; it involves the disposal of legacy systems and it is difficult to manage. Investment costs will be high and the potential savings attractive. Besides IT, external factors can produce unforeseen costs during the merger process; for example, unexpected credit and market losses, such as economic recession, volatile stock markets, the impact of the Asian crisis or the tragic effects of September 11. There are other well-known sources of value destruction in mergers, such as an unrealistic assessment of the opportunities resulting from the merger, clashes between senior executives, a slow integration process, and cultural differences. These are not necessarily destructive; some of them can be handled but not without difficulty. They may delay the benefits but will only destroy value if they cannot be resolved. Even public and bitter hostility between joint chairmen or chairman and chief executive can be resolved and the banks can be successful. Spain's BSCH and BBVA are examples of that.

Looking at increased but often hidden costs, the question remains as to whether value creation through mergers is really possible for banks, and if it is possible, what is the extent of the transformation needed to create such value on a sustainable basis? It is in fact difficult for banking analysts to assess value creation in this sense. A

---

[3] Steven I. Davies, 2000, *Bank Mergers: Lessons for the Future*. Basingstoke: Macmillan, p. ix.

comprehensive statistical analysis of the only hard data—the financial objectives or cost savings—is not possible, partly because of the general difficulties in a highly complex business to correlate certain specific causal factors with aggregate financial results. Indeed even the banks rarely keep a merger P& L for a long enough period to validate any hard analysis.[4] The market tends to value cost savings more highly than potential synergies, or even the aims and objectives of the merger.[5] It would, of course, be wrong to suggest that cost savings are irrelevant or that they are not a major matter of concern to banks considering an acquisition or a merger. The strategic goals banks set themselves play the crucial role.

The emphasis on cost savings almost to the exclusion of everything else fails to account for the context in which such mergers take place; it also overlooks the fact that banks have to respond to the changing circumstances and find ways to develop their business. The pressures on the banking industry can be summed up by looking at the way banks see their own situation: 'Traditional network banks feel under siege . . . Consumers are changing. They are getting more sophisticated, more value-conscious and more demanding. At the same time, new technologies enabled banks to offer new and more sophisticated services, and often for less cost. The problem is that there are more technologies available and they simply add more cost and proliferation of cost'.[6] Geographic expansion and industry pressures, which are leading banks to seek cost savings and scale are driving major mergers in the EU and will drive banks towards pan-European banks. One example is Banca Intesa:

> The changes in the financial services industry greatly impacted on the development and growth of Banca Intesa. The European-wide challenges posed by the internet, the EU push towards consolidation and the highly fragmented market in Italy *forced* Banca Intesa to adopt a specific growth model. This so-called *federal* was based on a bottom-up process of soft integration, without drastic reorganisations and bitter cost-cutting programmes. A large degree of operational autonomy was granted to the banks that joined Intesa. Internal forces amplified the drive to a federal model. Giovanni Bazoli and Carlo Salvatori, (then President and CEO of Intesa, respectively) experimented with a bottom-up, inclusive and consensus-oriented approach aimed at pulling otherwise reluctant small local banks into Intesa's reach, thus successfully managing dozens of friendly acquisitions and considerable growth.
>
> Banca Intesa is the largest bank in Italy with a network of more than 4,000 branches and over 700,000 employees. This success is mainly due to the rapid growth pattern driven by the federal model. However, as the competition increases and financial institutions no longer compete on the national level but on a European or even a global scale, the pressure is being felt from within. Intesa's shareholders are increasingly demanding better financial results and a more efficient firm.
>
> This is forcing the management to abandon the federal strategy in favour of a more effective integration process. The new strategic plan released in May 2000 calls for a fully fledged divisional banking model based on closer customer focus, rather than pampering to traditional shareholders' political interests. The distribution strategy will

---

[4] Steven I. Davies, 2000, *Bank Mergers: Lessons for the Future*. Basingstoke: Macmillan, p. ix.
[5] Richard Barfield, *The Banker*, July 1998, p. 24.
[6] David Rhodes, Do large-scale mergers make sense? *Retail Banker International*, August 1997, p. 8.

move from the traditional branch-based model towards a multi-channel approach with an ambitious €775 million investment plan for e-banking. The integration strategy of Intesa's latest acquisition BCI has also been deeply revised, and now aims at €1 billion of synergies of which about 50% are expected from cost reduction, lay-offs and divestment of physical branches. [7]

This process has made the bank the largest in Italy, but not perhaps in a position to look for cross-border acquisitions in Euroland. A bank's merger strategy may have less to do with cost savings and more to do with preserving and extending its position in the market.

It is clear that many leading bankers would understand and accept Banca Intesa's reasons for embarking on a series of domestic mergers of that kind, from which the bank has emerged as a strong and successful bank. Some have suggested that there are alternative strategies to growth through expansion. Some of the most profitable banks in the world, it is argued, are niche players, specialist banks: 'Utilisation rates, price, quality, customer focus and cross-selling must keep up to maintain throughput and profit margin as size increases. Otherwise the scale-related average cost reductions do not translate into profitability'.[8] In addition such large and diverse banks pose immense management challenges; many may feel called to the task, but few can fulfil it. The huge universal banks should dissolve into private banking, asset management, corporate banking and retail financial services as separate entities. Not only is recent history against such a development—niche players tend to be snapped up and become part of financial conglomerates—but existing, dominating players are unlikely to divest themselves of those aspects of a bank's operations which enable them to provide the full range of services and products to their existing clients as part of their means of retaining clients. Leading bankers do stress costs, but the costs are of quite a different kind. They are the costs of acquiring new clients. Several bankers pointed out that 'the cost of acquiring new clients is far too high'.

The purpose of acquiring a bank is to acquire a customer base at what bankers clearly regard is a much lower price than the painful and expensive work of acquiring clients by differentiating what the bank offers on the basis of the quality of service, competitive prices, the range of products and the effectiveness of advertising. Another banker claimed that 'it is impossible to bridge the gap between the cost of acquiring new clients and the return on equity. . . . The aim of merger and acquisition activity in the retail sector is to obtain a broader profit base, preferably one where synergies are possible'. Another banker pointed out that 'you cannot create growth through cost savings—saving another 10% is nothing. You have to work on the growth factor, and to achieve the nature of the company and build a strong company with the aim of improving the return on equity'.

The objective of growth may not always be achieved. One banker, whose bank has been through many mergers in his own country and in other countries, admitted that

---

[7] Bert Flier et al., 2001, The changing landscape of the European financial services sector. *Long Range Planning*, vol. 34, p. 181.
[8] H. Langohr, European banking: biggest is not best in Euroland. *The Banker*, January 1998, p. 26.

one of the domestic mergers had led to 'a decrease in market share after the merger'. The loss was, however, a temporary one, and in the longer term, the 'experience has been good, and we are very satisfied with it'. A further merger was 'a complicated operation, but it is working very well. The integration of the IT systems is completed, also without a loss of market share. We have been able to incorporate new people with new skills. The people who planned the merger have had a lot of experience in planning mergers, and almost all the strategic decisions were made at the right time. We have cut costs and improved efficiency, as well as seeing an increase in profits with two years of experience in the merged bank. We are poised for further growth and will play a major role in any pan-European expansion'. Another banker described his domestic merger as being 'powerful and effective, leading to substantial cost savings'.

One banker defined his 'goal' as becoming a 'leading European player'. Most bankers would agree that 'you cannot envisage being a significant player in the European market unless you have a strong position in the domestic market'. That is part of the reason for the claim that size matters. It matters in a variety of ways. For one banker, 'If you want to remain independent, you have to become a larger bank'. For another, 'Acquiring another bank is the cheapest way to acquire customers . . . [and] it is the only way you can get enough investment in technology. . . . It is possible to improve the cost base and expand through acquisition, and that is what we intend to do'. There was one dissenter, who entirely rejected what he considered to be an obsession with size: 'Size is neither a concern, nor is it relevant. In the retail market, it has never been demonstrated that this is a key factor for success'. But his bank, although it is efficient and successful, is constantly regarded as a takeover target.

Will They Merge Across Borders?

Asked to speculate about cross-border mergers, most bankers were hesitant to agree that pan-European banks would emerge. One rejected such a possibility outright, saying 'We don't need and don't want a large universal bank in another country'. The reasons offered were themselves interesting. One saw the possibility as essentially 'a political question. If it concerns France or Italy, the central bank or the government or both must agree'.

Other bankers argued that cross-border mergers were unlikely to occur, citing 'cultural and legal obstacles'. It is, however, difficult to see why these constitute obstacles to many of the leading banks in seeking to merge with another bank in another member state. Some of the leading banks are global banks and almost all have successfully merged with banks outside the EU. Some of the Italian banks have acquired banks in Central and Eastern Europe; the two leading Spanish banks have made extensive acquisitions throughout Latin America; the Nordic banks have acquired banks in the Baltic states and one, SEB, has acquired a German bank. Nordea has grown rapidly through acquisitions in the four Nordic countries and established itself as a well-managed, innovative bank. The Dutch banks are already global players, as are the leading UK banks. Clearly all the banks involved in such mergers and acquisitions had to overcome legal and cultural hurdles, and obviously decided that it was a worthwhile part of their strategy. Indeed such acquisitions are sometimes part of a longer-term strategy, that is, to provide a strong enough launching pad for acquisitions in Euroland. Such considerations may have led one banker to dismiss all the alleged obstacles in trenchant terms: 'There is no obstacle at all, either cultural or legal or in terms of staff, management or the shareholders. All that is needed is that you get it right. There are no legal obstacles to mergers in other sectors, so why should banking be any different?'

Other bankers sought to emphasise the extent to which retail banking is essentially domestic. In France one said, 'Retail banking will remain a domestic concern for the next five years or so. . . . Retail banking is a matter of local loyalties, of allegiance to the local bank'. Bankers refer to the 'stickiness of the relationship to the name you know'. Banks themselves are 'preoccupied with domestic issues'. Some bankers have begun to consider the issue of branding and the ways in which branding could be developed so that the 'domestic' or 'local' aspects of the bank could be maintained. One banker claimed that it would be possible to establish a single brand name. Indeed this bank is in the process of creating 'a global brand for some 60 million customers worldwide'.

Two other banks are looking at the approach adopted by the automobile industry and its sophisticated approach to branding. Perhaps the first point to notice is that customers are already familiar with global brands and trust them when it comes to purchasing a car. Banks would of course argue that the selection of a bank is much more important, that it has to be a relationship of trust, and that the relationship lasts much longer, possibly for the whole of an individual's adult life. It is indeed a relationship of trust, yet it is possible for banks to merge or for a bank to acquire another bank, but retain the brand and ensure that it still reflects the customer's approach to banking. The overall brand may remain, but the bank may select specific brand names within the overall brand or image of the bank, and each name would be designed to appeal to a particular range of customers. Nordea has just adopted a single brand for the whole of the Nordic region and has indeed changed its name more than once as the process of mergers and acquisitions has taken place over the past four years. All of this suggests that bankers are too concerned about the alleged domestic character of banking in an increasingly global world, and especially in Euroland, now their customers have euro notes and coins. What bankers should realise perhaps is the speed with which people abandoned their legacy currency and adopted the euro. That could be the real lesson for bankers. One or two bankers have bravely declared their intentions to seek a cross-border merger. ABN-AMRO has withdrawn entirely from 10 countries in a move which would release about €1 billion in capital and is looking for a substantial acquisition in European consumer banking. Having 'conquered' Latin America, both BSCH and BBVA have been eying up the rest of Europe with a view to reducing their risk exposure there. Central banks will eventually abandon their resistance to cross-border mergers, both banks believe. BBVA predicts 'the first cross-border merger will be friendly' but has not yet embarked on the process.

Bankers present a picture of themselves, shivering by the edge of a pool, waiting for one to plunge into the cold water and then they will follow. One banker summed it up like this: 'It will take one high-profile cross-border merger, and whether it is successful or not, others will follow. The number of large banks which could undertake such a merger or an acquisition is limited, so no one will want to be left out. Like sheep over the dam, once one merges, the others will follow'.

But who will jump first?

Appendix

Commerzbank

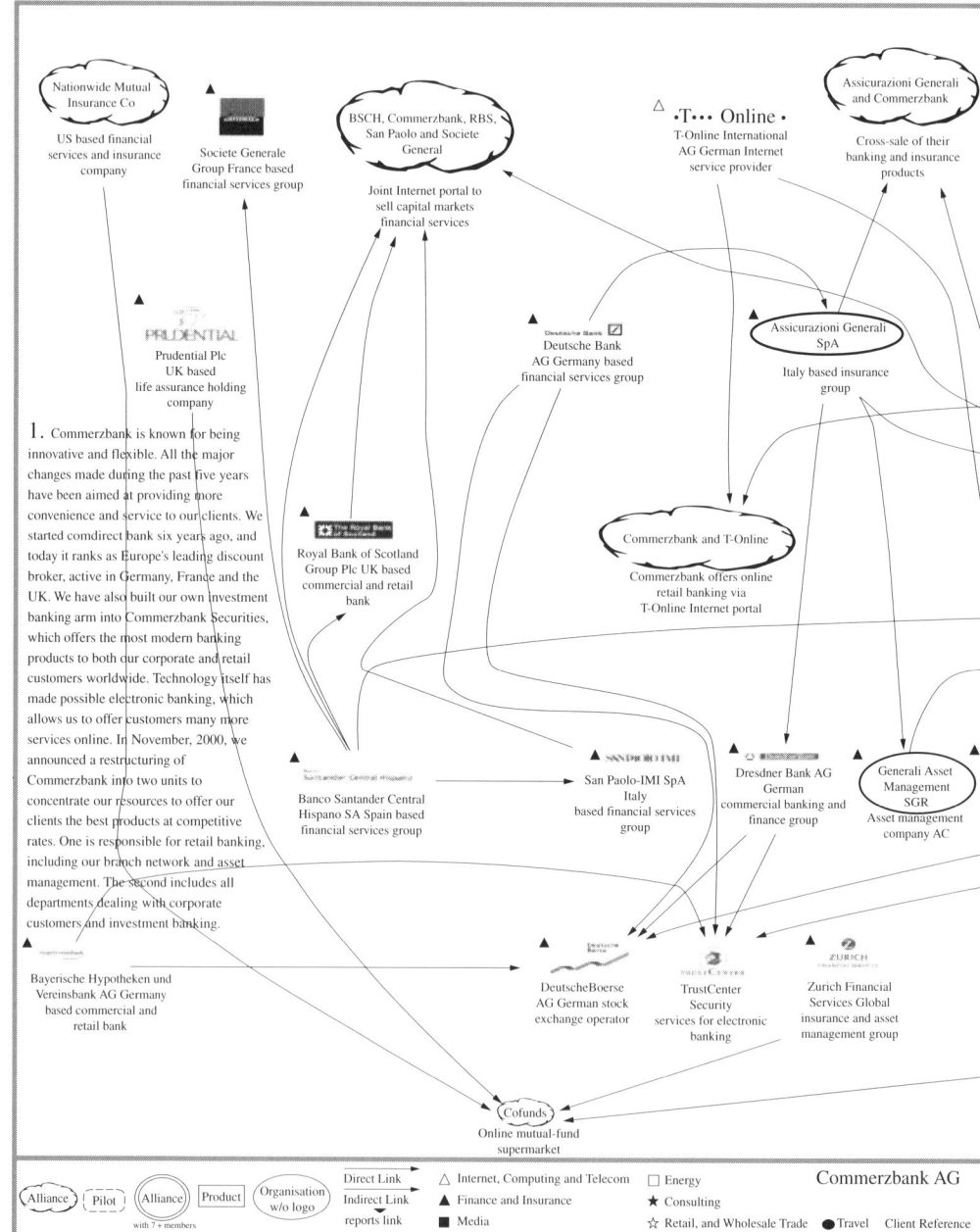

Nationwide Mutual Insurance Co

US based financial services and insurance company

Societe Generale Group France based financial services group

BSCH, Commerzbank, RBS, San Paolo and Societe General

Joint Internet portal to sell capital markets financial services

△ ·T··· Online ·
T-Online International AG German Internet service provider

Assicurazioni Generali and Commerzbank

Cross-sale of their banking and insurance products

PRUDENTIAL
Prudential Plc UK based life assurance holding company

Deutsche Bank AG Germany based financial services group

Assicurazioni Generali SpA

Italy based insurance group

1. Commerzbank is known for being innovative and flexible. All the major changes made during the past five years have been aimed at providing more convenience and service to our clients. We started comdirect bank six years ago, and today it ranks as Europe's leading discount broker, active in Germany, France and the UK. We have also built our own investment banking arm into Commerzbank Securities, which offers the most modern banking products to both our corporate and retail customers worldwide. Technology itself has made possible electronic banking, which allows us to offer customers many more services online. In November, 2000, we announced a restructuring of Commerzbank into two units to concentrate our resources to offer our clients the best products at competitive rates. One is responsible for retail banking, including our branch network and asset management. The second includes all departments dealing with corporate customers and investment banking.

The Royal Bank of Scotland
Royal Bank of Scotland Group Plc UK based commercial and retail bank

Commerzbank and T-Online
Commerzbank offers online retail banking via T-Online Internet portal

Banco Santander Central Hispano SA Spain based financial services group

San Paolo-IMI SpA Italy based financial services group

Dresdner Bank AG German commercial banking and finance group

Generali Asset Management SGR
Asset management company AC

Bayerische Hypotheken und Vereinsbank AG Germany based commercial and retail bank

DeutscheBoerse AG German stock exchange operator

TrustCenter Security services for electronic banking

ZURICH
Zurich Financial Services Global insurance and asset management group

Cofunds
Online mutual-fund supermarket

Alliance | Pilot | Alliance | Product | Organisation w/o logo
with 7 + members

Direct Link
Indirect Link
reports link

△ Internet, Computing and Telecom
▲ Finance and Insurance
■ Media

☐ Energy
★ Consulting
☆ Retail, and Wholesale Trade

Commerzbank AG

● Travel   Client Reference

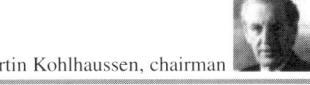

Martin Kohlhaussen, chairman

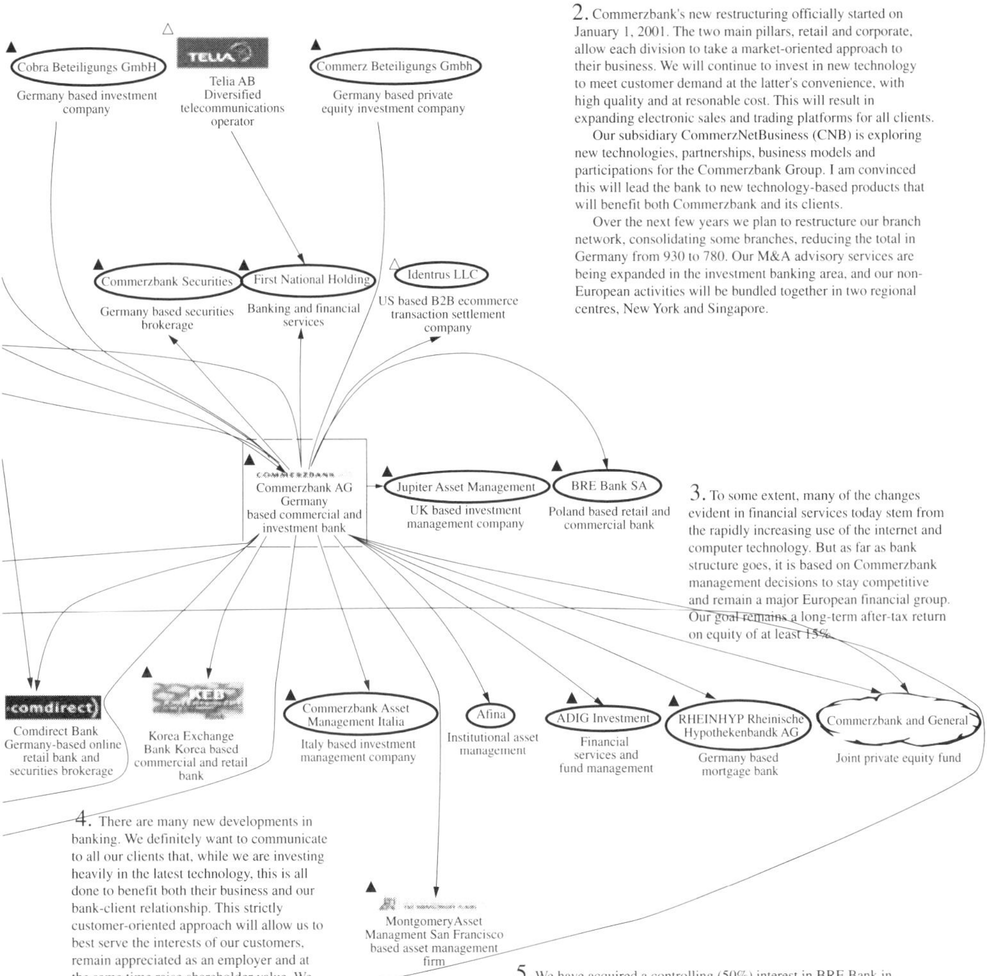

Cobra Beteiligungs GmbH

Germany based investment company

TELIA

Telia AB
Diversified telecommunications operator

Commerz Beteiligungs Gmbh

Germany based private equity investment company

Commerzbank Securities

Germany based securities brokerage

First National Holding

Banking and financial services

Identrus LLC

US based B2B ecommerce transaction settlement company

COMMERZBANK
Commerzbank AG
Germany based commercial and investment bank

Jupiter Asset Management

UK based investment management company

BRE Bank SA

Poland based retail and commercial bank

comdirect

Comdirect Bank
Germany-based online retail bank and securities brokerage

KEB

Korea Exchange Bank Korea based commercial and retail bank

Commerzbank Asset Management Italia

Italy based investment management company

Afina

Institutional asset management

ADIG Investment

Financial services and fund management

RHEINHYP Rheinische Hypothekenbandk AG

Germany based mortgage bank

Commerzbank and General

Joint private equity fund

MontgomeryAsset Managment San Francisco based asset management firm

2. Commerzbank's new restructuring officially started on January 1, 2001. The two main pillars, retail and corporate, allow each division to take a market-oriented approach to their business. We will continue to invest in new technology to meet customer demand at the latter's convenience, with high quality and at resonable cost. This will result in expanding electronic sales and trading platforms for all clients.

Our subsidiary CommerzNetBusiness (CNB) is exploring new technologies, partnerships, business models and participations for the Commerzbank Group. I am convinced this will lead the bank to new technology-based products that will benefit both Commerzbank and its clients.

Over the next few years we plan to restructure our branch network, consolidating some branches, reducing the total in Germany from 930 to 780. Our M&A advisory services are being expanded in the investment banking area, and our non-European activities will be bundled together in two regional centres, New York and Singapore.

3. To some extent, many of the changes evident in financial services today stem from the rapidly increasing use of the internet and computer technology. But as far as bank structure goes, it is based on Commerzbank management decisions to stay competitive and remain a major European financial group. Our goal remains a long-term after-tax return on equity of at least 15%.

4. There are many new developments in banking. We definitely want to communicate to all our clients that, while we are investing heavily in the latest technology, this is all done to benefit both their business and our bank-client relationship. This strictly customer-oriented approach will allow us to best serve the interests of our customers, remain appreciated as an employer and at the same time raise shareholder value. We need investors and clients to understand that new technologies can benefit them by making banking more convenient.

5. We have acquired a controlling (50%) interest in BRE Bank in Warsaw, plus we have purchased Jupiter Asset Management in London and Montgomery Asset Management in San Francisco during the past several years with no surprises in their structure. We prefer to give each unit's management a high degree of autonomy. These have all been good investments and we are planning with them for future expansion.

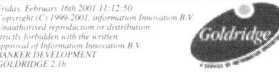

Credit Suisse Group

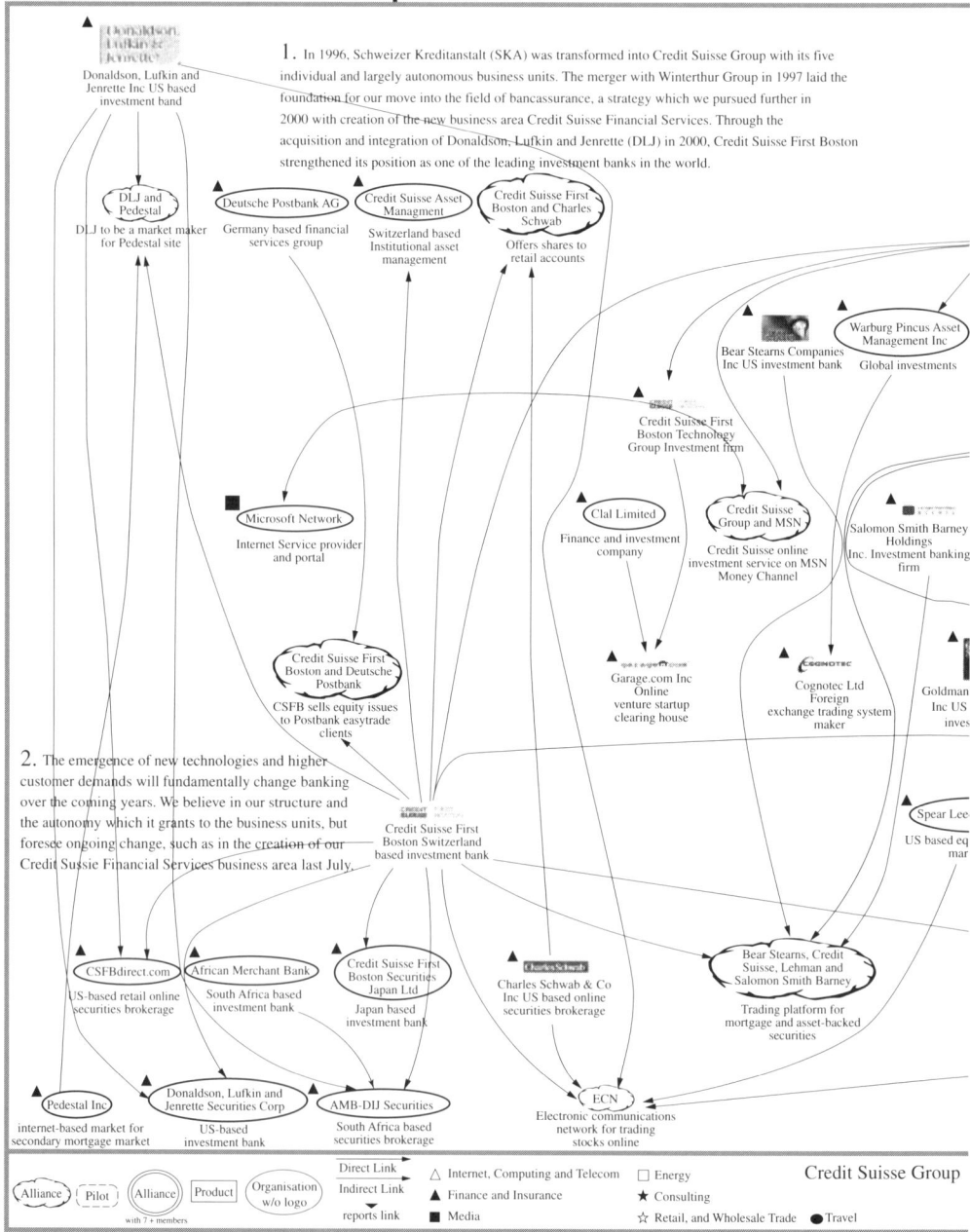

1. In 1996, Schweizer Kreditanstalt (SKA) was transformed into Credit Suisse Group with its five individual and largely autonomous business units. The merger with Winterthur Group in 1997 laid the foundation for our move into the field of bancassurance, a strategy which we pursued further in 2000 with creation of the new business area Credit Suisse Financial Services. Through the acquisition and integration of Donaldson, Lufkin and Jenrette (DLJ) in 2000, Credit Suisse First Boston strengthened its position as one of the leading investment banks in the world.

Donaldson, Lufkin and Jenrette Inc US based investment band

DLJ and Pedestal
DLJ to be a market maker for Pedestal site

Deutsche Postbank AG
Germany based financial services group

Credit Suisse Asset Managment
Switzerland based Institutional asset management

Credit Suisse First Boston and Charles Schwab
Offers shares to retail accounts

Bear Stearns Companies Inc US investment bank

Warburg Pincus Asset Management Inc
Global investments

Credit Suisse First Boston Technology Group Investment firm

Microsoft Network
Internet Service provider and portal

Clal Limited
Finance and investment company

Credit Suisse Group and MSN
Credit Suisse online investment service on MSN Money Channel

Salomon Smith Barney Holdings Inc. Investment banking firm

Credit Suisse First Boston and Deutsche Postbank
CSFB sells equity issues to Postbank easytrade clients

Garage.com Inc
Online venture startup clearing house

Cognotec Ltd
Foreign exchange trading system maker

Goldman Inc US inves

2. The emergence of new technologies and higher customer demands will fundamentally change banking over the coming years. We believe in our structure and the autonomy which it grants to the business units, but foresee ongoing change, such as in the creation of our Credit Sussie Financial Services business area last July.

Credit Suisse First Boston Switzerland based investment bank

Spear Lee
US based eq mar

CSFBdirect.com
US-based retail online securities brokerage

African Merchant Bank
South Africa based investment bank

Credit Suisse First Boston Securities Japan Ltd
Japan based investment bank

Charles Schwab & Co Inc US based online securities brokerage

Bear Stearns, Credit Suisse, Lehman and Salomon Smith Barney
Trading platform for mortgage and asset-backed securities

Pedestal Inc
internet-based market for secondary mortgage market

Donaldson, Lufkin and Jenrette Securities Corp
US-based investment bank

AMB-DIJ Securities
South Africa based securities brokerage

ECN
Electronic communications network for trading stocks online

Alliance	Pilot	Alliance
Product	Organisation w/o logo	
with 7 + members		

Direct Link
Indirect Link
reports link

△ Internet, Computing and Telecom
▲ Finance and Insurance
■ Media

☐ Energy
★ Consulting
☆ Retail, and Wholesale Trade

Credit Suisse Group

● Travel

Philip Ryan, CFO

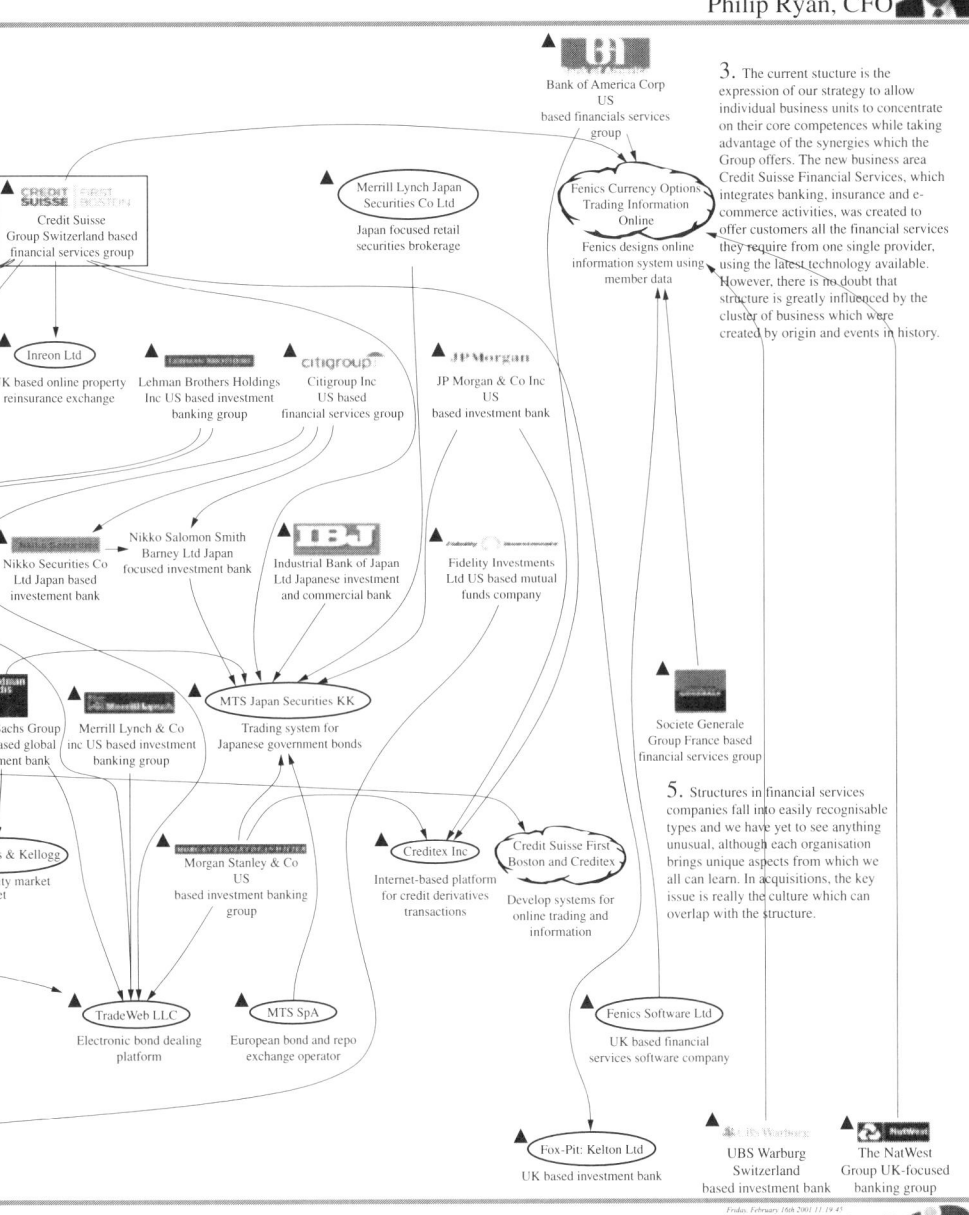

3. The current stucture is the expression of our strategy to allow individual business units to concentrate on their core competences while taking advantage of the synergies which the Group offers. The new business area Credit Suisse Financial Services, which integrates banking, insurance and e-commerce activities, was created to offer customers all the financial services they require from one single provider, using the latest technology available. However, there is no doubt that structure is greatly influenced by the cluster of business which were created by origin and events in history.

5. Structures in financial services companies fall into easily recognisable types and we have yet to see anything unusual, although each organisation brings unique aspects from which we all can learn. In acquisitions, the key issue is really the culture which can overlap with the structure.

Bank of America Corp US based financials services group

Merrill Lynch Japan Securities Co Ltd
Japan focused retail securities brokerage

Fenics Currency Options Trading Information Online
Fenics designs online information system using member data

Credit Suisse Group Switzerland based financial services group

Inreon Ltd
UK based online property reinsurance exchange

Lehman Brothers Holdings Inc US based investment banking group

Citigroup Inc US based financial services group

JP Morgan & Co Inc US based investment bank

Nikko Securities Co Ltd Japan based investement bank

Nikko Salomon Smith Barney Ltd Japan focused investment bank

Industrial Bank of Japan Ltd Japanese investment and commercial bank

Fidelity Investments Ltd US based mutual funds company

Societe Generale Group France based financial services group

Sachs Group based global stment bank

Merrill Lynch & Co inc US based investment banking group

MTS Japan Securities KK
Trading system for Japanese government bonds

ds & Kellogg uity market ket

Morgan Stanley & Co US based investment banking group

Creditex Inc
Internet-based platform for credit derivatives transactions

Credit Suisse First Boston and Creditex
Develop systems for online trading and information

TradeWeb LLC
Electronic bond dealing platform

MTS SpA
European bond and repo exchange operator

Fenics Software Ltd
UK based financial services software company

Fox-Pit: Kelton Ltd
UK based investment bank

UBS Warburg Switzerland based investment bank

The NatWest Group UK-focused banking group

UBS

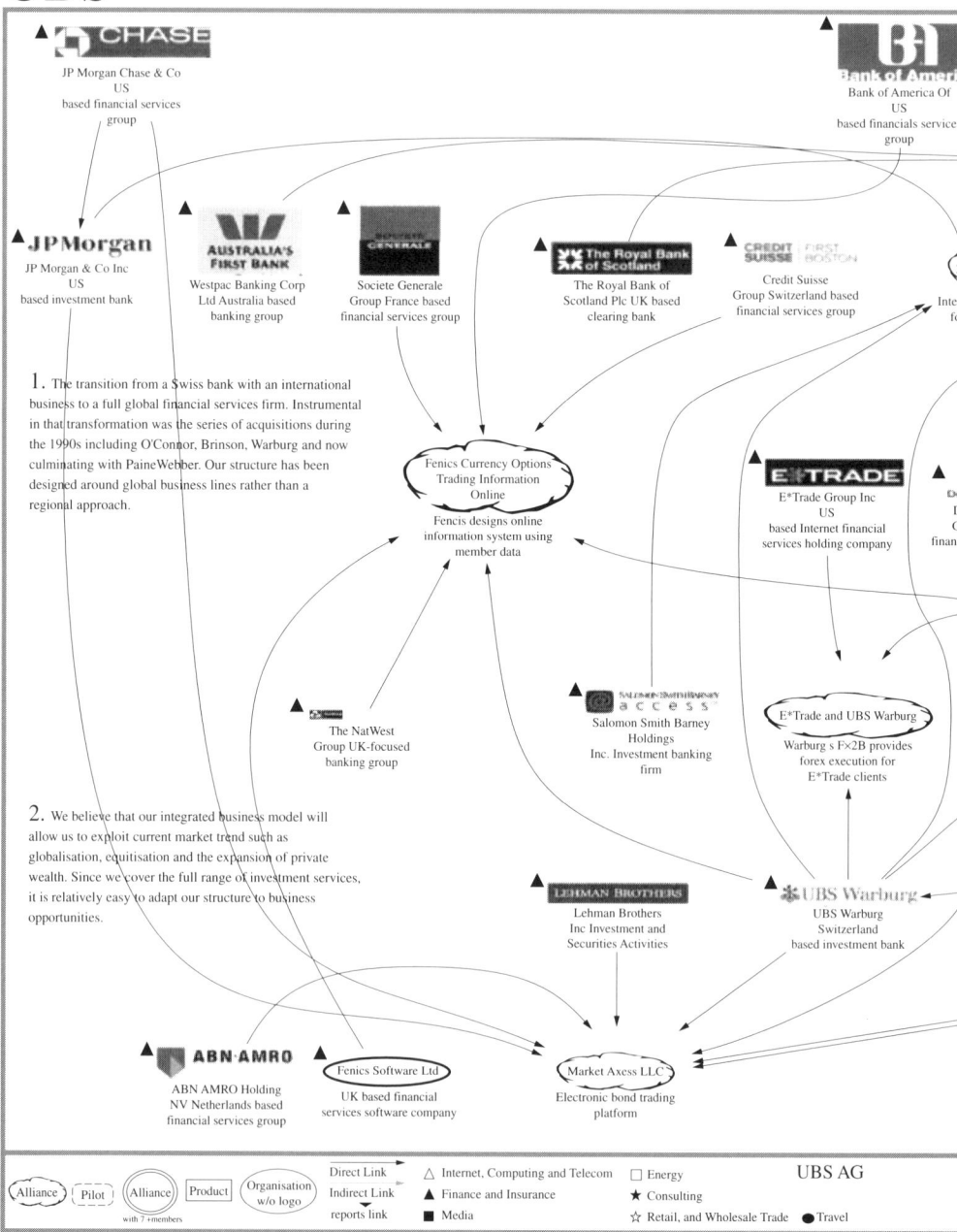

1. The transition from a Swiss bank with an international business to a full global financial services firm. Instrumental in that transformation was the series of acquisitions during the 1990s including O'Connor, Brinson, Warburg and now culminating with PaineWebber. Our structure has been designed around global business lines rather than a regional approach.

2. We believe that our integrated business model will allow us to exploit current market trend such as globalisation, equitisation and the expansion of private wealth. Since we cover the full range of investment services, it is relatively easy to adapt our structure to business opportunities.

Marcel Ospel, group chief executive

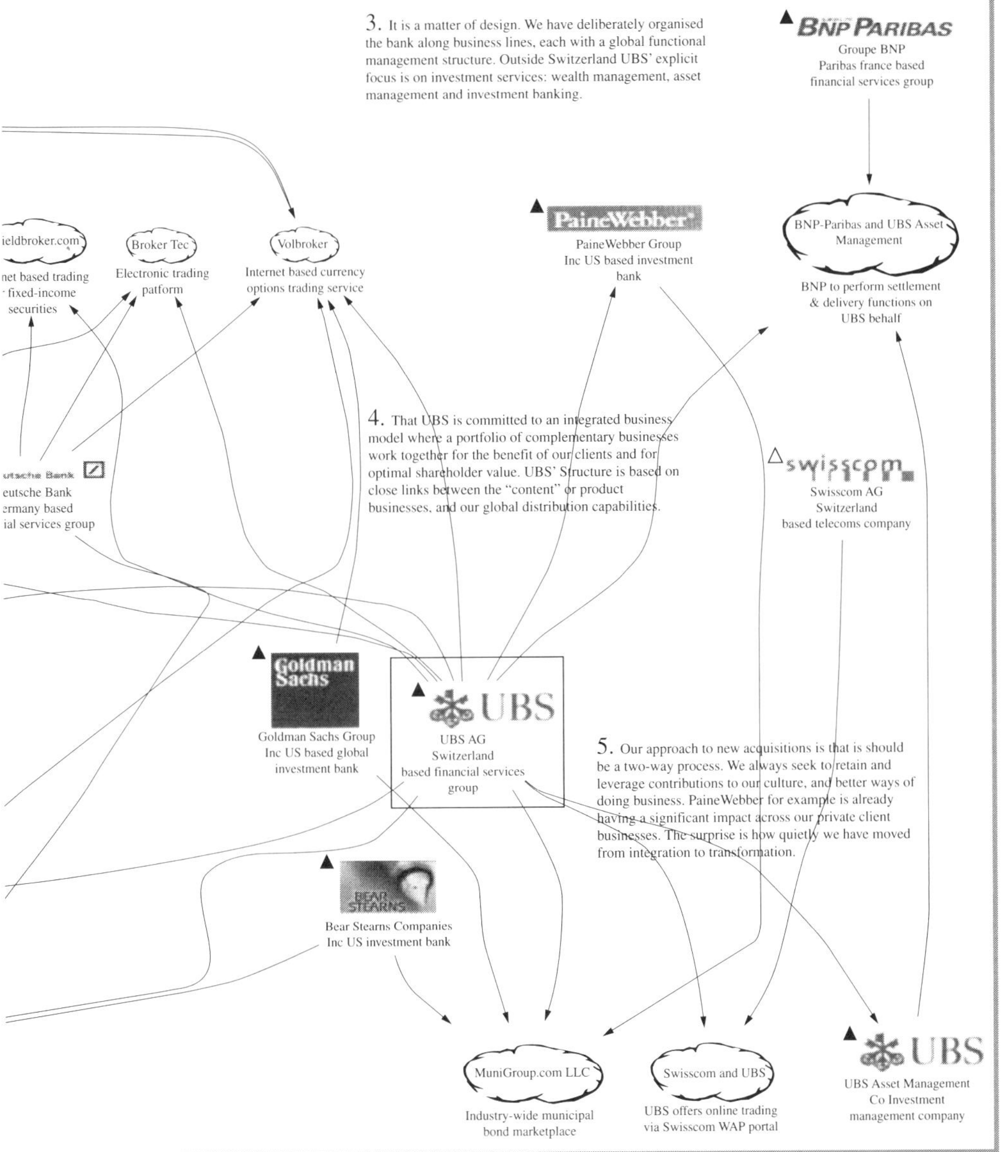

3. It is a matter of design. We have deliberately organised the bank along business lines, each with a global functional management structure. Outside Switzerland UBS' explicit focus is on investment services: wealth management, asset management and investment banking.

BNP PARIBAS

Groupe BNP
Paribas france based
financial services group

ieldbroker.com

net based trading
· fixed-income
securities

Broker Tec

Electronic trading
patform

Volbroker

Internet based currency
options trading service

PaineWebber

PaineWebber Group
Inc US based investment
bank

BNP-Paribas and UBS Asset
Management

BNP to perform settlement
& delivery functions on
UBS behalf

4. That UBS is committed to an integrated business model where a portfolio of complementary businesses work together for the benefit of our clients and for optimal shareholder value. UBS' Structure is based on close links between the "content" or product businesses, and our global distribution capabilities.

△swisscom

Swisscom AG
Switzerland
based telecoms company

utsche Bank

eutsche Bank
ermany based
ial services group

Goldman Sachs

Goldman Sachs Group
Inc US based global
investment bank

⚜ UBS

UBS AG
Switzerland
based financial services
group

5. Our approach to new acquisitions is that is should be a two-way process. We always seek to retain and leverage contributions to our culture, and better ways of doing business. PaineWebber for example is already having a significant impact across our private client businesses. The surprise is how quietly we have moved from integration to transformation.

BEAR STEARNS

Bear Stearns Companies
Inc US investment bank

MuniGroup.com LLC

Industry-wide municipal
bond marketplace

Swisscom and UBS

UBS offers online trading
via Swisscom WAP portal

⚜ UBS

UBS Asset Management
Co Investment
management company

Fortis

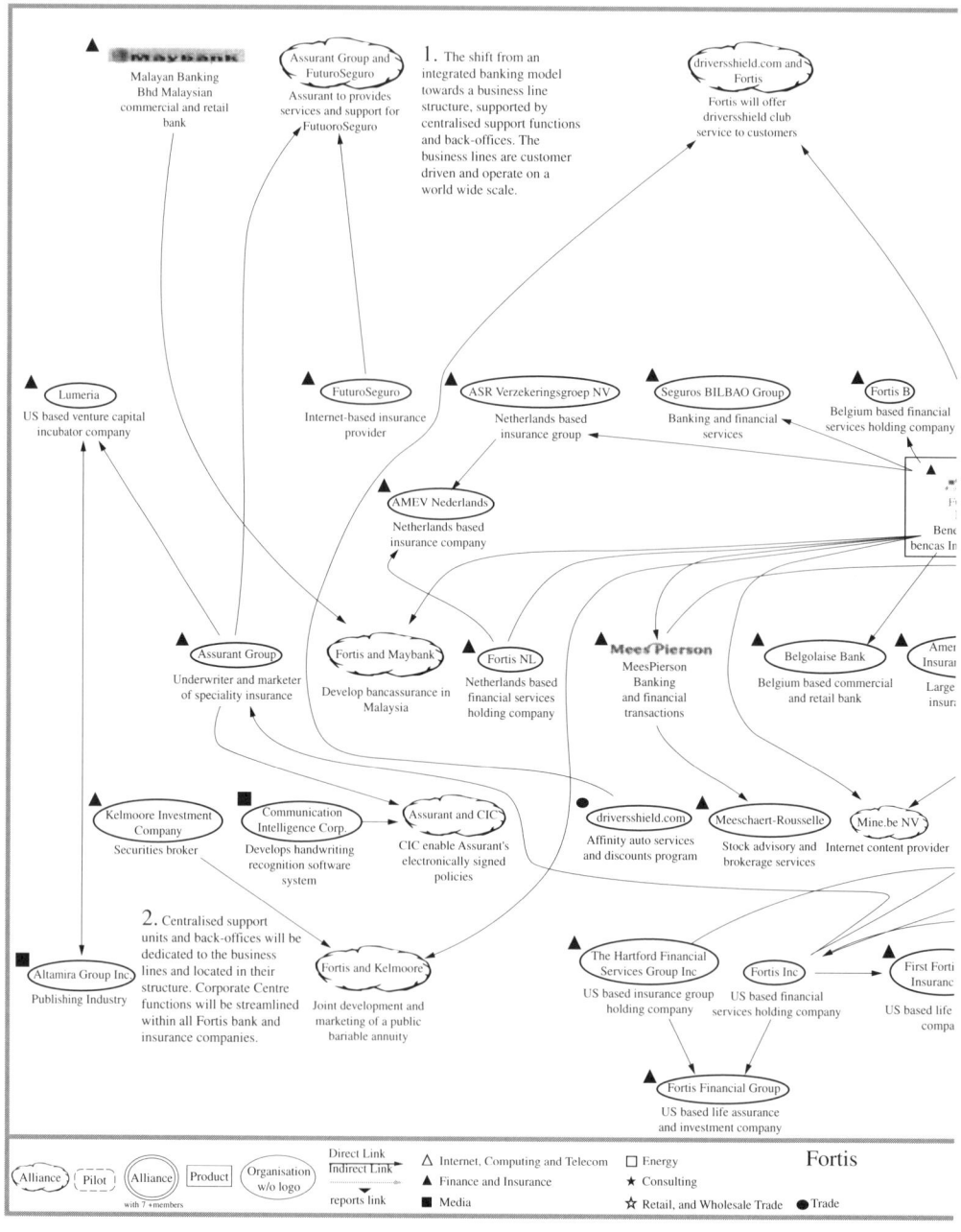

1. The shift from an integrated banking model towards a business line structure, supported by centralised support functions and back-offices. The business lines are customer driven and operate on a world wide scale.

Maybank — Malayan Banking Bhd Malaysian commercial and retail bank

Assurant Group and FuturoSeguro — Assurant to provides services and support for FutuoroSeguro

driversshield.com and Fortis — Fortis will offer driversshield club service to customers

Lumeria — US based venture capital incubator company

FuturoSeguro — Internet-based insurance provider

ASR Verzekeringsgroep NV — Netherlands based insurance group

Seguros BILBAO Group — Banking and financial services

Fortis B — Belgium based financial services holding company

AMEV Nederlands — Netherlands based insurance company

Assurant Group — Underwriter and marketer of speciality insurance

Fortis and Maybank — Develop bancassurance in Malaysia

Fortis NL — Netherlands based financial services holding company

MeesPierson — MeesPierson Banking and financial transactions

Belgolaise Bank — Belgium based commercial and retail bank

Kelmoore Investment Company — Securities broker

Communication Intelligence Corp. — Develops handwriting recognition software system

Assurant and CIC — CIC enable Assurant's electronically signed policies

driversshield.com — Affinity auto services and discounts program

Meeschaert-Rousselle — Stock advisory and brokerage services

Mine.be NV — Internet content provider

2. Centralised support units and back-offices will be dedicated to the business lines and located in their structure. Corporate Centre functions will be streamlined within all Fortis bank and insurance companies.

Altamira Group Inc — Publishing Industry

Fortis and Kelmoore — Joint development and marketing of a public bariable annuity

The Hartford Financial Services Group Inc — US based insurance group holding company

Fortis Inc — US based financial services holding company

First Forti Insuranc — US based life compa

Fortis Financial Group — US based life assurance and investment company

Alliance | Pilot | Alliance (with 7 + members) | Product | Organisation w/o logo

Direct Link
Indirect Link
reports link

△ Internet, Computing and Telecom
▲ Finance and Insurance
■ Media

□ Energy
★ Consulting
☆ Retail, and Wholesale Trade

● Trade

Fortis

Herman Verwilst, deputy CEO

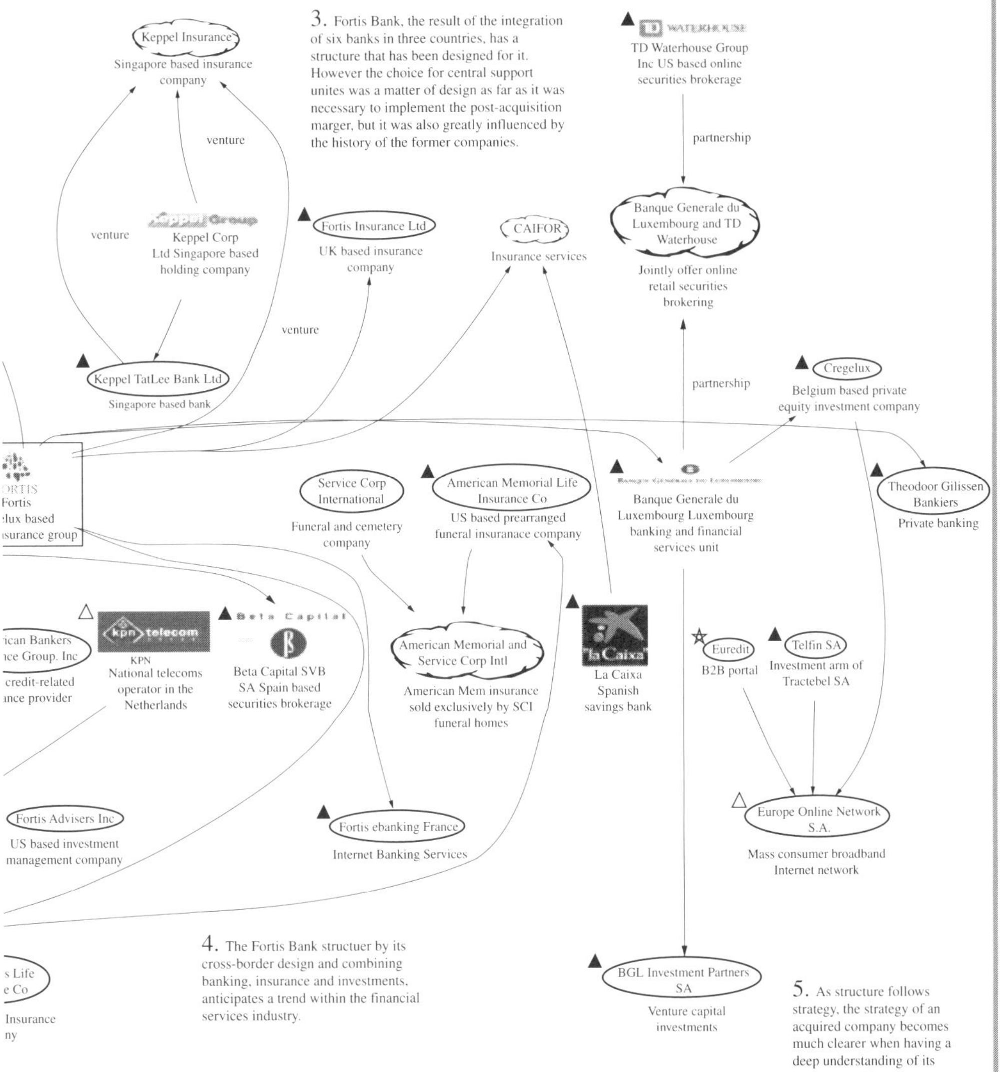

Keppel Insurance
Singapore based insurance company

venture

3. Fortis Bank, the result of the integration of six banks in three countries, has a structure that has been designed for it. However the choice for central support unites was a matter of design as far as it was necessary to implement the post-acquisition marger, but it was also greatly influenced by the history of the former companies.

TD WATERHOUSE
TD Waterhouse Group Inc US based online securities brokerage

partnership

Keppel Group
Keppel Corp Ltd Singapore based holding company

venture

venture

Fortis Insurance Ltd
UK based insurance company

CAIFOR
Insurance services

Banque Generale du Luxembourg and TD Waterhouse
Jointly offer online retail securities brokering

venture

Keppel TatLee Bank Ltd
Singapore based bank

partnership

Cregelux
Belgium based private equity investment company

FORTIS
Fortis
lux based
insurance group

Service Corp International
Funeral and cemetery company

American Memorial Life Insurance Co
US based prearranged funeral insuranace company

Banque Generale de Luxembourg

Banque Generale du Luxembourg Luxembourg banking and financial services unit

Theodoor Gilissen Bankiers
Private banking

ican Bankers
ice Group. Inc
credit-related
nce provider

KPN
KPN National telecoms operator in the Netherlands

Beta Capital
Beta Capital SVB SA Spain based securities brokerage

American Memorial and Service Corp Intl
American Mem insurance sold exclusively by SCI funeral homes

La Caixa
La Caixa Spanish savings bank

Euredit
B2B portal

Telfin SA
Investment arm of Tractebel SA

Fortis Advisers Inc
US based investment management company

Fortis ebanking France
Internet Banking Services

Europe Online Network S.A.
Mass consumer broadband Internet network

s Life
e Co
Insurance
ny

4. The Fortis Bank structuer by its cross-border design and combining banking, insurance and investments, anticipates a trend within the financial services industry.

BGL Investment Partners SA
Venture capital investments

5. As structure follows strategy, the strategy of an acquired company becomes much clearer when having a deep understanding of its structure and its governance.

ING Group

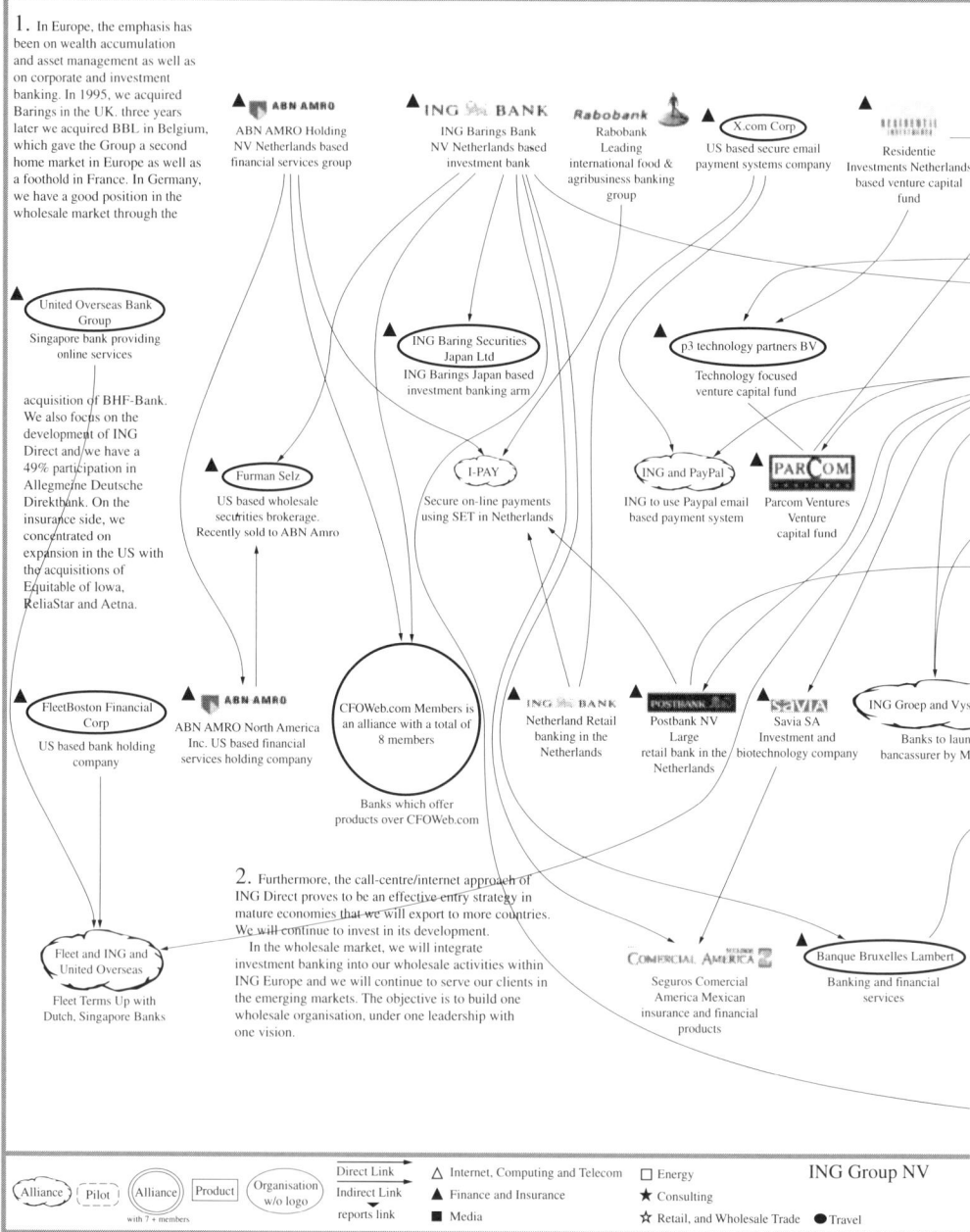

1. In Europe, the emphasis has been on wealth accumulation and asset management as well as on corporate and investment banking. In 1995, we acquired Barings in the UK. three years later we acquired BBL in Belgium, which gave the Group a second home market in Europe as well as a foothold in France. In Germany, we have a good position in the wholesale market through the

acquisition of BHF-Bank. We also focus on the development of ING Direct and we have a 49% participation in Allgemeine Deutsche Direktbank. On the insurance side, we concentrated on expansion in the US with the acquisitions of Equitable of Iowa, ReliaStar and Aetna.

ABN AMRO
ABN AMRO Holding NV Netherlands based financial services group

ING BANK
ING Barings Bank NV Netherlands based investment bank

Rabobank
Leading international food & agribusiness banking group

X.com Corp
US based secure email payment systems company

Residentie Investments Netherlands based venture capital fund

United Overseas Bank Group
Singapore bank providing online services

ING Baring Securities Japan Ltd
ING Barings Japan based investment banking arm

p3 technology partners BV
Technology focused venture capital fund

Furman Selz
US based wholesale securities brokerage. Recently sold to ABN Amro

I-PAY
Secure on-line payments using SET in Netherlands

ING and PayPal
ING to use Paypal email based payment system

PARCOM
Parcom Ventures Venture capital fund

FleetBoston Financial Corp
US based bank holding company

ABN AMRO North America Inc. US based financial services holding company

CFOWeb.com Members is an alliance with a total of 8 members

Banks which offer products over CFOWeb.com

ING BANK
Netherland Retail banking in the Netherlands

POSTBANK
Postbank NV Large retail bank in the Netherlands

SAVIA
Savia SA Investment and biotechnology company

ING Groep and Vys
Banks to laun bancassurer by M

2. Furthermore, the call-centre/internet approach of ING Direct proves to be an effective entry strategy in mature economies that we will export to more countries. We will continue to invest in its development.
In the wholesale market, we will integrate investment banking into our wholesale activities within ING Europe and we will continue to serve our clients in the emerging markets. The objective is to build one wholesale organisation, under one leadership with one vision.

Fleet and ING and United Overseas
Fleet Terms Up with Dutch, Singapore Banks

COMERCIAL AMERICA
Seguros Comercial America Mexican insurance and financial products

Banque Bruxelles Lambert
Banking and financial services

Michel Tilmant, group deputy chairman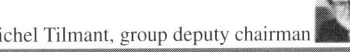

3. Our structure is carefully designed according to the principle: structure follows strategy. Since its creation, ING has regularly adapted its structure to match the requirements of its clients in insurance, banking and asset management, as well as to create cohesion along geographical lines, i.e. Europe, the Americas and Asia/Pacific.

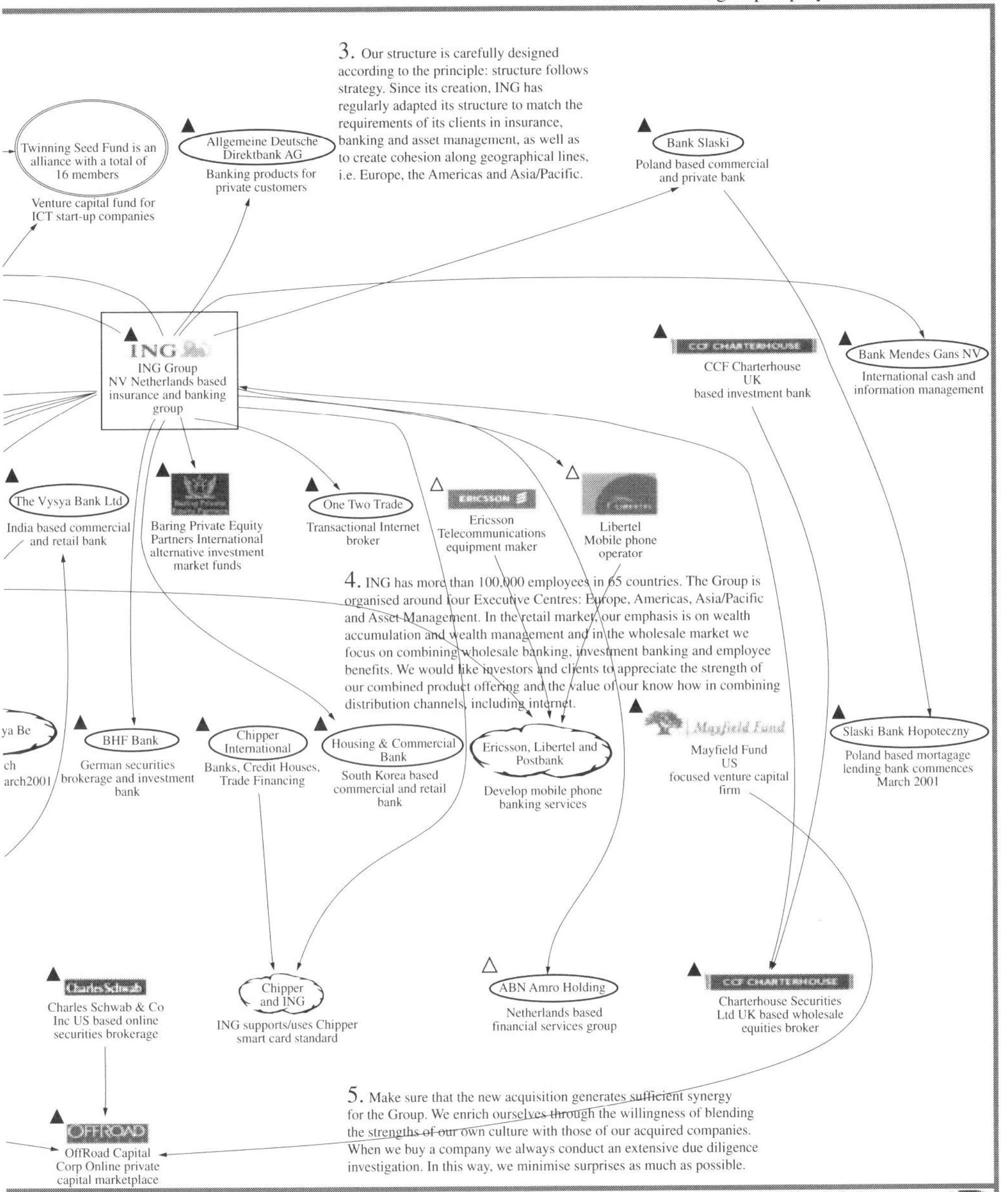

Twinning Seed Fund is an alliance with a total of 16 members

Venture capital fund for ICT start-up companies

Allgemeine Deutsche Direktbank AG

Banking products for private customers

Bank Slaski

Poland based commercial and private bank

ING

ING Group
NV Netherlands based insurance and banking group

CCF CHARTERHOUSE

CCF Charterhouse UK based investment bank

Bank Mendes Gans NV

International cash and information management

The Vysya Bank Ltd

India based commercial and retail bank

Baring Private Equity Partners International alternative investment market funds

One Two Trade

Transactional Internet broker

ERICSSON

Ericsson Telecommunications equipment maker

Libertel

Libertel Mobile phone operator

4. ING has more than 100,000 employees in 65 countries. The Group is organised around four Executive Centres: Europe, Americas, Asia/Pacific and Asset Management. In the retail market our emphasis is on wealth accumulation and wealth management and in the wholesale market we focus on combining wholesale banking, investment banking and employee benefits. We would like investors and clients to appreciate the strength of our combined product offering and the value of our know how in combining distribution channels, including internet.

ya Be

ch
arch2001

BHF Bank

German securities brokerage and investment bank

Chipper International

Banks, Credit Houses, Trade Financing

Housing & Commercial Bank

South Korea based commercial and retail bank

Ericsson, Libertel and Postbank

Develop mobile phone banking services

Maxfield Fund

Mayfield Fund US focused venture capital firm

Slaski Bank Hipoteczny

Poland based mortgage lending bank commences March 2001

Charles Schwab

Charles Schwab & Co Inc US based online securities brokerage

Chipper and ING

ING supports/uses Chipper smart card standard

ABN Amro Holding

Netherlands based financial services group

CCF CHARTERHOUSE

Charterhouse Securities Ltd UK based wholesale equities broker

OFFROAD

OffRoad Capital Corp Online private capital marketplace

5. Make sure that the new acquisition generates sufficient synergy for the Group. We enrich ourselves through the willingness of blending the strengths of our own culture with those of our acquired companies. When we buy a company we always conduct an extensive due diligence investigation. In this way, we minimise surprises as much as possible.

Banca Intesa

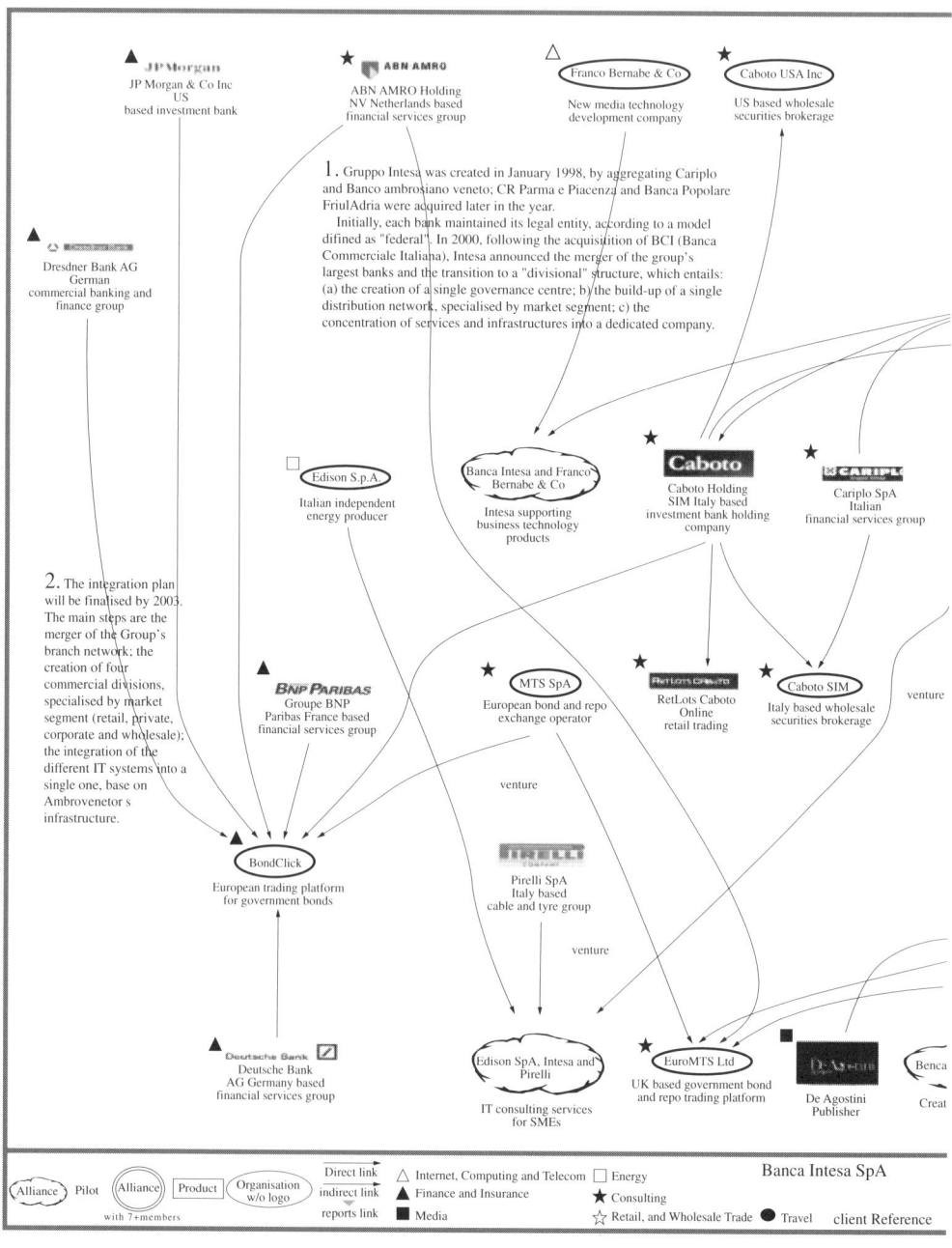

JP Morgan
JP Morgan & Co Inc
US
based investment bank

ABN AMRO
ABN AMRO Holding
NV Netherlands based
financial services group

Franco Bernabe & Co
New media technology
development company

Caboto USA Inc
US based wholesale
securities brokerage

Dresdner Bank AG
German
commercial banking and
finance group

1. Gruppo Intesa was created in January 1998, by aggregating Cariplo and Banco ambrosiano veneto; CR Parma e Piacenza and Banca Popolare FriulAdria were acquired later in the year.
Initially, each bank maintained its legal entity, according to a model difined as "federal". In 2000, following the acquisition of BCI (Banca Commerciale Italiana), Intesa announced the merger of the group's largest banks and the transition to a "divisional" structure, which entails: (a) the creation of a single governance centre; b) the build-up of a single distribution network, specialised by market segment; c) the concentration of services and infrastructures into a dedicated company.

Edison S.p.A.
Italian independent
energy producer

Banca Intesa and Franco
Bernabe & Co
Intesa supporting
business technology
products

Caboto
Caboto Holding
SIM Italy based
investment bank holding
company

CARIPLO
Cariplo SpA
Italian
financial services group

2. The integration plan will be finalised by 2003. The main steps are the merger of the Group's branch network; the creation of four commercial divisions, specialised by market segment (retail, private, corporate and wholesale); the integration of the different IT systems into a single one, base on Ambrovenetor s infrastructure.

BNP PARIBAS
Groupe BNP
Paribas France based
financial services group

MTS SpA
European bond and repo
exchange operator

RetLots Caboto
Online
retail trading

Caboto SIM
Italy based wholesale
securities brokerage

venture

BondClick
European trading platform
for government bonds

venture

PIRELLI
Pirelli SpA
Italy based
cable and tyre group

venture

Deutsche Bank
Deutsche Bank
AG Germany based
financial services group

Edison SpA, Intesa and
Pirelli
IT consulting services
for SMEs

EuroMTS Ltd
UK based government bond
and repo trading platform

De Agostini
Publisher

Benca

Creat

Alliance Pilot   Alliance   Product   Organisation w/o logo   with 7+members

Direct link
indirect link
reports link

△ Internet, Computing and Telecom
▲ Finance and Insurance
■ Media

☐ Energy
★ Consulting
☆ Retail, and Wholesale Trade ● Travel

Banca Intesa SpA

client Reference

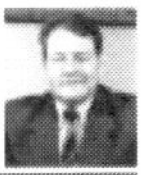

Christian Merle, CEO

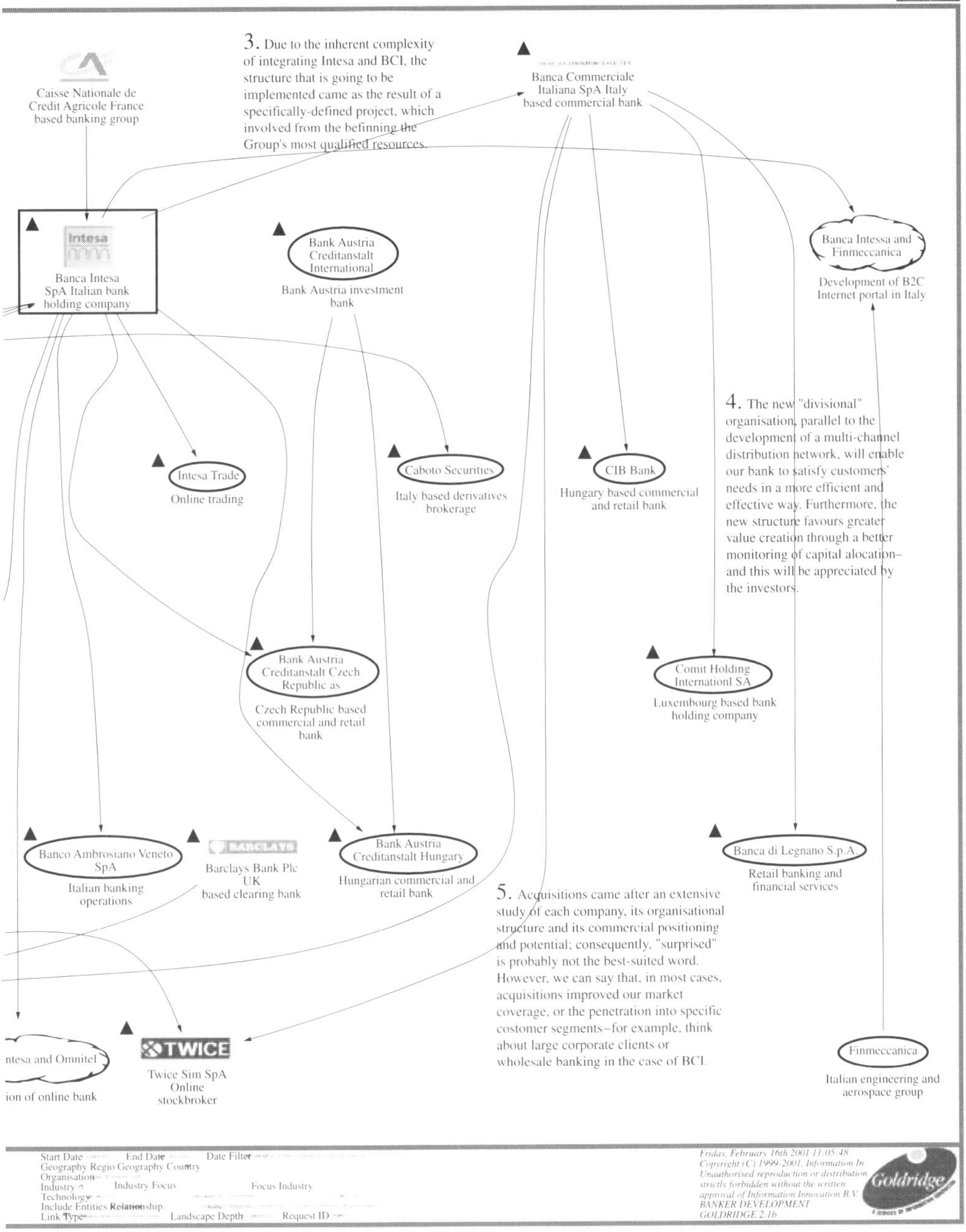
Caisse Nationale de Credit Agricole France based banking group
Banca Intesa SpA Italian bank holding company
Bank Austria Creditanstalt International
Bank Austria investment bank
Banca Commerciale Italiana SpA Italy based commercial bank
Banca Intessa and Finmeccanica
Development of B2C Internet portal in Italy
Intesa Trade
Online trading
Caboto Securities
Italy based derivatives brokerage
CIB Bank
Hungary based commercial and retail bank
Bank Austria Creditanstalt Czech Republic as
Czech Republic based commercial and retail bank
Comit Holding Internationl SA
Luxembourg based bank holding company
Banco Ambrosiano Veneto SpA
Italian banking operations
Barclays Bank Plc UK based clearing bank
Bank Austria Creditanstalt Hungary
Hungarian commercial and retail bank
Banca di Legnano S.p.A.
Retail banking and financial services
ntesa and Omnitel
ion of online bank
TWICE
Twice Sim SpA Online stockbroker
Finmeccanica
Italian engineering and aerospace group
Start Date End Date Date Filter
Geography Regio Geography Country
Organisation
Industry Industry Focus Focus Industry
Technology
Include Entities Relationship
Link Type Landscape Depth Request ID
Friday, February 16th 2001 11:05:48
Copyright (C) 1999-2001, Information In
Unauthorised reproduction or distribution strictly forbidden without the written approval of Information Innovation B.V.
BANKER DEVELOPMENT
GOLDRIDGE 2.1b
Goldridge

3. Due to the inherent complexity of integrating Intesa and BCI, the structure that is going to be implemented came as the result of a specifically-defined project, which involved from the befinning the Group's most qualified resources.

4. The new "divisional" organisation, parallel to the development of a multi-channel distribution network, will enable our bank to satisfy customers' needs in a more efficient and effective way. Furthermore, the new structure favours greater value creation through a better monitoring of capital alocation– and this will be appreciated by the investors.

5. Acquisitions came after an extensive study of each company, its organisational structure and its commercial positioning and potential; consequently, "surprised" is probably not the best-suited word. However, we can say that, in most cases, acquisitions improved our market coverage, or the penetration into specific costomer segments–for example, think about large corporate clients or wholesale banking in the case of BCI.

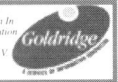

Index

Index compiled by Annette Musker